D1372878

Trophies of the Heart

Trophies
of the Heart

by
RUSSELL THORNBERRY

THE DERRYDALE PRESS
Lanham and New York

THE DERRYDALE PRESS

Published in the United States of America by
The Derrydale Press
4720 Boston Way, Lanham, Maryland 20706

Distributed by NATIONAL BOOK NETWORK, INC.

British Library Cataloguing in Publication Information Available

Library of Congress Cataloging-in-Publication Data

Thornberry, Russell.
    Trophies of the heart / Russell Thornberry.
       p. cm.
    Includes bibliographical references (p.   ).
    ISBN 1-58667-012-3 (cloth : alk. paper)
    1. Big game hunting—North America. 2. White-tailed deer
  hunting—North America. I. Title.
    SK40 .T56 2000
    799.2'6'097—dc21

                              00-031611

To my grandchildren
*who may never know the wonderful
wild places I have known and loved.
I fear that such places are being gobbled
up in the name of "progress." It is my
prayer that some will remain for you.*

Contents

Preface

It seems like only yesterday when I was a junior high student contemplating my future. The only thing I was sure of back then was that I was wholly smitten with a passion for the great outdoors—so much so that I couldn't imagine an applicable college major. I couldn't find a "hunting" or "fishing" major anywhere. All I knew was that I wanted to follow my passion. I read ads in the back pages of hunting magazines that offered careers as forest rangers, gunsmiths and taxidermists, but those offered little appeal to a kid who just wanted to hunt and fish. I still remember dashing to class as the morning bell rang, with duck and goose feathers still stuck to my hunting boots. I hunted before school, after school, and yes, upon occasion, during school.

Oddly, it was music that both took me away from the outdoors and eventually led me back to it. Back in the 1960s, I was captivated by folk music. Before I knew it, I was clanging around on an acoustic guitar and writing songs. Shortly thereafter, I did a stint with the New Christy Minstrels and several other lesser-known folk groups. It was while performing in Hawaii that I came down with the Asian flu and lost my voice. Back in Los Angeles, my doctor told me to get out of the smog for awhile so my sinuses could heal. So I headed to Saskatchewan to visit Rob Kingsland, the only Canadian I knew. I was quite sure the air would be better there than in L.A. One week's Canadian vacation turned into two and I met a pretty, blue-eyed Alberta maiden named Sharleen Gibson who stole my heart. Sharleen and numerous musical offers kept me lingering in Canada until we were married in 1969. After that, Canada became home.

Though immersed in the world of music, television, concerts and recording, I was only an arm's length from those alluring wilds of western Canada. My first moose hunt, back in 1970, changed my life. It set me on a course in the guiding and outfitting business that spanned nearly 20 years. In addition, it was the catalyst that prompted me to write my first hunting story about that incredible first moose hunting experience in northern Alberta. Little did I know when that first story was published, that I was tapping into my destiny.

My life in the outdoors begs to be written. First, because I have been so blessed with opportunities to travel and experience a life that is a dream to most outdoorsmen, and second, because it seems that wherever I go, something most unusual happens that makes the experience unique. Those who know me marvel at how I always seem to end up in either just the right or just the wrong place at the right time. Sometimes those rare and unique experiences have to percolate for awhile before the amusement outweighs the pain, but, in the end, they always seem to make fascinating tales.

I consider myself a most fortunate storyteller who gets more than his fair share of inspiration—both as a hunter and as a former outfitter/guide. "Trophies of the Heart" represents the cream of the crop of my memories of a lifetime pursuing big game all over North America, and occasionally over seas, both for my personal amusement and as a professional hunter trying to help a client realize his or her dream.

While I have thrilled at the experience of hunting many regal creatures on this planet, when it's all said and done, the whitetail remains the single most captivating animal I have ever pursued. I dedicate a goodly and justifiable portion of this book to my pursuit of moose, elk, caribou, sheep, bear and other wonderful animals, and finish off with memoirs of whitetails that remain as vivid in my memory as the instant I laid eyes upon them.

I don't know why God creates some such as I, so consumed with the beauty and the mystery of the wilds—so captivated by nature's intoxicating allure. But I'm glad that I am among that number. It is my hope that on the pages that follow, I will justly convey the marvel, the passion and the gratitude I feel for wild places and the creatures that inhabit them.

SECTION I

The Antlered Giants

ONE

A Moose for the Tenderfoot

*W*hen I was still a small child, too young to read, I remember asking my mother to buy a sporting magazine from the newsstand at the grocery store. I wanted her to read me the story about a bear hunt advertised on the cover. The picture of the bear on the magazine cover had completely captured my imagination. That was back before "sporting" magazines were ashamed of hunting—before they turned their emphasis to bird watching features and RV columns. Hunting was not politically incorrect in those honest days, when bear hunting could be a cover story. From then on, I was intrigued by the thought of experiencing the vast wilderness areas described in the magazine article and the thrill of hunting big game. As I grew up in south Texas, I hunted all there was to hunt— from cottontails to whitetails, javelina and feral hogs.

In the fall, when the geese passed overhead at night, I watched from my window as they swept across the moon on their long flight from Canada. There was always something mysterious to me about Canada, and I read all I could find about the Great White North. I became captivated by the idea of someday going to Canada and experiencing the mystery for myself. Years later, at age 25, I ended up marrying and settling in Edmonton, Alberta, Canada.

While driving in Edmonton one afternoon, I saw a truck carrying a monstrous set of moose antlers in its bed. When I looked closer, I realized that there was a whole moose in that truck, field-dressed and apparently en route to a locker. I don't know how long I stood there stunned by the size of the moose, but I still remember the shock of seeing what must have been an animal weighing upwards of 1,000 pounds. Actually, it was only an average bull. But it seemed so huge compared to the small Hill Country whitetails from Texas that I had hunted. A seed was planted that day, and I knew I would not rest until I experienced moose hunting for myself.

For the next two years, I went through the time-consuming agony of seeking out all the moose hunting information I could find. I hunted in many areas, but always managed to be in just the wrong spot at the wrong time. The first two seasons I hunted moose, I missed the calling season, which occurs from mid-September to about Oct. 10. I wasn't so concerned at first, because I didn't know how to call a moose anyway; nor did anyone I knew. In the fall of my third season in Canada, I was invited to go on a moose hunt with two fellows who owned an all-terrain vehicle that would get us deep into moose country and enable us to transport our game, should we be so fortunate. Horses or some type of terrain vehicle are essential to moose hunting. It is not a simple matter to pack a moose out of the bush on your back, no matter how small the pieces you've cut.

We left Edmonton and pulled the ATV behind the car on a trailer as we headed north to the Wandering River area of north central Alberta. We spent the first night in a motel. Early the following morning, we set out for the final leg of the trip. We were beyond the last paved highway and into the big timber country. The golden aspens glittered against the deep greens of the tall spruce. The sweet-and-sour smell of decaying leaves and frost-ripened wild cranberries mixed with the intoxicating perfume of the evergreens and drifted on a crisp fall breeze. The sky was an endless blue.

We pulled off the gravel road onto an old logging road that was barely visible beneath the undergrowth that had hidden it through the spring and summer. We loaded up the ATV with all our gear and the three of us (Doug Hutton, Lloyd Gordon and myself) jumped in and started down the logging road into the dense timber. Doug was driving, and as we made each turn through the trees, penetrating deeper into the forest, we all silently expected to see that trophy bull about which we had dreamt. The traveling got rougher as we crossed washed-out creeks and sank into seemingly bottomless muskeg bogs. We somehow managed to crawl through them. After a couple of hours and about 10 miles into the tall timber, we hit a small slough and really had to put the machine through its paces to cross it. As we crawled out on the other side, we picked up the logging trail and Doug suddenly hit the brakes. A tremendous bull moose was standing in the trail about 70 yards ahead of us. He stood there and stared at us for a second before vanishing into the trees.

"There's your bull," Doug whispered. We jumped off of the ATV and began unpacking our rifles. Doug suggested we pick up the bull's tracks where he'd crossed the trail and follow him into the timber. We hurried on foot and, in minutes, found the fresh tracks.

Not more than 100 yards into the trees, everything broke loose at once. Doug spotted the bull and signaled me toward him with his hand. As I tried to edge silently toward Doug's position, I snagged a bootlace crossing a fallen log and went right over on my face.

By the time I clambered back to my feet, Doug and Lloyd were farther into the timber. I heard the boom of a rifle and Doug yelling excitedly. I followed the sounds and finally caught sight of them. When I reached them, they were standing proudly beside the bull that was supposed to be mine. Doug had connected with his 7mm Mag.—a perfect heart shot—and the bull was his.

In spite of the mishap that cost me my first bull moose, it was really thrilling just to be there. After all, we hadn't even made camp yet!

Doug and I field-dressed the bull and estimated his weight at about 900 pounds. The rack was not as big as it appeared when the animal was still on the hoof, but they seldom are. At any rate, it was a proud moment for any man. We marked the trail so we could find the animal easily the next day and left him there to cool for the night. By that time, it was late afternoon and the coolness of the day presented no threat of spoiling the meat. We traveled another three miles or so that first afternoon and finally set up camp for the night.

Doug decided that he would take the moose out of the bush the following morning and asked which of us would like to help. Some vote that turned out to be! Lloyd and I both wanted to stay and hunt. I won the toss, and it was agreed that the next morning I would leave camp early to hunt and Doug and Lloyd would head back and transport the moose to Lac La Biche. I asked them to be sure and leave my bedroll, my .22 rifle, ammo and matches. Then they would return as soon as possible. In the meantime, I was to tend camp.

The next morning, before the others awoke, I dressed and left camp in the dark. I hunted the area east of our camp and found fresh moose tracks everywhere, as well as deer and bear tracks. I also found a single rodent-chewed palm of a cast moose antler from the previous year. The squirrels, mice and porcupines had chewed the edges away for the calcium it contained. The sight of the huge palm spurred me onward. By 10 a.m., I noticed that the sky was darkening in the north. There was a strange stillness hanging in the air as black clouds began swallowing what was left of a distant blue sky. The chattering of the squirrels and Whiskey Jacks ceased, and a light snow began to fall. Though it wasn't snowing hard at first, the flakes were as big as silver dollars. Although I was new to the north, I sensed trouble and decided that I'd better head back to camp.

By the time I made the mile-and-a-half trek, the snow was being swept down by a strong, biting wind, and I knew I was in for a bad storm. The first thing I noticed when I arrived at camp was that my sleeping bag, .22 cartridges and matches were gone. When Doug and Lloyd packed up that morning, one of them had inadvertently packed my gear on the ATV. A great sinking feeling settled in my heart. My primary sources of warmth were gone, and I was 15 miles from the nearest traveled road. The snow was already piling deep on the ground and visibility was nearly zero. As little as I knew of such matters then, I realized I was trapped in a full-blown blizzard. My choices were to try to walk 15 miles back to the Fort McMurray highway, or try to tough it out under a tree. I wasn't sure I could survive either of my options, given the serious conditions at hand.

I was standing under the canopy of a big spruce tree, trying to decide what to do next, when a movement caught my eye. I stared through the blur of wind-swept snow and, to my utter amazement, saw a short little man walking through the trees toward me. He was wearing a faded red wool shirt and a red hunter's cap, and he was carrying an ancient lever-action Savage Model 99 rifle. Appearing as if in a dream, he walked straight up to me and spoke without disturbing the dampened butt of a "roll-your-own" hanging in the corner of his mouth.

"Yer a long way from home ain'tcha?" he asked.

"Yessir, I guess I am," I stammered.

"Your friends won't be back for a spell 'cause of the storm," he said.

"How did you know I came with friends?" I asked.

"I live here, and I heard you boys coming. Then this mornin' I saw 'em leaving. Don't know where they went with that little machine, but it'll never make it back through the kinda snow like we're about to get. You'd better follow me if you wanna get outta this weather." This was my introduction to Marion Diesel, a 63-year-old trapper and bushman extraordinaire.

I was only too willing to follow him through the timber. It was obvious that he knew every tree as if they were old friends. A half-mile later, we arrived at his cabin. I was surprised at the picture it made, snuggled there in the trees with snow piling up on the roof. The little log house was a piece of history. Marion made a fire in the old wood stove and before long it was as comfortable as the Hilton. I was truly in another world—a world that I had read about as a child but never expected to experience. Snowshoes and fur stretchers hung on the walls. In the thin plastic windowpane at the head of his bed were five small holes, each plugged with spent .22 cases. Marion explained that they were all bullet holes and each one represented a bear that attempted to get a better look at the inside of his cabin. Instead, they each received a .22 bullet between their eyes. Marion believed in keeping the bears outside.

The old man was weathered and tough, but he had a personality and a sense of humor that were unique. I had always presumed that trappers were introverted types who sought a place in the wilds to escape society. In my mind's eye, I viewed them as reclusive hermits. Marion quickly dispelled any such notion. He was simply delighted to have company and dearly loved people. He explained that his lifestyle was not an effort to escape anything, but rather the only thing left that he could do and still remain in the peace and serenity of the wilds that he loved.

Marion showed me his treasures from the forest, which consisted of various formations and growths from the trunks of trees. Some looked like figurines and others like faces. His collection represented many years of watching and appreciating the wonders of nature.

Of greatest interest to me were the never-ending tales Marion could tell about his years prospecting in the Yukon and trapping in the Northwest Territories. The things that he had lived were true history, and I was spellbound by each tale. He had piloted paddlewheel steamers on the McKenzie River back in the '30s. He had tangled with a big grizzly on a beaver dam and crossed Great Bear Lake by compass in a raging blizzard with a team of dogs. It was obvious that his 63 years hadn't been easy ones by modern standards, but it was also obvious that he was showing no signs of weakening. The years were on his face, but they hadn't yet begun to reach his soul.

We talked far into the night as the embers snapped in the old stove. I asked questions that I had always pondered concerning the habits of wolves and wolverines. He had seen and experienced them all. He was a living encyclopedia of nature.

The next morning it was still snowing, but fortunately, not as hard as the previous day. Marion made me a pile of pancakes on the wood stove and added maple syrup, slices of fried moose backstrap and strong black coffee. I ate until I could barely move. With my first bull moose still in the forefront of my mind, I asked what he thought of trying to hunt moose in the snow. He said it would be good as long as the snow was fresh and quiet to walk in. I could make good use of the wind, and tracking would be fairly simple. I asked him if he wanted to join me, but he said he had a few things he had to do to get his traps ready for the upcoming season.

I had walked only about a quarter of a mile when I crossed moose tracks so fresh that I could see the grass still lying down in the bottom of the tracks. The snow was still falling and would cover the tracks in a matter of minutes, so I knew the animal could be no farther than five minutes ahead of me. The terrain ahead gradually inclined, and the tracks were headed straight uphill. I could see that eventually I would hit a ridge. At the crest of the ridge, there was a large windfall, which offered cover as well as a perfect shooting rest. From the top of the ridge, I would be able to see several hundred yards clearly. The area beyond was open, with just a few sparse clumps of poplars. The clearing and the snow would make a moose easy to spot from my vantage point. As I neared the crest of the ridge, I edged toward the windfall for cover and moved cautiously forward for my first look into the opening beyond.

Suddenly, a crashing sound erupted from the log pile only 15 feet from me. I jumped back, shouldering my rifle, and up from the windfall emerged a large black bear. I could see nothing but a black blur in my scope at that range. I was still frantically backing away from the bear that was obviously no less surprised than I. In his haste, the bear lost his footing momentarily and slipped back down among the logs. By then, I was beginning to make out the bear in my scope, and my heart was throbbing so loud I could hear it.

At the very second that the bear cleared the top of the windfall, and at the precise time I should have shot, I heard a crunch behind me. In my panic, I glanced over my shoulder to see what else I had to encounter. A cow moose was high-tailing it into the timber. It was over before I knew it. I stood shaken and dismayed, not having fired a single shot—the bear going one way, the moose going another. My knees were knocking, and I felt a little light-headed.

After my nerves settled, I decided to see if I could follow the bear's tracks in the snow. I wasn't after a cow moose anyway, and that was the first live bear I ever had seen outside of a zoo. Thankfully, at Doug's suggestion, I had purchased a bear tag. The tracks led into a thick stand of young pines, obviously a new growth where a forest fire had recently burned the older timber. The saplings were just a bit higher than my head, extremely thick and covered with a deep layer of fresh snow. Visibility was occasionally 15 yards at best, but more often a matter of feet rather than yards. I could follow the bear's tracks easily enough, but I was keenly aware that I could quite possibly bump into this critter before I could see him.

I slipped along quietly, listening intently and watching for a trace of black among the snow-covered pine boughs. The bear's tracks finally led up onto a large fallen log. I followed them to the end of the log where they simply disappeared. It took me 10 minutes to figure out that the bear had walked back down the log in his own tracks. I suddenly had the feeling that he was playing with me. The hair on the back of my neck stood up as I crept forward, still following his tracks. I looked down to check his tracks and saw something that made my blood run cold. It was my own boot print in the snow with the bear's track on top of mine. The bear had made a circle and now was following me. At that point, all I wanted to do was get back to the cabin as fast as my legs would carry me. Thoroughly disgusted and unnerved with my performance, I made my retreat. This "northern hunting" was turning out to be a lot more than this tenderfoot had bargained.

When I got back to the cabin, I told Marion my woeful tale, and he had a good laugh about it. Then I told him of my misfortune two days earlier when I had muffed my chance at the bull Doug killed. He asked me if I'd ever shot a moose before, and I admitted that I had not. "Oh, I see." he said. "We'll have to change all that."

As we ate lunch, he told me that he would call up a nice bull for me later that evening. He said it so matter-of-factly that I was a little doubtful at first, but who was I to question him? He didn't strike me as a boastful man, or one who would say anything he didn't mean.

At 4:00 that afternoon, Marion dug out his calling horn—a long slender megaphone-shaped roll of birch bark. It looked like the calling horns I'd seen in so many pictures. I grabbed my rifle and asked him if he thought we had a good chance. He looked outside.

"Yep, the wind and snow have stopped," he said, explaining that when the air was completely still, the call could be heard for miles by the moose.

Marion said that he had killed and field-dressed a moose several days earlier near the windfall where I'd seen the bear. The bear had probably dragged the remains into the log pile and was feeding on them when I surprised him that morning. He decided we should give the same area one more try.

When we reached the top of the ridge where all the excitement had taken place, Marion stopped and climbed into the windfall. He directed me to continue across the clearing some 300 yards and find a spot to hide and wait in the edge of the timber. After I was settled in a clump of willows with my back against a hollow birch, I heard the eerie bawling of Marion's call. I almost laughed to think that this odd noise was going to attract a big bull moose. I listened as the strange sound penetrated the stillness of the evening. Marion would call three or four times in succession, wait 10 minutes or so, then call again.

"Aaaaaaaaaaaaaahwugh!"

"Aaaaaaaaaaaaaahwugh!"

Silence.

As I sat quietly, I became entranced by the silence of the forest. A small field mouse was eating a blade of grass at my feet. I was amazed at how human-like he was. He used his tiny hands to pull a blade of grass over, then held it down and chewed on it as if it were an ear of corn.

In the distance, I heard a crashing sound as if a tree had fallen. I held my breath, straining to hear more. A long silence passed and I became aware that my lungs were burning for another breath. I breathed deeply, then heard the crashing sound again. This time it sounded closer. I inhaled deeply and again held my breath. I heard a crazy sound like the croaking of an overgrown frog. Again the crashing sound echoed from within the green timber and I realized that it must have been a moose! The sound was coming from the north, and it seemed to be approaching the clearing from the end where I was hidden. Then the sound of antlers raking against saplings became audible. Again I had to remind myself to breathe.

Then, to my surprise, I heard much the same sound coming from the south. Could it be that there was yet another bull coming to the same call? I heard the sound in the distance, then the bull from the north hooked the poplars again. The north bull was obviously the closer of the two, and I was fully prepared to take the first one I saw. I had visions of the two meeting in front of me!

I turned, facing the direction of the closest bull. He would stop and hook the trees, bellow loudly, then charge ahead a few more yards and repeat the process. My heart was pumping like a steam engine. I could hardly hold my breath, even to listen. Behind me, I could still hear the other bull. There seemed to be little doubt about which bull was going to arrive first. The moose in front of me stopped hooking the bush and I listened between heartbeats for any sound. Then I heard the "Chh . . . chh . . . chh . . . " of his hooves as he moved in the foot-deep snow. Suddenly, he was directly in front of me, pawing the ground with his head low and swinging from side to side as he hooked the poplars around him with his antlers.

For a time, I was simply spellbound, then something in the back of my mind reminded me that I had spent a dangerously long time watching him and that at any second he might notice me and be gone. I carefully released the safety on my rifle and raised it to my shoulder. I breathed as deeply as I dared and let go of half my breath. I felt the trigger and began slowly squeezing. The moose was facing me directly, and I could only see the top of his shoulder hump above his head, which was still low and thrashing from side to side. When he raised his head, I centered my crosshairs in the middle of his massive chest and felt the rifle lurch as it shook the still air. Under the jolt of the recoil, I lost sight of the bull. I watched breathlessly to see if there was any movement and finally eased out of my hiding place toward the spot where the moose had been standing. I silently prayed that I had not imagined all this or, worse yet, missed him. I bulldozed my way through the poplar saplings toward where I thought he had been, and there he laid—the biggest moose I'd ever seen. He had slumped forward in his tracks, still upright, and yet the top of his shoulder hump reached my waist. His antlers were still as large as I had thought them to be. I had my first moose! I whooped with joy, and Marion soon appeared with a big smile and congratulated me.

"That's the way a feller's s'posed to get those big ones," he grinned. The bull field-dressed close to 1,000 pounds. I'm sure he wasn't the biggest moose in Marion's backyard, but I couldn't have been prouder.

The storm that originally threatened to finish my hunt turned out to be a blessing in disguise. Another day passed before Doug and Lloyd returned. Their machine had broken down altogether, and they had to borrow another to return for me.

The September blizzard had been a record-setter for Alberta. In the outside world, roads and schools had been closed and power lines were down. But life had continued without a hitch at Marion's cabin. Coal oil lamps and wood stoves don't skip a beat when the conveniences of modern living fail. The stay with Marion had been an education for me. I was thrilled about bagging my first moose, but equally thrilled to get to know and experience this amazing man of the north.

I bid Marion farewell after spending four of the greatest days of my life with him. In truth, he might have saved my life. I often wonder what would have happened to me if he hadn't appeared at that bleak moment when the fateful storm hit.

"Now that you know where I am, you better come back!" he said.

It was an invitation I would accept many times in the years to follow.

POSTSCRIPT

I made many trips back to visit with Marion Diesel, and we became good friends. We eventually joined forces in a guiding and outfitting operation for moose and bear hunters. The chapters that follow make reference to our joint venture and subsequent adventures. It was under the tutelage of Marion Diesel that I embarked on a career as an outdoorsman, guide and outfitter, which eventually led me to a second career as an outdoors writer. I will forever be in Marion's debt for all that he taught me about the Canadian North, its creatures, their habits and habitat.

TWO

Moose Fever

My chance meeting with Marion Diesel described in the previous chapter resulted in our joining forces in a moose hunting operation for several years afterward. Marion taught me how to call moose well in those days of my Canadian guiding and outfitting infancy. What follows are some humorous and entertaining incidents that I experienced while guiding moose hunters in the early '70s.

If the sight of a 150-pound deer can rattle a man, imagine the shock of seeing a moose for the first time. A moose, after all, is as big as a horse, and it might have a rack the size a bulldozer blade. My years of guiding hunters have shown me that while buck fever is bad, it's nothing compared to moose fever.

You wouldn't believe the things that have happened.

One sport I guided had never seen or heard a moose. On the first morning out, he watched in disbelief as I grunted and coughed out my best bull moose imitation through my birch bark calling horn. He obviously didn't think I had both oars in the water. When I grunted again, the guy smiled. "You kidding me?" he asked. He just couldn't accept the fact that a love-stricken bull moose makes sounds like regurgitated hiccups. I wondered vaguely what he thought he was paying me for and called again.

I heard a bull answer from a long way off and nudged the hunter to be sure he'd heard it too. "A moose!" he exclaimed, staring blankly at me for a suspended moment. Then he began to chuckle. Then he laughed. The next thing I knew he was out of control, rolling on the ground. I began to call louder, trying to cover the madness of the situation. Quickly the bull was on us. We heard it coming through the brush, bellowing and hooking the birch saplings with a hollow clatter of heavy palms. The moose was cooperating to the best of its ability, but laughing boy, writhing at my feet, was doing his dead-level best to botch the opportunity. I could hear the determined beast moving closer, and I didn't know what to do. Nothing like this had ever happened to me.

Suddenly, the bull appeared in the open, 50 yards distant. Instinctively, I clouted the guy across the brow with the birch bark calling horn and hissed, "Take him!" To my amazement, the sport jumped to his knees, drew quick aim and dropped the bull in its tracks with a high shoulder shot. From then on, he was as rational as any veteran moose hunter.

"Do you know you went a little bit nuts on me when that bull was coming in?" I asked later at camp.

"Nuts? What do you mean, 'nuts?'" He asked. He had absolutely no recollection of his hysterics. I wasn't going to waste time convincing him it had happened. I chalked it up for what it was—moose fever.

That same season, I called another bull moose for a hunter from Minnesota. It, too, came in well. When it reached the edge of a thicket of red willows, my hunter was able to squeeze off a perfect lung shot. A moose with its adrenaline up seldom drops on the spot, however, and this one bolted and charged into the willows. My hunter was already mourning a miss, but I'd been watching with binoculars and had seen hair fly from behind its shoulder. Trying to reassure him, I told him to follow me through the willows where we'd no doubt find the fallen bull. At the thicket's edge, though, the hunter stopped fast. "Oh my god," he gasped, staring up at the willow tops, which reached ten feet in the air and were smeared with blood. "Never realized how big those monsters really are," he muttered, stepping back. I chuckled and explained that the bull had pushed the willows down as he ran through them. The blood from the wound had painted the tops red before they could spring up again. He was still not convinced that the bull wasn't the size of a dinosaur, and I had to do some more selling before he would go any farther. It was only when he actually saw the moose, lying stone dead 40 yards ahead, that he was sure it wasn't 15 feet high at the shoulder.

It's odd the way the big north woods spook some people, although they are really safer there than in any large city. I once guided a hunter who was moose-sized himself—as big as an NFL tackle. On a late, gray September morning, I walked him into a low-lying area where the muskeg threatened to swallow us with every step, and I began calling. Nothing happened. Just as I decided to change locations, we heard what sounded like the beating of large wings drawing closer. I looked up, expecting to see a raven or a hawk. The sound grew louder and movement caught my eye in the timber ahead. Before I could comment, a pack of timber wolves were standing alert in a semicircle around us. What we'd heard had been the panting of running wolves. They obviously thought they'd found a cow moose and were coming in for breakfast.

The wolves realized we were humans as quickly as we realized they were wolves and quickly faded like passing shadows into the forest. I was surprised but not afraid, for I know how much they fear man. My hunter, however, might have been big enough to tackle pro running backs, but wolves were another matter entirely. The rest of the day he remained certain they were going to get him, and he kept a close watch of his backtrail.

By the third day, his jumpiness had subsided and we found ourselves with the kind of crisp, cold weather that lets a call echo for miles through the timber. Although I called all afternoon from the cover of a large deadfall, we got no answers. It started to get dark and I whispered to the hunter that it was time to head back. He nodded, then we both heard the distinct snap of a branch behind us. Aware that bulls sometimes tiptoe to the call without a sound, I advised my hunter to chamber a cartridge and to prepare himself. We strained to listen, but we heard nothing more. It was almost too dark to see, so in a last-ditch effort, I lowered the muzzle of my birch bark calling horn to the ground and made a faint call, hoping to disguise our exact location. As if from out of space, a huge black bear reared up on its hind legs no more than six feet in front of us. My hunter screamed in horror as he let a wild one go with his .300 Mag. I just sat there in complete amazement. I wasn't carrying a gun. If I had been, I would have been too stunned to shoot. The bear vanished as mysteriously as he'd appeared, and my hunter danced a jig of uncontrollable fright, half crying and half laughing.

At camp, I tried again and again to convince him that both incidents were extremely rare and that at no time were we in any real danger, that both bears and wolves want no part of humans. They had simply miscalculated. I could see he wasn't buying it.

I hoped the next day he'd get a nice, normal crack at a moose and take his trophy home and brag about his prowess. But things didn't work out that way. He got himself a sneaker. It's another rare event. The guy was getting more than his share, I know. But only once in perhaps 50 times will a moose come in as quiet as a mouse.

The hunter was sitting against a dead stump at the intersection of five major game trails. I was 100 yards from him. I figured the moose would follow my call and the hunter would intercept it en route to me. When the bull stepped out behind the hunter instead, I was amazed. The hunter was looking at me, and the moose, about 15 feet behind him, was also looking in my direction. I dared not move a muscle. I remember how silly it looked to see my hunter sitting there straining for a hint of the animal, which stood looming above him. To make things worse, it was a huge animal, black as midnight. This one really seemed as big as a dinosaur.

For what seemed like an hour, it was a standoff. I allowed only my eyes to blink, and the hunter stayed frozen, too. Eventually the moose took a small step and a piece of deadfall crunched beneath him. The noise sounded like an explosion to me from 100 yards away, so I understood perfectly why the poor man flew off the ground as if shot from a cannon. He somehow turned in flight and fired a shot, which startled the unsuspecting moose. The big bull whirled around in a circle, trying to figure out things. They stood there staring at each other from a distance of 10 feet. I held my breath waiting for another shot. After what seemed like another hour, a second shot echoed through the woods. If a twig snapping had seemed like an explosion, that shot sounded like an H-bomb. As I sat there blinking, to my wonder, both man and moose dropped to the ground in unison—the moose dead, the man fainted. I was beside him within seconds and was greatly relieved to find him alive. He trembled and had trouble speaking for a few minutes, but he finally got himself together. He could only describe the termination of his hunt as pure relief. He had experienced all the excitement he could stand.

Most of the strange reactions to moose fever are understandable. Hunters are awed by their first sight of a creature so big and imposing, and they find themselves dumbstruck. Usually, a nudge or two is all that's needed to break the trance.

One of the weirdest moose fever reactions I ever witnessed happened to a very savvy hunter from Michigan. He was a veteran, fitted with equipment that reflected his experience. But he'd never hunted anything larger than whitetails.

I called for 30 minutes before the first sound of the bull's approach became audible. We could hear his cautious footsteps on the bed of dry aspen leaves as he came closer. The tension was apparent in the hunter's face. Finally, a small bull stepped into the opening and my sport swiftly shouldered his rifle and fired. The moose fell in his tracks as if struck by lightning. I turned with a shout of congratulations. To my amazement, the guy wasn't there. He had leapt to his feet and was racing through the forest, tripping and falling and scrambling along the way. "What the heck are you doing?" I yelled.

At my shout, he stopped, panting and pointing to a spot in the woods. "I'm going to cut him off. He went that way!" By then I had reached his side, and I led him back to the fallen moose. He looked down at it, then turned to me and said, "I'll be . . . I coulda swore I saw him take off thattaway."

My guess is that he was expecting a miss. The fever got him, and he hallucinated his expectations. Moose fever is undoubtedly the result of tension, anxiety, nervousness, stress and a host of other $2 psychological terms that your average first-time moose hunter wouldn't understand. But then, your average psychiatrist probably wouldn't understand moose fever either.

THREE

Bowhunting the Yukon Giants

$\mathcal{A}$ visual treat greeted me when I arrived in the central Yukon in early September 1986. Against a backdrop of an endless bluebird sky were the flaming crimson canopies of the arctic birches, interspersed with golden-crowned aspens and the patchwork greens of balsam and spruce. I felt almost dizzy as I tried soaking up all that met my eyes. As I stepped off the little Cessna at the landing strip along the foot of Two Pete Mountain, Dave Coleman, my outfitter, was there to greet me and the other incoming hunters. While baggage was quickly hustled to the appropriate cabins, dinner was on the table in the log kitchen.

The next day, on horses saddled and packed beforehand, hunters and guides rode off into the mountains in search of various game. Some were hunting sheep. Both Dall's and stone sheep are plentiful in Dave's area. Other hunters struck out for grizzlies. I was among those who had come for caribou and moose. I had longed to bowhunt the Yukon's huge moose, which are considerably larger than those in my former home province of Alberta, Canada.

Dave and I left base camp at noon with two saddle horses and two packhorses. We set up our spike camp at the timber's edge, just below the summit of Two Pete Mountain. With two hours of daylight remaining, we rode the last mile up to the summit's rock crown to glass for game. As we approached the top, we encountered a small group of curious and somewhat comical caribou cows. They circled us, getting ever closer, until they were less than 50 yards. I was able to snap several photographs before they hoisted their stubby tails and strutted off into the rocks.

We tied the horses and climbed the last 100 yards to the rocky summit. We had barely settled behind our spotting scopes before we noticed a big bull moose bedded down within 100 yards of the trail we'd traveled just minutes earlier. He was a dandy bull, too, better than 60 inches wide. I couldn't believe he'd let us ride right by him. He sure wasn't as spooky as the moose I was used to hunting. Little did I know just how different this moose was going to be.

I was concerned about the location because he was lying in a hollow choked with thick willows and arctic birch. There was absolutely no way to approach the critter quietly. I pointed out my concern to Dave, who simply said, "We'll just ride the horses right up to him." It sounded pretty crazy, but I had no better ideas.

"We'll have to hurry because we only have 30 minutes of shooting light left," Dave said as he hopped into the saddle.

He took my reins and led my horse so my hands would be free. I felt like a little kid on his first pony ride as Dave led me through the tangle of willows toward the bedded bull. The horses made a terrific racket as they plowed through the brush. I couldn't imagine that moose just lying there calmly, listening to all that approaching noise. Dave finally pulled the horses to a stop and turned to me. "The bull is just over this rise. Get ready to jump off your horse and make your shot," he whispered.

I nodded dubiously. He kicked his horse ahead, and our two-pony caravan advanced cautiously.

"There he is!" Dave snapped.

I couldn't see the moose at first because I was right behind Dave's horse, so I bailed out of the saddle and stepped quickly aside of the horses. The huge bull stood facing us, his ivory-colored palms freshly stripped of velvet. He looked like a four-legged, black boxcar. I was frantically trying to nock an arrow when he turned broadside, offering the perfect target. Adrenaline poisoning caused me to rush the shot, however, and I watched my arrow skim over his back.

"I blew it," I moaned as the bull bolted forward, unscathed.

Dave ordered me back into the saddle, so I climbed back quickly as he spurred the horses forward, still leading mine by the reins. The moose was obviously trying to circle downwind of us to see what this was all about, but Dave rode in a semicircle to keep us downwind of the bull, instead. The move seemed to confuse the great animal. He stopped and watched us intently as if to see what our next move would be.

Dave pointed out a deep ravine that wound its way beneath the rise where the bull was standing. He told me to dismount and hightail it through the ravine while he kept the bull's attention. At that moment, I was so baffled by the whole episode that I was merely taking orders. This was more like a rodeo with bow and arrows than anything I had ever experienced in the name of hunting. Still, Dave's confidence kept me trying in spite of my doubts.

I ran the 250 yards through the ravine and, as I arrived below the ridge where I last saw the moose, I could hear him grunting and thrashing the willows above me and to my right. I could also hear Dave and the horses moving back and forth behind me. Dave was yelling, telling me where the moose was headed. It was all too crazy! I hesitated, caught my breath and tried to pinpoint the moose's location.

Then I saw him. He was following the ridge above me, stopping after every few steps to thrash more willows. He was definitely behaving as if he were rutting, which was to my advantage. When he disappeared behind a small clump of balsam, I jumped the small creek and dashed up the ridge another 50 yards. I froze amidst a clump of willows as the bull appeared almost immediately. As he lumbered directly above me, I nocked an arrow, stepped out of my hiding place, "guestimated" the distance and released an arrow—just as the bull took his last step in the open. The shot was too low, and the sound of the arrow clattering through the willows sent the moose stampeding down the ridge and out of sight.

I'm not sure whether I actually uttered the words or just thought them, but I clearly remember what went through my mind: "Thornberry, how could you miss a barn door-sized moose at 40 yards?"

What a beginning! I'd been hunting less than an hour and already missed the same bull twice! The opportunity presented itself so suddenly and the approach was so unlike anything I had anticipated, I was just caught off guard. I felt as bad for Dave as I did for myself. He'd provided me with a great opportunity. I just blew it. Thankfully, however, he took it all in stride. I remembered doing the same when one of my hunters blew the chance of a lifetime. I think it's called diplomacy, at least when in the company of the hunter. "Screw-up" is the term that comes to mind after the hunter goes home!

The following day, we spotted two bulls on a small lake at the base of the next mountain. We broke camp and made the ride in four hours. The first evening after we'd changed locations, we rode up the side of the mountain to a high point where we could observe the entire lake below us. We saw one excellent bull, two smaller ones and several cows. With darkness closing in, we decided against trying a stalk that night.

We spotted our big bull the next morning as he bedded down in a willow flat. We made our move down through the timber and carefully inched up to the bull's bed only to find him gone. Something had gone wrong; he had given us the slip. Then it was another climb up the mountain to locate him again.

That evening, we saw him and tried another stalk through the jungle of tall willows. But, once again, he was not to be found when we got there. It was discouraging, because it took a tremendous effort to go up and down that mountain.

This bull, unlike the first one on Two Pete Mountain, was as spooky as any white-tailed buck. The willows where he was living were 10 feet tall and so thick that a quiet stalk was impossible.

After two days of this spot-and-go-seek game, Dave and I were nearly worn out from all the climbing. We had planned for a five-day hunt, and we were down to our last rations. Either the moose was going to have to make a mistake soon, or we were going to have to go back to base camp for more supplies. On the fifth morning, from our mountainside vantage point, we spotted our slippery bull. We also saw a second bull that was considerably larger than the first. The new bull's antlers were so big for his body size that he looked front heavy, like he might tip over on his nose. He was easily the best bull I had ever seen, and renewed excitement inspired our weary bones to try again.

From high on the mountain we watched him in the valley below until he finally bedded. Down through the jungle of timber we went again into the towering willows that grabbed at clothing and bowstrings like claws. The stalk ended in nothing more than a warm, yet very empty moose bed. The climb back up the mountain was a quiet one. These bulls were obviously not into the rut yet and, until they were, it seemed impossible to get on them. We tried calling them in, but they weren't yet in the mood.

From the mountaintop later that evening, we spotted the big bull again. He was in the timber, midway up the next mountain. There was no way to approach him. A nasty rain and snowstorm, combined with our dwindling grub supply, led us to the decision to return to base camp and regroup. As we rode back in the blackness of night, a hollow, nagging feeling formed in the pit of my stomach, telling me that I would never see the great bull again.

The next morning, after a big breakfast and a good night's sleep, Dave decided to send me to Earn Lake where he expected numerous bulls to be congregating in preparation for the rut. He had some inflatable boats and outboard motors there, as well as a spacious camp facility. It would be a different style of hunting. Maybe it would change my luck. I was ready for a change after a week of plowing through willows on horseback, holding my bow up over my head to keep it out of the never-ending tangle of willows. My bowstring was already showing some serious wear from the continuous abrasion.

My new guide, Quincy Barrett, and I arrived at Earn Lake late on the afternoon of Sept. 11. We organized ourselves, inflated a 12-foot Zodiak and added a 20-horsepower outboard. We made a quick tour of the end of the lake near camp as the sun was setting. We saw one small bull feeding in the lake at dusk, and I was encouraged about the potential of the boat. It is legal to shoot a moose from a boat in the Yukon, so our plan was to try to find a decent bull along the shoreline and paddle into bow range.

Quincy and I arose at 5:30 the next morning to find ourselves enveloped by fog. We couldn't see 50 yards, so we went back to bed. At noon, the veil of fog lifted and exposed one of the most glorious days I have ever seen in the wilds. The 16-mile-long lake was mirror calm, perfectly reflecting the inverted images of the surrounding mountains on the water. I made a dozen or so practice shots and pondered the wear on my bowstring. I decided to risk it one more day, the last day of my hunt. Changing strings would mean resetting my sights. Surely it would last for one more day. Famous last words!

Quincy and I toured the lake and I photographed the spectacular scenery. I did some fishing, too, and found the arctic grayling to be virtually suicidal. As quickly as my little yellow-bellied goofus bug settled on the water, a greedy grayling inhaled it. After a shore lunch of fresh fish, we agreed to head back to camp and take a nap. We would go out again during the evening, when the moose were more apt to be moving. I got an early start, lying down in the bottom of the Zodiak. I drifted off to sleep as the motor droned toward camp.

When Quincy suddenly cut the throttle, I sat up to see what was happening. He was looking at a grass bed on the near shore. One peek through my binoculars showed me why. There were a bull and cow, feeding belly-deep in the lake a mere half-mile distant. I looked at my watch. It was 3 p.m. Right there in the brightest part of a bluebird day was a respectable bull!

Quincy idled us to within 400 yards of the moose before stopping the motor. The bull was standing broadside to us. He stood statue-still for a long time, gradually swinging his big, lazy head toward us, then back to check on his lady friend. Eventually, satisfied, he resumed his statuesque, broadside pose.

Quincy grabbed a canoe paddle and began the painstaking job of edging us into range. We moved so slowly that I don't think the bull even realized we were moving. In a matter of 15 minutes, Quincy closed the distance to less than 100 yards. I could see the bull roll his eyes toward us, without moving his head. He knew something was afoot.

When we were at 60 yards, he rolled his eyes our way again and grunted. The cow also stopped feeding and stared at our boat. After a few seconds, she seemed satisfied that we were not a problem and resumed feeding. The bull maintained his position without moving so much as a whisker. The wind was dead calm.

At 50 yards, he grunted softly at us again and I saw the whites of his eyes, as large as saucers, as he rolled them back to observe us.

"Ten more yards," I whispered to Quincy, as he paddled toward the bull in slow motion.

At 40 yards, I slowly raised myself off the bottom of the boat into a kneeling position and drew my arrow. The bull grunted and rolled his eyes again, but he remained standing broadside. I put the 40-yard pin in the middle of his ribs, behind his muscular shoulder, checked my anchor point one last time and let the string slip from my fingers. The arrow hit with a resounding thump, catapulting the bull into high gear in one great leap. The shot was certain to be fatal, but, meanwhile, both moose were running for shore.

Quincy urged me to take another shot to try and get the bull down before he made it into the muskeg and dense timber along the shoreline. I already had another arrow on the string, so I drew quickly, leading the bull about four feet. Suddenly, there was a hollow snap and my arrow fell helplessly into the bottom of the boat. The willow-worn bowstring had given up the ghost. We were overcome by a feeling of utter helplessness as we watched the two moose splashing their way through knee-deep water toward the bank.

I was powerless, unable to shoot another arrow. What if the first shot didn't stop him?

Relief flooded through me as the bull began to stagger and slow. His knees wobbled and he stopped for a moment, then toppled over just 20 feet from the bank. I breathed a great sigh of relief and watched the cow disappear into the timber.

Quincy and I just sat and regained our composure for a few minutes as we discussed the wild sequence of events. It was the last day of the hunt for me and obviously the last arrow of the trip. You can't cut it any finer than that.

I had my moose, but by the skin of my teeth. Schwartz's Law had prevailed until the last possible moment. What? You haven't heard of Schwartz's Law? Okay, I'll explain: Schwartz's Law says Murphy was an optimist.

At the airport in Whitehorse, I met my friend, Robert Wiebe, who had just flown in from Alberta for a moose hunt with Dave Coleman. I told him about the huge bull I had hunted on Two Pete Mountain and suggested that he go back and try for him. He did. He and his guide, Neil Sorkin, stood on the shoulder of the same mountain where I had first spotted the bull and located him a mile down the valley. Neil called, and the bull (now fully in rut) responded and marched right to them. Rob dropped the bull with a single shot from his .308!

ONE YEAR LATER

The Zodiak floated as lightly in the current as the armada of new fallen aspen leaves. The Hess River snaked magically through sandbars and gravel banks lined with golden cottonwoods and yellowing willow thickets. Rising overhead was the high country: green mountain shoulders topped with a mantle of snow rising above the timberline. Up there, on top of the world, were stone sheep and caribou, but down here in the golden glitter of the river valley were the giant

Alaska/Yukon moose—the largest antlered animals on earth. Sept. 18, 1987, was off to a beautiful start.

Dave Coleman held the inflatable boat in midriver with a canoe paddle and we drifted silently in the chilled morning air. There was little conversation as we strained to listen for the grunting cough of a rutting bull around every bend.

The river straightened for a half-mile stretch and paralleled a willowy sand bar island to our right. Midway down the sandbar, we heard the low chugging sound for which we'd been waiting. Dave nodded in the direction of the sound and gently paddled the Zodiak toward the bank. We could hear the bull thrashing the brush with his antlers and grunting furiously. "He's really into it," Dave whispered.

"So am I!" I said as my pulse quickened.

The light breeze was in our favor as we headed straight toward the bull, easing quietly through the 10-foot willows.

We saw two sets of grizzly tracks in the soft sand. One was very large, the other about average. The sign of their presence added unexpected questions to the stalk. Were we the only ones after this bull? If not, would there be a conflict among the hunters?

The bull grunted again, now only 70 or 80 yards ahead of us. Dave climbed up on a log pile for a better view. "I see him," he said as he stretched his arms wide, indicating the width of the antlers. "He's got to be a 65-incher!" He pointed toward the bull and motioned for me to move into the lead so I could be ready. Slowly, I inched forward 20 yards to an opening. I could see the white pans of massive antlers above the willows. I guessed the distance at 60 yards. Somehow, I had to get closer and find a hole through which to shoot. I nocked an arrow, crouched low and began slowly circling below the bull – which was still grunting and ripping willows out of the ground. He was obviously in another world and had no idea he was being hunted.

As I crept quietly around him, I was utterly amazed at his size. The tips of his pans had to be 11 to 12 feet high to be visible above the willows. I thought of how ancient hunters must have felt as they approached the great hairy mammoths with spears. How small they must have felt. How small I felt.

I closed to within about 40 yards, but I still could not see the opening I needed. I could smell the bull's musky odor as I studied the situation. The willows seemed to form a protective wall around him. All I could do was hold my position and wait for him to make the next move. Resting on my knees, I waited with my heart in my throat. Within seconds, the bull started moving. He was coming out of the willows, heading back toward the river along a path that would take him within 20 yards of me. I quickly checked my tackle. All was ready. Antlers bobbed above the willow tops as the bull literally plowed through the wall of tangled shrubs. He grunted with every step. I could even hear him breathing.

Suddenly, he slammed to a stop. I could tell that he was looking my way. The tops of two huge pans stood motionless, flattened toward me. My heart sank into my boots as I felt a slight breeze on the back of my neck. With only 30 yards between us, I knew it was finished. Then came the explosion in the willows as the bull turned on his heels and bolted for the timber. I dropped my bow and dashed for the back channel just in time to see him cross. He was awesome. His antlers were so massive that he looked awkwardly front-heavy, characteristic of truly huge-antlered bulls. Even at 100 yards, I knew that he was, by far, the best bull I had ever seen. "Too bad," Dave groaned from behind me. "He's a book bull if I ever saw one." I nodded in silent agreement, trying to control my disappointment. Dave suggested we brew a pot of tea to warm up before continuing. It was just what I needed to settle the trembling inside, a combination of the crisp morning air and the electric excitement of being so close to a monstrous bull.

Dave pushed the Zodiak back out into the current as the morning sun peeked over the mountains and settled on the river. It felt good, and a shiver ran across my shoulders as the warmth penetrated. We floated through a gradual bend, less than a mile from where we made our play on the big bull. As soon as the river straightened again, to my amazement, another bull emerged from the river and shook himself on the bank about 400 yards downstream. The grin on Dave's face told me we were on red alert, and we quickly beached the Zodiak on the gravel bar. The bull was grunting, now only 200 yards from us. He was unaware of our presence as he stood there in plain sight on the gravel bar. We waited for him to decide what he was going to do. In less than a minute, he walked away from the river into a thin strip of sparse willows. It was perfect! I nocked an arrow and quickly closed the distance to 50 yards. The bull was grunting away and pushing the willows around with his antlers. The light breeze was in my face as I moved along the outside edge of the hedge of willows growing parallel to the river. There was clean sand underfoot, granting me a silent approach.

At 30 yards, I could see the bull, standing with his back to me, but willows still obscured a clear shot. The bull turned parallel to the willow hedge and began walking away from me. It was my chance. I would get ahead of him on the opposite side of the hedge, find a hole and wait for him to pass. I was in mid-step when I glanced through the willows and saw two huge eyes pinned on me at a mere 15 yards. I held statue-still while mentally kicking myself for misjudging his position. He was trying to get my scent, but the gentle breeze was in my favor.

After a 15-second stare-down, he turned away from me and began trotting farther down the gravel bar. Before I could gather my wits, he was 50 yards away and gaining speed. Instinctively, I grunted like a bull moose. With a crash, the bull plowed through the hedge of willows and stopped broadside to me with not so much as a blade of grass between us. I knew opportunity when it knocked. I locked the 50-yard pin behind the bull's shoulder and set an arrow free. The fluorescent red vanes sunk out of sight into the coal-black hair behind his shoulder. The bull immediately bolted for the river approximately 80 yards distant. Since I realized that he was going to cross, I dashed after him, hoping for another shot. He showed no sign of weakening until he hit the river's edge. As soon as his feet hit the water, he seemed to realize how sick he was. His legs began to wobble, and he knew that he couldn't make the swim. He stopped and looked back to see me closing in on him. In a valiant effort, he turned to face me and swung his huge head in a threatening manner. I stood my ground and waited. As he continued to weaken, he made a quarter turn back toward the river. I placed a second arrow low behind his last rib. As the arrow found his heart, the bull collapsed and died in the ankle-deep water of the Hess River.

Dave's whoop echoed down the river and broke my trance. The reality of my good fortune flooded through me as he grabbed my hand and congratulated me. It took a few seconds to shift mental gears from the intensity of the hunt to the appreciation of the tremendous trophy that lay before me. Many years ago, I had committed myself to bowhunting for a true trophy-class Alaska/Yukon moose. Now that dream was fulfilled. The experience was mind-boggling. Two huge bulls in less than a mile! My bull was 55 inches wide with 14 points on the right side and 12 on the left. Pan length on the right side was 43 inches; 40 inches on the left. Both pans were 14 inches wide. His green Pope and Young score was 186 3/8, which ranked him at No. 69 for Alaska/Yukon moose in the P&Y records at that time. After examining his antlers and teeth, we figured he was past his prime, an older bull of perhaps 10 or 12 years. He was definitely smaller than the bull that gave me the slip earlier that morning, but then that's hunting. What would the future hold if the big one didn't get away sometimes?

I returned to base camp at Earn Lake the following morning. My 11-year-old son, Darren, was waiting for me. He had been occupying his time catching grayling and listening to the wild tales of the other guides and hunters. The small Float plane that transported Dave, the inflatable boat and me wasn't big enough to include him. Now, however, with my moose behind me, we could just hang out together, do some fishing and just enjoy life. One afternoon, we took a Zodiak and went touring around Earn Lake. We spotted a young bull bedded on the lakeshore and, just for fun, paddled in to see how close we could get to him. We were less than 35 yards from the 40-inch bull when he finally stood up and glared at us. "Boy . . . I wish I was old enough to have a license," Darren whispered. After a long silent staring contest, the bull turned and walked into the timber.

An hour later, as we were passing a little willow-covered point that jutted out into the lake, we heard the unmistakable hollow grunting sound of a rutting bull moose. We killed the motor and listened. The bull grunted again. I answered him with a mournful cow call and immediately we heard timber cracking. "Here he comes," I whispered. Next we saw the huge white pans of his rack floating above the stunted tamaracks, and then he stepped out of the timber and faced us. There was only 50 yards between us.

I grunted at him, as one bull would challenge another. As soon as he heard my challenge, he marched defiantly to the lake's edge, now only 30 yards distant. He stood there, larger than life, swinging his head to and fro, grunting and slobbering like some deranged behemoth. I grunted at him again and this time he stepped up his routine. We were close enough to see the whites of his big eyes as he drove his massive head into a large willow bush and ripped it out of the ground. Finally, he stood there staring directly at us in our puny little rubber boat, with the entire willow dangling in his rack, as if to say: "Do you want to be next?" With that, we paddled farther out in the lake away from shore. He was a grand spectacle, at least 60 inches wide, maybe more, and a far better bull than I had taken on the Hess River the previous day.

We told the story of the huge bull back at camp. But, as fate would have it, all the hunters with moose licenses were tagged out. Well, almost all of them. Joni McKinnen, our cook, had a resident moose license. What's more, she was a bowhunter! She had her bow with her at camp, so we immediately went about getting her tackle in order for the challenge at hand. She had a mismatch of shafts and broadheads in her quiver, but we sorted them out and I screwed on my extra broadheads so that all her arrows would match. She took a few practice shots and all was ready. The next morning, we'd see if we could find that same bull again.

An hour or so after breakfast, we stopped the Zodiak off the same point where Darren and I had seen the bull the previous day. I made a bull call and got an immediate answer. "He's still here!" I announced to Joni. "Better get an arrow on your string." I called again and, this time, got two answers from two different bulls. This complicated matters. I figured that the rutting bulls were either fighting or they were herding a hot cow. In either case, it would be unrealistic to expect a bull call to draw them out of the timber. I decided to try a cow call to see if I could separate them. Just as my long whining cow call was trailing off, I heard timber snap about 60 yards down the shoreline. "Here he comes . . . Better get ready!" I whispered to Joni. She was in the front end of the Zodiak, I was in the back, and Darren was sitting on the right rear pontoon.

To our surprise, instead of a bull, a cow and calf came trotting out of the timber and right into the lake. When I saw them, I knew we were in business. "Okay Joni, the bull will be right behind that cow." No sooner had I uttered those words than we saw the same wide, white pans of the huge bull's rack emerging from the timber. It was the same bull. He followed the cow and calf out into the lake a few yards and then turned toward the boat, facing us. I grunted as belligerently as I could, and he started marching to us. The water was no more than six or eight inches deep, and the bottom was solid rock, so the bull literally towered above us feeble humans hunkered in our rubber boat. He came with a determined stride, grunting every time his front feet hit bottom. It appeared that he was coming to do some serious business with this black, inflated creature floating in the shallows of his domain. The bull was now 30 yards out and still coming, and things were getting tense. Joni glanced back over her shoulder at me with eyes that silently asked: "What the heck are we going to do?"

"Twenty-five yards," I announced. She turned back to face the oncoming bull. At a distance of 20 yards, he turned broadside and stopped dead still. Never in my hunting career had I ever witnessed a moose giving a hunter this kind of reception. It was a bowhunter's dream.

Joni, still rattled by the bull's ominous march, let her first arrow fly and somehow managed to shoot over the bull's back, completely missing her barn door-sized target. Her arrow plunked helplessly into the lake on the far side of the bull. "Shoot again!" I whispered, hoping the bull would be patient with us. Joni was visibly shaken as she fumbled to nock another arrow. I glanced back at Darren to see how he was holding up. What I saw almost made me laugh out loud. He had taken his red wool stocking cap off his head and stuffed it into his mouth to muffle the scream of tension that wanted so desperately to escape from his young lungs. I smiled at him and put a finger to my lips to remind him of the importance of our silence. He nodded. Meanwhile, Joni got another arrow on the string and took aim. I knew she was rattled, and didn't blame her for taking some extra time in aiming, but we were running out of time. Finally I noticed her shaking unnaturally. A closer look revealed the root of her problem. Somehow, she had managed to hang her broadhead up on one of her sight pins. She was hung up and couldn't get loose. I felt a sinking sensation inside, realizing that Schwartz's Law was again at work. Surely Schwartz wasn't going to rob us of this incredible opportunity.

Finally, with a desperate surge of strength, Joni pulled the broadhead free from her sight pins and tried to line up again on the amazingly cooperative beast. With muscles exhausted from holding at full-draw for so long, she released arrow No. 2 and hit the bull too far back, probably in a kidney. When the arrow struck, the bull whirled away and took off running back down the lakeshore in the direction from which he had come. On a lark, I splashed a canoe paddle in the water loudly and grunted at the bull with my most convincing challenge call, trying my best to sound like another bull in the lake. To our amazement, the bull skidded to a stop and turned, still in six inches of water, and started back toward us once more. Again he came stomping and grunting directly at our little rubber boat. This time I was concerned that he might not conduct himself so gentlemanly. Joni was vibrating by now, wondering if she was going to have to go hand-to-hoof with the huge beast. She nocked another arrow and, at about 20 yards, the bull turned his other broadside to us and stopped just as he had previously done. I couldn't believe my eyes. There, at no more than 20 yards, without so much as a twig between us, was a vital zone the size of a garbage can lid begging for an arrow. Joni's nerves were obviously as strained as her muscles by this time and her third arrow flew so wide that I thought she'd missed the bull completely. But instead, it struck the huge animal in the hock of his left rear leg, just above the knee. The bull never even flinched, but rather chose to stand there like a coal-black statue, glaring at us with eyes that looked like bloodshot, hard-boiled eggs. The broadhead cut the big femoral artery, and every time the beast's heart beat, a stream of blood shot three feet out into the lake.

"Keep shooting, Joni," I coached, now praying that the bull wouldn't decide to stomp us into the rocky lake bottom. A feeble attempt sent arrow No. 4 to never-never-land. Joni was finished. Now it was all up to the bull. After a spellbinding wait that probably lasted a minute, the bull swung his huge head around toward the shore, as if looking for somewhere else to go. He finally staggered to the bank and dropped on the only high ground on the point. It was over, much to the relief of all concerned. I have been either the hunter or the guide during some incredible experiences in my life, but none that could rival the episode with that huge Yukon bull. His rack was over 60 inches wide—a considerably nicer bull than my own.

FOUR

A British Columbia Bowhunting Odyssey

*F*light delays out of Vancouver put my hunting partner, Michael Lynn of Perry, Fla., and me several hours late arriving at Fort St. John, British Columbia, on the east side of the Canadian Rockies, near the Alberta border. Sharon Jackson of Horseshoe Creek Outfitters was there to meet us and drove us the remaining 90 miles to our base camp. Michael and I were licensed for black bear, whitetail, mule deer and elk. The two other bowhunters in camp, Pete Meeuwsen and Van Stanley, "Cheese Heads" (I use the term affectionately) from Wisconsin, were looking for trophy mule deer, moose and black bears. They were great company, as long as Van didn't get to sleep ahead of us. His snoring could rip the stitching out of the sturdiest wall tent ever made.

Our outfitter, Ray Jackson, announced that bacon and sausage were suddenly off the menu, thanks to a marauding bear that raided his camp earlier that day while everyone was out hunting. In addition to 10 pounds of bacon and 10 pounds of sausage, the bear had also polished off a whole case of apples. Then, after his free lunch, he left his calling card on the ground right in front of our tent. Who says bears have no sense of humor?

Thanks to our late arrival, the first night was a short one. We had a cup of coffee and headed for the sleeping tent. Four o'clock in the morning came too soon. While Pete and Van were ready to go hunting, Michael and I were still unorganized. I hadn't even screwed a broadhead on an arrow, much less shot my bow to check my sights, so I decided not to hunt that first morning. I would stay in camp and get organized.

Pete and Van left camp in the dark with guides Bret "Mac" Thorpe and Chris Franke. Bret's nickname is an abbreviation for "macaroni," which, when mixed with cheese, is the only dish we're sure he knew how to make. It seemed somehow appropriate that a guide named after macaroni should be paired with two "Cheese Heads." Macaroni and "Cheese Heads" . . . get it? A match made in Heaven.

The camp came to life well before dawn as hunters and guides scurried around preparing for the day's hunt. Michael and Ray were going to see if they could locate a black bear worthy of an arrow. After breakfast, they were gone.

As darkness gave way to dawn, I sat by the campfire and sipped coffee from a tin cup, soaking up the wonderful solitude of the Peace River Valley. It was good to be back in western Canada. The sunrise was breathtaking. Greater Canada geese lifted off the Peace River only a hundred yards below our camp and barely cleared the aspens as they passed overhead, cackling and honking. It was a beautiful sight against a cloudless, new September sky. No sooner had they disappeared than I heard the shrill squeal of a bull elk bugling on the other side of the river. A scratching sound caught my attention, coming from the roof of the old dilapidated log cabin only 10 yards behind me. I turned to see a Boone and Crockett-class pack rat sitting up on the roof, looking down at me suspiciously. I had never seen a pack rat of that magnitude. He had jaws like a pit bull, and I remember thinking a rat that size could make off with your saddle. After we stared at each other for a minute or two, he disappeared through a hole in the roof, back into the sanctuary of his own private log cabin. How great it was to be out of the city, back in the splendor of the wilds. I was lost in the marvel of it all – still only halfway through my first cup of coffee. I looked around camp, now seeing it in the daylight for the first time. The aspen leaves were turning gold and fluttering in the cool of the morning breeze. The fresh smell of spruce and pine filled the air. Fireweed and Indian Paint Brush bloomed scarlet in marked contrast to the deep green of the wild grasses, yet untouched by the season's first frost.

My bow was lying on a wooden bench beside me, along with arrows and broadheads, which I planned to assemble when there was enough light. I happened to glance toward the kitchen area to see if the burner was still lit under the coffeepot. A tarp was stretched over a ridgepole to keep things out of the rain, but otherwise the kitchen was an open-air arrangement. When I looked at the little Coleman camp stove, something caught my eye that looked out of place. In fact, there were two somethings that looked out of place—two furry ears poking up behind the stove.

How quietly the bear had appeared, never making a sound. He was back to finish off the grub that he had discovered the day before, and it was obvious that he wasn't expecting company. I sat stone still to see what he would do next. After waiting for a couple of minutes, he turned and walked back to the corner of our sleeping tent about 10 steps away, plainly casing the joint. When he turned his back on me, I slipped an arrow on my string and dropped to my knees to stay out of sight. Soon he was back behind the stove. One more step and I'd have a clear shot at about eight yards. As I considered the angle of the shot, I realized that my arrow, which would surely pass through the bear, would then go right through Jackson's brand new snow-white sleeping tent. The medium-sized, light brown bear turned and walked back to the corner of the tent for one last look. As he did, I shifted to my left. When he turned back toward the kitchen area, he was facing me and I was already at full draw. I centered my top pin on the white patch on the center of his chest and, with a thump, accomplished two things: I filled my bear tag and stopped the grocery thief in his tracks.

As I suspected, the arrow zipped through the bear, entering his chest and exiting through his backside. He snarled as the arrow bit him, whirled around and dove off the little bluff toward the river. His legs melted under him and he piled up a mere 40 yards from where I shot him. He moaned a couple of times and gave up the ghost. How ironic! Jackson and Michael were out looking for a bear. I was there minding my own business, and the bear came to me. I chuckled at the circumstances and went back to have that second cup of coffee. As I sat there by the fire, thinking about the bear, my warped sense of humor kicked in and a plan was born. When I finished my coffee, I took a rope down to the bear and tied one end in a loop around my hips and the other around the bear. By walking backward slowly and digging in my heels, I could drag the bear a few feet up the bluff at a time. Fifteen minutes later, I had him lying beside the campfire. Then I hoisted him up in one of the old wooden chairs right beside the one I'd been sitting in when he arrived. I propped one hind foot up on a firewood stump and one front paw on an axe handle. I put my bowhunting cap on his head, fashioned a cigarette out of a piece of rolled up paper and stuck it in the corner of his mouth for effect. To top it all off, I put a tin cup of coffee beside his other front paw. He looked perfectly at home and very relaxed. When Jackson and Michael came rolling in about 11 a.m., they found the bear and me sitting side-by-side having coffee. They got pretty excited about the whole thing. Michael couldn't believe his eyes. "I'm out looking for a bear and you sit here in camp and shoot one while you're having coffee!" he exclaimed.

"Precisely," I replied.

"Good," Jackson growled. "That'll be the end of our bacon shortage."

My hunt had started with a bang—or should I say, "twang." I had my first critter only halfway through my first cup of coffee, only minutes after dawn.

That evening, Van arrowed an excellent black bear that was considerably larger than mine. He reported seeing no less than 19 bears. It was a great first day.

For the next couple of days, Michael and I hunted two huge mule deer bucks that Ray had been monitoring for nearly the entire month of August. But, as fate would have it, when Michael and I showed up, the bucks didn't. They seemed to have vanished. We saw many other bucks we could have taken, including some very respectable 4x4s, but we knew they were young bucks destined for greater things, so we let them walk.

One morning Ray suggested we go for an exploratory walk (which we now fondly refer to as a "Jackson death-march") through the forest to the backside of an oat field to see if the bears were in the oats. After the 40-minute hike, we broke out of the timber and instantly saw several cow elk in the cool morning haze. Their breath rose above them like a cloud. What a sight it made!

The elk were heading toward the far end of the mile-long oat field. When we turned our attention to the field, we were astounded to see a huge cloud of steam rising from the southwest corner. The white cloud rising above the oats appeared as if the whole end of the field was on fire. Suddenly, the matriarch cow elk lifted her head above the shoulder-high oats and we realized the corner of the field was packed with elk! Eventually they saw us and stampeded into the timber, barking as they went. It was a rare and incredible sight that shall forever remain vivid in my memory.

In addition to the elk, the bears were also feeding heavily in the oats. As we walked single file along the bear trail, beaten deep into the soft earth where the timber met the oat field, I noticed an unusually large aspen tree riddled with claw marks. It was obvious that many bears had been climbing it. I nudged Michael and whispered, "There's the perfect tree for your treestand. Looks like the bears will climb right up for a visit."

Michael studied the tree for a contemplative moment and then nearly jumped out from under his hat. "There's a bear!" he hissed, pointing higher up the tree.

Sure enough, sprawled in a large forked limb was a black bear, sound asleep. We watched him through binoculars, trying to decide if he was a taker or not. Since we couldn't see his head, we decided to wake him up. Jackson and Michael stood ready, and I eased in and slapped the tree trunk with the back of an ax. The bear sat up and looked around at the world with a sleepy, comical daze. We decided he was a bit on the small side, so we left him in the tree and continued our morning of scouting.

About midday, we found a hay meadow about a half-mile long and a quarter-mile wide, tucked back in the timber. One thing was immediately obvious: The elk had been spending lots of time there. As we walked the perimeter of the meadow, we realized that there was not a square foot of earth without an elk track in it. In most places, there were tracks on top of tracks. There were also plenty of moose and deer tracks. Networks of trails cut through the forest, entering the meadow every few yards. While we were speculating about which trail to hang a stand over, a cow and calf elk walked out of the timber on the opposite side of the meadow and began to feed. We backed out of the area quietly so we wouldn't spook them and came back the next day at midmorning with a portable tree-stand. The trail on which the elk had emerged earlier was red hot and obviously being used by a number of animals. The trail made a "Y" split about 50 yards back in the timber, forming two emerging trails entering the meadow about 30 yards apart on either side of a large cottonwood tree. Beneath the tree, the ground was literally peppered with elk tracks upon more elk tracks. The choice was clear. I hung the stand 30 feet up in the cottonwood and was back promptly at 4:30 that afternoon to man my first shift.

At precisely 5:30, a 5x5 bull entered the meadow about 300 yards west of me, leading four cows out to a hidden water hole in the center of the meadow. It was a regal sight. They drank, the cows fed for a few minutes, then the bull bugled and herded them back into the timber. I sighed, realizing I was probably on the wrong trail after all. But it was still early, and, if nothing else, I had seen a shootable bull elk. That alone was worth the price of admission.

An hour passed and several mule deer does and yearlings entered the meadow and began to feed. About 6:30, I heard something moving in the timber behind me and to my right. It sounded like a large animal, too big to be a deer. A few minutes passed and then the shrill bugle of a bull elk rocked me in my tree-stand. He was coming quickly now. I turned my head slowly to look and a fat bull with twin two-foot long spikes stepped into view. My heart sank. He wasn't legal. I wouldn't have shot him if he were. He passed me at 20 yards en route to the meadow where he began feeding.

I mentally rehashed my choice of stand locations and wished I'd been farther west. Then I heard another crunch in the timber, this time behind me and to my left. Now the spike bull was watching the timber intently. In seconds, a cow elk poked her nose out right under my left hand. Satisfied that all was well, she stepped out and began feeding right under my stand. One by one, three more cows emerged and fed under me. I could have dropped a rock on any of them.

Now the air was super-charged with anticipation. The spike bull was keeping his distance from the cows, so I was suspicious that there was another, larger bull nearby. Another crunch in the timber turned my head just in time to see a big, muscular 5x5 bull step out of the timber 35 yards to my left. As soon as he cleared the trees, he tipped his nose up and bugled. My hair stood on end, and my heart rate tripled. He was standing there, quartering toward his cows and me. I couldn't risk moving a muscle yet. He would have to come farther out into the meadow before I could shoot anyway because of a cottonwood limb that blocked the shot.

Then, the unthinkable happened. He turned and began walking straight away from me along the edge of the timber. I couldn't believe it. So close, and now he was leaving! At about 50 yards, he stopped and looked back over his shoulder at the cows. "C'mon baby," I whispered under my breath. "Come on back."

As if he heard me, he turned obediently and started walking back toward the cows. As soon as he cleared the ill-placed cottonwood limb, I drew and held on him until he stopped perfectly broadside. I wasn't sure of the distance, but when my sight pin felt right, I touched the trigger on my release and watched my arrow make a shallow arc in the golden afternoon sun. My green fletchings dissolved into the dark auburn hair behind the bull's right shoulder. Upon impact, he lurched forward and stopped. The cows raised their heads momentarily to see what made him jump, then resumed feeding. I knew it was a perfect heart shot. It all seemed too good to be true. The bull turned west and plodded slowly in a half circle for a short distance and bedded down. His head began to droop until his chin rested on the ground. He rolled over on his side and kicked up a huge dust cloud. He was finished. When I climbed down from my stand, I could see more than 25 elk in the meadow. I paced off the distance to where the bull had been standing when I took my shot. It was 63 yards.

In retrospect, it was quite an amazing episode. Though not my first elk with a bow, it was different to be resting in a treestand instead of puffing up mountainsides where the air is skinny. This was relatively flat land at an elevation of a mere 3,500 feet. All things considered, it was a pretty gentlemanly elk hunt. When we delivered the carcass to the butcher, minus guts, head, hide, lower legs and backstraps, he still weighed over 500 pounds. Elk dress 60/40 according to the butcher, making this an honest 900-pound bull!

I should mention that a large percentage of Jackson's hunting territory is private land, and he has hunting access to several huge game-rich ranches on which we were privileged to hunt.

Back at camp, I learned that Van had scored again—this time on a bull moose. During the process of packing the moose out, a possessive black bear showed up and challenged the hunting party for the rights to one of the moose quarters. It added a memorable twist to the moose hunt and cost the daring bear his life. The hunt was only half over, and our party of four already had three black bears, a bull elk and a bull moose! As they say in Canada: "Not bad, eh?"

By now, Michael had committed himself to a big bear he'd seen in the oats. It was a case of musical bear trails. No matter which trail he covered, the bear he wanted would come out on a different trail, just out of bow range. Though he had bears under him each day, which he could have taken, he was still holding out for the big brown one that kept taunting him.

At lunchtime on the last day of the hunt, Van, Pete and Bret came in from a morning of hunting mule deer on the river breaks. As they discussed their morning, Bret mentioned to Ray that he had watched three large mule deer bucks bed down in the middle of an open field in a small patch of buck brush, seemingly impossible to approach. Ray ordered Michael and me to grab our bows and we were off to investigate. As we approached the little patch of brush, we spotted a high-tined 3x3 buck in velvet, beating his antlers against a small bush, obviously attempting to shed his velvet. The buck was so preoccupied with the task at hand, Michael was able to sneak to within 20 yards. He couldn't get a shot, however, because of one ill-positioned bush. At that moment, an unseen bedded 4x4 buck exploded out of the brush, and the 3x3 followed him on the run. They crossed the grassy field and entered the thick aspen timber above a creek bed. Ray hurried us down into the creek bottom to try to intercept them. To our utter amazement, both bucks skylined themselves simultaneously on the ridge above us and stood there wondering what to do next. They realized that we had cut them off. They must have felt safe in the cover of the thick aspens because they just stood there like statues. I found a hole to shoot through and watched my arrow find its mark behind the tall 3x3 buck's left shoulder. Before I could even speak, I heard Michael announce a perfect hit on his buck. Both bucks piled up within 30 yards of each other, and Michael and I stood flabbergasted at our good fortune. The crew back at camp was also shocked when we returned with two bucks taken right in the middle of the day.

That evening, Michael didn't see the big brown bear with which he'd been playing peekaboo, but he did arrow a beautiful six-foot black bear right under his treestand. From beginning to end, it had been an incredible hunt, perhaps the most rewarding and exciting bowhunt of my experience for a mixed bag of antlered game and black bears. Michael and I were already planning our return visit before we were halfway through the hunt. Ray and Sharon Jackson and their crew deserve top marks for effort, attitude, expertise and a hunting area teeming with game. And to The One, who arranged 10 days of glorious, cloud-free weather, I am truly grateful. Rarely does a hunt measure up to all that one anticipates beforehand. In this case, we couldn't have dreamed of better.

FIVE

Caribou of the Central Canadian Barren Grounds

*T*he Twin Otter on floats soared above the barren landscape on the one-hour flight from Yellowknife, the capitol of the Northwest Territories, to our hunting outpost at Warburton Bay. The dull gray granite was sprinkled with pale yellow caribou moss and lichens of red and brown. Clumps of stunted balsam struggled out of the rocky ground and seldom stood as tall as a man.

The intimidating expanse below us appeared devoid of life. Water was scattered across granite in thousands of small ponds and lakes, and everywhere we looked were the narrow trails made by meandering caribou.

The central barren ground caribou is a relatively small animal, at least in proportion to his antlers. A mature bull weighs less than 300 pounds on the hoof, something like a mature western Canadian white-tailed buck. But the caribou are built altogether different. Unlike deer, which are slab-sided critters, the caribou are stocky, spindly-legged, pot-bellied creatures with large rounded, cloven hooves that click and clatter on the granite when they walk. Their hair is hollow, which helps keep them floating high as they swim across bodies of water along their migration route. They seem to be as at home in the water as they are on land, and they are tremendous swimmers.

I strained my eyes, trying to spot a caribou, but I saw nothing but granite and tundra that extended all the way to the Arctic Ocean.

The Twin Otter finally swung down, lit on the water and taxied up to the dock in front of the tiny outpost camp. Warburton Bay is a remote arm of water connected to MacKay Lake, a 100-mile-long, sprawling body of water lavished among granite ridges and outcroppings, forming the barren grounds of central Canada. This is the range of the central barren ground caribou, the most recent member of the caribou family to be granted specific category status by both the Boone and Crockett and Pope and Young clubs.

Hunting laws in the NWT forbid hunting on the same day you fly so, without hesitation, I commandeered a boat and a guide and spent my first afternoon fishing for the ever-willing lake trout of Warburton Bay.

There's nothing quite like seeing the tundra's Arctic birch framed in flaming crimson, set against an azure-blue September sky. It makes a person pinch himself to be sure it's not a dream. An awesome sense of gratitude wells up inside one's heart for the opportunity to breathe the pure air of this pristine world.

I was the guest of the late Benton & Brown Firearms Inc. The object of the exercise was to put the then new Benton & Brown rifles to the test while hunting caribou. It was indeed a nasty job, but someone had to do it. When the invitation came at the 1994 SHOT show in Dallas, Texas, I considered it for about 2.5 seconds before accepting. My lightweight B&B rifle was chambered for .300 Weatherby Magnum and topped with a Leupold 3x9 scope. It shot like a dream.

On our first morning, Mike Benton and I paired up as hunting partners. Our native guide, Bobby Migwi, navigated the 16-foot aluminum boat along the lee side of islands and shorelines through waters that had suddenly forgotten the calm of the previous day. After a jarring, hour-long boat ride, which was definitely not for the faint of heart, we pulled up on shore below a towering granite rise. Part of a dock and the remains of an old wooden tent frame stood near the shore as a monument to previous hunts. We followed Bobby uphill to where we could survey miles of surrounding tundra with binoculars and spotting scopes.

Bobby spotted a group of bulls three-quarters of a mile distant. Mike won the coin toss for the first shot, so he and Bobby took off on foot and were soon swallowed up by the creases in the rocky landscape. The caribou they were after kept moving as only caribou can, and the hunters never caught up with them.

Meanwhile, I had spotted several bulls, perhaps some of the same ones they were originally stalking. While we were still discussing their stalk, Bobby spotted an excellent bull heading our direction and motioned for me to take cover and prepare for a shot. I was too slow, still scrambling for the cover of a large boulder, when the bull topped a rise and spotted me. As quickly as he appeared, he was gone.

Minutes later, I spotted a group of bulls about 2½ miles distant. Through the spotting scope at 40x, it appeared that one of them was exceptional. His overall rack appeared to be wide with good tops. Mike and Bobby looked at him through the spotting scope and agreed he was worth pursuing.

The bulls were feeding in a grassy depression on the far side of a small bay. It was apparent that we could close the gap faster by boat than on foot, so we scampered back to the boat, ate a quick lunch and crossed the bay, closing the distance to about a mile. When we found the bulls again, they were feeding their way along the opposite side of a long ridge, which would soon hide them from our sight. That was to our advantage, since the ridge would give us the cover we needed to make our move.

The ridge was about a half-mile long, perhaps a bit longer. We wanted to move to the far end as fast as we could in hopes of intercepting the bulls as they fed. We gave it our best, all but running the whole distance. But, as we learned again and again, caribou cover more ground at a casual walk than a man can cover on the run. By the time we topped the far end of the ridge, we spotted the bull I wanted. He was already several hundred yards past us on a little rim at the end of a small lake out in the middle of nowhere, feeding with another bull. There was no more cover and no way to get any closer without being seen by keen caribou eyes.

It was not my first encounter with open-range game. I had hunted mountain sheep in North America and Mongolia, as well as prairie antelope and prairie whitetails. Years ago, I had made a study of using my crosshairs as a range-finder. It's a dandy means of knowing just how far away an animal is when there are no landmarks or relative objects in view. In anticipation of this kind of situation, I had mounted a short bipod on the forend of my rifle. I crawled over to a large flat rock, flipped the bipod legs down and snuggled in behind the rifle. After studying the range, I felt confident that I could make the shot. Holding two feet above his shoulder, I squeezed the trigger. The report of the Weatherby sounded impotent in the vast emptiness of the tundra. The bull staggered at the shot, took a couple of steps forward, then backward before toppling. The 150-grain bullet had centered the bull's lungs.

After we took photographs, Bobby performed a field-butchering session the likes of which I had never seen. With a long-bladed, Old Hickory butcher knife, he took the bull apart with surgical precision. In the traditional manner of his ancestors, he made a large carrying pouch of the caribou hide and placed every ounce of edible meat within it, drew it up and cinched it closed to protect the meat from getting dirty. Then he slung it over his back and held it in place with a strap around his forehead and carried the unbelievable load back to the boat. I was astounded. All I had to carry was the caribou head and my rifle, and I was dog-tired when we were finished. I tip my hat to one tough guide!

The next day was stormy. Rain mixed with sleet rode a relentless north wind and made hunting conditions miserable, to say nothing of the hazards of navigating a small boat through crushing whitecaps. It appeared that fall was making way for serious wintertime in the north. Perilous waters limited our travel and it looked like we might spend the day in camp. If there was one place we didn't want to be, it was in the icy waters of Warburton Bay where, if we didn't drown outright, we'd last about five minutes before hypothermia finished us.

Bobby managed to find the lee side of a long island that offered us enough shelter to travel in relative safety. As we motored along cautiously, Mike spotted a great bull feeding right above us at less than 100 yards. The roar of the wind somehow kept the caribou from noticing the sound of the motor, even though we were close. Bobby swung the boat around and headed downwind in search of a sheltered cove where we could tie up the boat away from pounding waves and granite boulders. It was tricky business, but we finally found the spot. We pulled the boat almost completely out of the water and tied it to a stunted, weather-gnarled spruce tree.

The wind was in our faces as we worked our way back toward the caribou, nearly a half-mile distant. It was 30 minutes before Mike and Bobby peeped over the outcropping above the caribou, which was feeding in a small stand of stunted spruce trees.

"Is he a good bull?" Mike whispered.

"Not bad for your first bull," Bobby answered casually.

I'm no expert on caribou, but I had seen enough to convince me this bull would make B&C with plenty to spare. Mike made the 80-yard shot with ease. His .270 barked into the wind, and the bull dropped in his tracks. Scoring a whopping 378⅞ (the B&C minimum is 335), it was a tremendous trophy. Not bad at all for one's first bull!

The next day, Rob Dunham and I hunted together and Mike paired off with Robert Charles Brown. Rain mixed with sleet, still being pushed by a bitter north wind, continued to limit boat travel. After some intense navigation, however, we managed to land in a promising area. Early in the hunt, we spotted some good bulls and pursued them on foot as hard as we could go, but we never caught up with them. Again, I emphasize the unbelievable speed that caribou can travel. It's hard to imagine how they can disappear in a landscape so barren, but they do.

As we headed back to the boat, after walking an estimated 12 miles in freezing rain, we spotted two bulls. One of them was a keeper. We made our stalk to within 150 yards and, again, I searched out a flat rock on which to rest my bipod. The bull had a single shovel that eliminated his chances for the record book, but with the weather getting worse each day, I decided to take him while I had the chance. He had long tines on top and was a worthy trophy by any measure.

The ride back to camp was brutal as the waves threatened to swallow our little aluminum boat. Whitecaps crashed over the bow and drenched us with deadly ice-blue water. By the time we made it to the dock we were all running on fumes and desperate to get to our warm cabins. We grabbed our gear and ran for cover. The fire in the little wood-burning stove was Heaven-sent. It took me hours to get the chill out of my bones. It had been a challenging day. In addition to the caribou I shot, Robert Charles had bagged his first bull.

I went looking for my caribou head and rack the next morning, but no one seemed to know where it was. We finally determined that it had accidentally been left on the dock overnight. Since it was no longer there, we concluded that it had been carried off by a barren ground grizzly. After an hour of scanning the landscape with binoculars, I spotted antlers protruding from a pile of rocks across the narrows from camp. I took a boat and went to investigate. Sure enough, the grizzly had carried the head off and had eaten all but the top of the skull to which the antlers were attached. I pulled the antlers out of the rocks and took them back to camp. That night was clear and calm, and the moon was full. Just before going to bed, I looked out the front window of my cabin and saw the bear. He was quite big for a barren ground grizzly, probably a 400-pounder. I estimated him to be over seven feet in length. He was prowling around the dock, looking for more caribou meat. It was an awesome sight to see the great hump-backed bear there in the bright moonlight. He sniffed around for 15 more minutes, then swam across the narrows and disappeared into the night. We didn't see him again.

The following day, Mike Benton bagged his second bull and Rob Dunham shot a bull that scored in the 390s, near the top of the heap for central barren ground caribou. The world record stands at 433⅝.

Our hunt had produced six excellent bulls, three of which qualified for the Boone and Crockett record book.

There was yet a fifth member of our party, Dan Helgenberger, a dedicated Texas bowhunter who bagged a fine Pope and Young-class bull as well as a second that also qualified for the Boone and Crockett records. He also missed a shot at a wolverine, which disappointed him. Still, it was an incredible hunt. There is nothing quite like hunting in the barren grounds of the Canadian north. At first sight, its rather bleak landscape appears alien. But the longer you stay, the more it grows on you and the more you feel at home—at least until winter comes. Then it's time to leave it to the caribou.

SECTION II

Bears and Scares

SIX

Bears Along the Peace

Dave tested the depth of the water with an oar and slid over the gunnels of the 14-foot Jon boat. I followed, and we began towing the boat over the gravel bar in 10 inches of icy spring water. We picked a spot on the south bank where the river brakes rose vertically from the river. There was a sandbar there with a clump of willows to which we could tie the boat. After lunch, we would climb up the brakes and photograph the miniature cactus and wild onions growing mysteriously on the steep banks of the mighty Peace River in northern Alberta, Canada.

The bottom of the aluminum boat ground against the gravel bar when the water got shallow. I grabbed the rope and took my first step toward the sandbar when suddenly the willows parted 20 feet ahead of us, under the weight of a charging bear. It was coming at us at full throttle, as if shot from a cannon. There was no time to contemplate the next move. I dropped the rope and reflexively snatched the .30-06 from the top of the duffel bag and crammed a shell into the chamber as I turned to face the bear. As soon as the bolt snapped shut, I fired into the black thunderbolt as it closed the remaining inches between us. There was no time to get ready — just shoot, dodge and hope for the best. And hope we did! The bear rolled through the spot I was occupying only a second earlier and cartwheeled into the water. Dave was doing the St. Vitas dance along the sandbar, looking for a blade of grass to hide behind or climb. As the bear landed in a heap and groaned his last, the gravity of the situation settled into our shaken nerves. In the span of no more than three seconds, we had seen the bear for the first time, realized we were in the line of his charge, and responded with precisely zero seconds to spare.

The bear was dead and we were safe, but the boat was gone. By the time we had the bear episode under control, our boat was 50 yards downstream in deep water. It might as well have been 50 miles. The water on the Peace River in early May is a deathtrap. The ice packed along the bank was still 10 to 12 feet thick in most places, so we watched the little boat drift freely out of sight. And with it went our food, shelter, clothing, camera gear and our precious matches.

During the next two days, we walked from 4 a.m. until midnight through wilderness that had little love for men in trouble. Dave carried the rifle, and I carried the bear skin around my shoulders. It served as a blanket, our only protection from the freezing nighttime weather. We huddled together and wrapped it around us, fur side inward, and praised the hide of the same bear that created our predicament.

With trembling knees and swollen feet, we eventually found a farmhouse and an end to our ordeal. We were safe. Luckily, our boat had been spotted and picked up by bear hunters miles downstream. A boat on the drift with no occupants spells trouble, so the hunters towed the boat back to civilization and reported the incident to the Royal Canadian Mounted Police, who were organizing a search when we appeared and explained what had happened.

That was my first experience on the Peace River. Dave Reidie and I were combining a newspaper assignment about the Peace River with a spring bear hunt when we encountered the unexpected. Dave was the photo editor, and I was the outdoor columnist for the *Edmonton Journal* at the time. Two days earlier, Dave had collected a beautiful cinnamon-colored black bear, and I was holding out for a larger bear or an unusual color phase such as cinnamon or blonde. Naturally, I settled for the one that charged. In retrospect, I don't believe the bear was charging with intent to attack us. Although I can't prove his motive, I believe the bear waded down the gravel bar and into the willows and went to sleep. When our boat clanged against the gravel, I suspect that the bear woke with a start and tried to escape our uninvited company via the only route available—the gravel bar where we were standing. The bear had its back to the vertical, icy wall of the riverbank. My guess is that he was doing the only thing he could. The problem was that I had no opportunity to discuss the matter with him. Like the bear, I too did the only logical thing I could think of under the circumstances.

It wasn't until we were safely back in Edmonton, Alberta, nursing our swollen feet, that we realized just how amazing our week had been. Our unexpected interruption had broken things up a bit from our planned schedule, but it was an adventure just the same. We returned to the Peace River for several spring bear hunts after that incident and were always successful. While we never encountered another bear problem, we knew it could happen and maintained a healthy respect for every bear we saw. That first trip ended with the charging bear, and while that was a pretty hard act to follow, the events that preceded that untimely encounter are certainly worth mentioning to anyone who has ever hunted or considered hunting bears.

The Peace River drains down from its origin in north central British Columbia and crosses the border into Alberta at Cherry Point. It then continues northwest as it traverses through deep and rugged shoulders of poplar forest, which mixes occasionally with spruce and birch. The steep river brakes rise over 200 feet above the river in many places and creates an almost mountainous topography. Many rugged canyons wind their way down the valley to the river. The area harbors moose, mule deer, whitetails and a great number of black bears. The Peace River, between the British Columbia border and its confluence with the Slave River, is probably the best black bear country in the world. In the spring, after the snow melts away from the river brakes, the open knolls above the river give birth to tender spring grasses a full two weeks before any other part of the surrounding countryside.

During the first weeks after the bears emerge from hibernation, they feed exclusively on new grasses and fresh poplar buds. Since this essential diet is available first along the river brakes, there is a tremendous concentration of bears there during that period. After the rest of the country catches up with greenery of its own, the bears disperse. What this means to bear hunters during that period is the opportunity to see an unusual concentration of bears. Fifty percent of the bears in the area are black; the other 50 percent in color phases other than black, such as chocolate, blonde and cinnamon. They are all black bears, regardless of their color phase.

Reidie and I made our plans to float from the British Columbia border into Alberta about 160 miles to the famous Dunvegan Bridge near Fairview. We arranged for a driver to drop us off at Cherry Point and return our vehicle to Dunvegan, where we would finish the trip. It was the 4th of May when we slipped the Jon boat, filled with camping and hunting gear, into the icy river. We had a 10-horsepower motor in case we needed upstream power, but, for the most part, we just drifted downstream and guided our drift with oars. The Peace River moves along at about 10 miles per hour, which is faster than it seems. It's wide, flat and appears lazy. From the quiet drift, we could spot the bears on the brakes above us. We were still getting settled in the boat no more than a half-mile from our departure point when we saw the first bear. It was a medium-sized black that did not interest me because I had already taken a good black bear a few years earlier. It was, however, tempting Dave when it finally walked into the timber and made the decision for him. Sometimes bears can be seen for a mile or more from the river bottom and the hunter must be able to assess the position of the bear relative to the wind and surrounding timber and decide what his odds are of making a successful stalk.

In the remaining four hours of daylight that first day, we saw six more bears, all blacks and small. We passed them up and made our first camp on a sandy bank. The days were already growing long, and, by the time we finished supper, it was 11 p.m.

Early the following morning, we were on the river and drifting lazily in the thick morning light. We scanned the little green knolls among the poplar trees, which were showing a faint green haze as their buds began to open. A gangly cow moose stood at the river's edge and we drifted within 25 feet of her. She was a mournful sight as only a moose in the springtime can be. Her long winter coat looked like it had been stored in a moth-infested closet—bald spots intermingling with shaggy winter hair that clung in patches. A beautiful blonde bear strolled into an opening in the timber 400 yards above us. We glassed her only to discover three cubs at her side. Female bears with cubs are protected, so we continued scanning the brakes.

At 11 a.m., a big cinnamon bear peaked over a ledge as we passed beneath him. Dave and I spotted him simultaneously. The bear ambled into the timber and then onto a grass-covered slope, partially hidden by thick poplars. I swung the boat ashore 10 yards downstream and checked the wind. The bear was working his way along the hillside toward us and the wind was crossing his path from our general direction. We had to intercept the bear and make a shot before the wind betrayed us. Wind is both a blessing and a curse when hunting bears. If it's in your favor, you can get in close. But if it catches you upwind of a bear's keen nose, he will vanish like magic.

We agreed that it was Dave's bear as we clambered through the ruthless underbrush that tangles the river bottom. By the time we could see the bear, he was 50 yards to our left and 75 yards above us. Knowing that as soon as he was directly above us the wind would betray us, Dave leaned into a fallen poplar tree for steady aim and waited for the bear to come into view again. He ambled forward and stopped to chew the spring grass, then he moved nearer. When at last he was broadside and nearly directly above us, Dave found him in his scope. I was to offer back-up support if necessary, but I was unable to see the bear from my position. When Dave's .30-06 spoke, I stood up to see nothing but a cloud of dust rolling down the side of the slope where the bear had already vanished. I asked Dave how he felt about his shot. He thought it was good. Cautiously, we pushed our way to the base of the hillside where we had last seen the bear. The brush was so thick that we knew we would find the bear (dead or alive) at pointblank range. Fortunately, we found him dead in his tracks. Dave had made a perfect heart shot. It was a beautiful buff/cinnamon-colored bear with fur so thick that it stood straight upright. It was the 12th bear we had seen in less than 24 hours. While we were attending to the necessary skinning and caping chores, I noticed little green stems rising slightly above the grass around us. I pulled one out of the ground and realized that it was a wild onion. I took a small bite and was amazed at how hot it was. We picked a few for seasoning, and Dave made another discovery. Springing to his feet from his perch on the hillside, he promptly pulled a little prickly pear cactus pad from his posterior. Wild onions and miniature cactus! Who would have expected to find them growing that far north?

We saw many bears during the next two days. Some were small; some were unapproachable because of their positions; and some simply eluded our attempts to stalk them. By the end of the fourth day, we had seen no less than 49 bears, including a fair number of cubs. We had seen at least 10 good trophies and had collected one excellent bear.

By the end of day four, the bluebird weather began to turn cold. A drizzle and snow were threatening as the temperature dropped. With only an hour of daylight left, we were feeling the sting of the cold night air and not particularly enthusiastic about a night in the rain. We were looking hard for a suitable campsite when we entered a series of small islands where the river braided through a long sweeping bend. As we drifted around the tail of the last and largest island, there stood a log cabin that could not have chosen a more perfect time to appear. We both whooped with delight at the possibility of getting out of the weather. The little 10-horsepower motor struggled against the current in the tail wash of the island, but eventually we landed on the bank below the cabin. We secured the boat to a tree and raced up the bank to examine the livability of the cabin. It was perfect, and the front door was unlocked. Inside were bunks and a large wood-burning kitchen stove. On the porch was a pile of firewood. It seemed as if someone was expecting us. We lit the coal oil lamp and found a logbook on the table. The book explained that the cabin was the property of the River Rat Jet Boat Club from Fairview. They left the cabin available to all comers who might need it, and asked only that it be left as it was found. Pages of signatures proved that it had been used by many hunters throughout the years. It also contained many comments about the bears seen and harvested along the way. One signature claimed to have seen 50 bears in two days! By then we knew that was possible.

We moved into the luxury of the log walls and a real roof over our head and cooked our supper on the wood stove. It was a pleasant night. We slept like babies while the sleet and snow pelted the outside world.

We slept in until 10 a.m. and woke rested and ready to continue. After a leisurely breakfast, we packed up and left the comforts of the River Rat Cabin behind us. Our trip was more than half over, and we decided to start concentrating on the photo story we had agreed to do for our hometown newspaper. We were to record the events for an adventure/travel feature when we returned.

Soon into our journey, we spotted a sow and two cubs walking single file along the river's edge. Cameras out, we collected some wonderful photos before the old mother hustled her babies into the timber. I recalled the wild onions I had seen growing on the river brakes when Dave shot his bear. I thought the onions warranted a photo, and Dave reminded me of the miniature cactus, which he had found most accidentally with the seat of his pants.

We decided to look for a steep slope on the south bank where the sun would linger for our photo session—also a likely spot for the plants we wanted to photograph. A large canyon yawned in the distance. Upon closer observation, we could see a gravel bar below a steep canyon wall at the river's edge. The gravel bar was topped with a sandbar, and it looked like a perfect place for a lunch stop before we climbed up the brakes for the photos. "That's a perfect spot," I said. "There is even a clump of willows where we can tie the boat . . ."

SEVEN

The Three Bears

*I*f I've been lucky at anything in life, it's been bowhunting for big black bears. *For some reason, they come to me like iron filings to a magnet. In three consecutive hunts, I've bagged three record book black bears, including the British Columbia record. This is how it happened.*

MAY 1987: QUESNEL, BRITISH COLUMBIA, CANADA

Off to my right, at the edge of the ravine, I heard a twig snap. From my perch in the pine tree, 25 feet above the ground, I craned my neck in the direction of the sound. What I saw stunned me. It was the largest black bear I had ever seen. He was chocolate brown with a wide, yellow chevron emblazoned across his massive chest. This was not the bear I was expecting, but he would certainly fill the bill!

Shuffling along slowly, he stopped every few feet as if he were contemplating things. His massive head bobbed up and down like one of those toy dogs you see in the rear windows of cars. His lower jaw hung open in a silly looking grin. He was right on the trail leading from the ravine to the edge of the winter wheat field that passed within a few feet of my treestand. My heart was doing a tap dance in my chest as I watched the huge bruin inch his way toward me. If he stayed on the trail, he would walk a mere nine yards from my tree.

Still at a distance of approximately 25 yards, the bear did something totally unexpected. He flopped down on his belly like a big dog, facing the wheat field through the timber. He was within easy bow range except for one problem: There was a small pine tree between us and, naturally, it was blocking a clear shot at his vitals.

"So close and yet so far," I thought as I watched his huge form lying there below me.

Meanwhile, 100 yards away on the far side of the winter wheat field, nestled behind a large boulder and a small bushy pine tree, my guide, John Blackwell, and my camera crew, Bill Skok and Ray Jackson, were wondering what on earth was happening. We were there to try to film a bowhunt for black bears for a video project entitled "Bowhunting the Monarchs of the North." We had seen a medium-sized black bear feeding in the field the evening before, and now we were set up to film my taking of the bear if he returned. I had climbed into my stand at 5 p.m., and it was now 8:00. I was supposed to signal the camera crew if I saw a bear approaching so Bill could power up the video camera. I had waved to them as soon as the big chocolate bear rolled into my view. Now they were on red alert and wondering why they couldn't see the bear. I could see them hunkered in hiding, peeking out between the boulder and the tree, obviously wondering what was happening. I had no signal to describe what the bear was doing, so all I could do was point silently and hope they would understand.

Time dragged on and the bear just lay there studying the winter wheat field. I began to fidget internally, wondering if this bear was indeed going to come past me, or if he had just happened along and decided to stop here for a rest. What if he didn't follow the trail past my tree? Would this episode end in a coincidental peek at such a monster, with no opportunity for a shot? All these unanswered questions tormented me, but there was nothing I could do but wait for him to make his move.

The more I watched the massive bruin, the more impressed I became with his size. For years I had guided black bear hunters up on the Peace and Smoky Rivers in northern Alberta, and some of them bagged bears in excess of 400 pounds. But this animal was in a class of his own. I "guestimated" him at well over 500 pounds, perhaps as high as 600. Blackwell had told me that a friend of his reported seeing a huge, brown-colored black bear in that area. He said it was as large as a good-sized grizzly. But bear stories, as a rule, lean toward exaggeration, so Blackwell hadn't taken the story very seriously. There was no doubt in my mind that this had to be the same bear. At a glance, he could easily be mistaken for a grizzly!

Over half an hour passed and I spent my time watching both the patient bruin and my comrades across the field, waiting and wondering what was happening.

The wind was perfect, blowing in their faces. The bear, if he ever decided to cooperate, would never know of their presence. I kept pointing at the bear to assure them that it was not over yet. In the meantime, a rainstorm blew in and fell in torrents upon Blackwell and the camera crew. The old pine tree in which I was sitting acted as a natural umbrella, so I sat in relative comfort while the others bit the bullet and got soaked. I believed the bear was waiting for dark before he came out to feed. In British Columbia, daylight hangs on until 10:30 at night during the month of May.

My emotions ran the gamut while the wait continued. I would find myself beginning to shudder and shake uncontrollably, and it wasn't because it was cold. I'd literally have to talk myself back down to earth. I vacillated between relative calm and internal hysteria for what seemed like a lifetime, and finally the bear stood. My heart and my breath stopped in unison.

I glanced at my watch; it was 9:10 p.m. He just stood there at first, lower jaws still agape and head bobbing. For all the world, it appeared as if he were trying to decide what to do next. I held my breath as I waited for his decision. Finally, he turned toward me, grunted and began walking toward the field. In seconds, he was right beneath my stand, but there was one misplaced branch that prevented me from taking a shot. The bear stopped and again seemed to be considering matters. I glanced nervously over my shoulder at the crew and I could see Bill's face glued to the camera. I knew he was already filming.

"He must be wondering what I'm waiting for," I thought as I looked back at the giant bear. After an agonizing wait of probably no more than a minute, the bear took another calculated step forward and began sniffing the ground where I had walked to my stand. I knew he was on to the fact that a man had been there. I had an arrow on the string and waited in electrifying suspense for his next move.

After a long examination of my tracks, he swung his huge head away from me and stood still, offering me a broadside view of his ribs. I had been waiting for that. I quickly drew and placed the top pin in the center of his ribs, behind his left shoulder, and let the bow string slip through my fingers.

The bear bellowed and instantly bolted sideways at the sting of the arrow. The shot was perfect, as well it should have been at a mere nine paces! The broadhead penetrated his left lung and passed through his heart as it angled downward. The big bear made a sudden dash into the winter wheat field and then looped back toward the timber from which he came. His legs were buckling as he hit the tree line, and he piled up about 20 yards from my tree, not more than five or six seconds from the time the arrow found its mark.

I sat there, stunned that it was all over and that the huge bear was now mine. Blackwell and the camera crew arrived just as my feet hit the ground. We stood in silent awe over the bear, each man knowing that this was no run-of-the-mill black bear. I was congratulated for being the luckiest bowhunter in British Columbia, a fact that I could not deny. But that's the way hunting goes. So often the greatest trophies are simply gifts and have no bearing on the hunter's ingenuity.

The four of us did our best to lift the bear into the back of my truck, but we couldn't even get his head as high as the tailgate. He was indeed an awesome creature. His hide was as prime as could be, without so much as a single rub. It had been unusually warm in the Quesnel area, and we were worried that the bears might be rubbing early as a result. But not this one; he was perfect. After the skinning was done, we measured the hide. From nose to tail, he measured eight feet and seven inches. Across the back, from front claws to front claws, he measured an even eight feet. Blackwell, who is well known for the huge grizzlies he had produced for his hunters, estimated the live weight of the bear at 600-plus pounds. After the required 60-day drying period, the skull was officially measured at $20^{11}/_{16}$ inches, $2^{11}/_{16}$ above the minimum score for the Pope and Young Club (only $\frac{5}{16}$ of an inch short of the B&C minimum). According to the Big Game Records of British Columbia, my bear was the No. 1 bow-and-arrow kill in the province, surpassing Peter Halbig's $20^{5}/_{16}$ black bear taken on the Queen Charlotte Islands in 1960. It ranked No. 12 in the British Columbia book among all black bears, most of which were killed with firearms. Oddly enough, it is the only black bear on record in the B.C. book from the Quesnel area. According to the third edition of the Pope and Young records, my bruin tied four other black bears at the No. 69 position.

I must add one intriguing comment as a footnote. The same man who told John Blackwell about my huge chocolate-colored black bear also told him of a black-colored blackie in the same area, even larger than the one I killed. He was right about my bear, so no telling how big that other bear must have been. If he were appreciably larger than the one I killed, he must have been a true giant.

MAY 1997: ATHABASCA RIVER, ALBERTA, CANADA

For the next decade after killing my B.C. bow record, I considered myself retired from black bear hunting. It seemed ludicrous to expect to ever see another bear to rival the one I shot near Quesnel. Then, in May of 1997, I was invited to bowhunt black bears up on the Athabasca River, northwest of Wandering River, Alberta. I was intrigued by the offer since that was the exact area where I had begun my own outfitting career back in the early '70s. It would be interesting to go back and see if the country had changed. That, combined with the fact that it was my longtime friend, Ryck Visscher, who was inviting me, made it irresistible. So in mid-May of that year, I started the pilgrimage back to my old stomping grounds where I had begun my guiding career. Twenty-five years earlier, that country was full of moose, black bears and timber wolves, but that was about all that could survive the deep snowfalls that were typical of the area.

Once again, a video project emerged. I was backed by cameraman Gene Bidlespacher, who is no stranger to bears. He used to raise them back in his native Pennsylvania. Unlike my video effort of 10 years ago, Gene would be in the tree with me, looking right over my shoulder. There would be no misunderstood hand signals this time.

Ryck's tent camp was right at the river's edge in a little meadow. The country looked the same as it had all those many years ago when I was young and eager to discover the wonders of the great North Woods. The single greatest difference was the proliferation of whitetails along the river valley. They were everywhere. In the mid-1970s, a whitetail was as rare as hen's teeth in that country. It amazed me that they could survive the deep snow and continual predation of the wolves and bears.

The day after our arrival at camp, our guide announced that he was going to take us to an area where they had been seeing a huge black bear for the last three years. "He's one smart bear," the guide announced. "For three years, our hunters have been trying to get him. But he outsmarts them every time."

"What's he doing that makes him so tough?" I asked.

"Well, he comes down off the ridge above the hunter on his well-worn trail. Then he stops and looks to see if there's a hunter in the stand. If there is, he walks to the bait (a beaver carcass), keeping a large tree between him and the hunter. Then he stands behind the tree, reaches around it to grab the beaver and pulls it back on his side of the tree. Then he rips the beaver off the wire and leaves with the tree still between him and the hunter."

I had to agree: That was a smart bear. Since Visscher's bear hunts catered to bowhunters, the bear could get away with that trick. A rifle hunter probably could have picked a shot through the brush, but a bowhunter couldn't. The fact was that the bear had patterned the hunters perfectly. He knew which tree they would be in, and he knew exactly how to stay out of their reach.

Gene and I were bringing in a second stand to place in the tree for him to use while filming. When we heard the incredible story of the bear and how he'd patterned the hunters successively for three consecutive years, I glanced at Gene out of the corner of my eye and he smiled knowingly. We were on the same wavelength. We both figured the bear had inadvertently created his own pattern in the process of patterning hunters. The "ol' change-of-pace" plan would likely be his undoing.

When the jet boat landed on the riverbank, we followed the guide to the fateful tree where so many hunts had been foiled. While the guide was explaining where the bear would come from, Gene and I were already scouting for an alternate tree. We assured our guide that we could set up the extra stand by ourselves, so he bid us farewell and promised to return at dark. As soon as he was gone, we snatched the existing treestand down and out of the predictable tree and relocated it 30 yards to the north. Then we set up Gene's stand on the opposite side of the tree. About an hour later, the task was complete and we were sitting 30 feet up a cottonwood, waiting for the cunning bruin. I happened to look up the ridge above us and saw the black form of the bear passing between two white birch trees. Soon we would know who would outsmart whom.

"Here he comes," I whispered to Gene. He powered up his video camera and we waited.

About an hour later, the bear appeared at the top on the trail leading to the bait. Halfway down the hill, he stopped and peered around a tree, looking straight at the tree that normally held a hunter. When he realized it was vacant, he marched boldly down the trail to take possession of another free lunch. He had no idea we were anywhere in his world until my 31-inch arrow zipped through him. He ran about 75 yards uphill and died in his tracks. The whole episode took two hours from start to finish, and Gene captured it all on video. We simply used the bear's conditioned response against him, and it worked like a charm, and in record time.

The big black weighed about 450 pounds and scored 19$^{9}\!/_{16}$ inches according to the Pope and Young Club, well past the 18-inch minimum score required for black bears taken with bow and arrow. It also turned out to be the largest bear taken in Visscher's camp that year. I told you I was lucky when it came to big bears.

MAY 1998: CREIGHTON, SASKATCHEWAN, CANADA

My friend Arnold Holmes, a guide and outfitter from Saskatchewan, Canada, called me in the winter of 1997 to tell me about a new black bear hunting area he was pioneering on the central eastern side of the province, near the Manitoba border. He offered me first pick of dates if I wanted to bring a camera crew and some hunters in for a hunt. I had several friends looking for a good black bear hunt, so we decided on the last week of May 1998.

I told Arnold that I'd be coming along as a camp helper, and I wouldn't be hunting. I had already taken two exceptional record-book blacks, so I had mentally retired from hunting them—for the second time. It seemed ludicrous to expect to find yet another monstrous bear comparable to the two I had already taken. The odds were about as plausible as winning the lottery three times in a row.

But when Holmes emphasized the fact that the area had never been hunted, it awakened the gambler in me. Experience has taught me that when you find a good population of black bears in an area that has not been exposed to hunting pressure, the percentage of mature bears in that area will be high, and the real bruisers are less likely to be nocturnal.

I must admit there is little in the world of hunting more exciting than seeing a huge boar walk out of the timber with that massive, muscled-up front end, a head like a cinder block and a body so deep that it looks like he has no legs. I decided to take my bow along—just in case.

I felt that tingling anticipation again when our video cameraman, Gene Bidlespacher, pointed out a huge track in some loose gravel on top of a timbered ridge. Gene knows more about black bears than most black bears, and the track was as he said—that of a very big boar. The location had been set up for a rifle hunter, so we had to reorganize a bit to make it work for bow and arrow. Once stands were set up within bow range of the bait, I was ready to live there until I saw the big guy that made those giant tracks.

Meanwhile, the other hunters were also setting up near promising locations. Camp life was something like a summer vacation. Since our camp was right beside a lake, fishing for pike and walleye was standard procedure every morning. Black bear hunting over baits is very much an afternoon and evening endeavor, so the fishing added a wonderful addition for those long Canadian spring days. We caught pike weighing up to 18 pounds and walleye up to 6. As they say in Canada: "Not bad, eh?"

My first afternoon on stand produced a close look at a medium-sized sow. She was obviously not the one that had made the giant pad marks in the gravel, so I let her dine for free. I returned to camp at dark to find that Harper Turner had retired his bear tag on a beautiful black boar. Harper, a native son of Prattville, Ala., and Buckmasters' Jimmy Little of Autaugaville, Ala., were set up in a clump of spruce trees overlooking a beaver pond, about 150 yards from the bait site. Jimmy was going to capture the moment of truth with Harper's video camera.

Everything went according to plan until the bear appeared, at which time Jimmy shot some interesting video footage of his hunting boots, the sky, the ground and other inconsequential surroundings, none of which contained Harper's bear. Oh well, bear hunting is intended to be exciting. The good news is that in spite of the adrenaline rush, Harper made a great shot, anchoring the bear in its tracks.

Jimmy bagged a beautiful blonde/cinnamon bear at a picturesque site along a lakeshore, and once again Gene captured the entire event on video.

Next, my hunting pal, Ted Keaton of Greensboro, N.C., arrowed one of two big black boars that came into bow range together. The next day, from the same stand, Ted Jr. (otherwise known as T.K.) put a single 225-grain bullet from his .35 Whelen right on the money and tagged the other bear when it returned to the bait site.

Buckmasters' Tim Martin also fulfilled a dream when he let the hammer down on an ancient, grizzled black bear with his .300 Win Mag. Cameraman Elliott Allen was perched behind him and captured the drama on video. Tim was thrilled with his trophy, and the scads of northern pike he caught after his hunt was finished.

On the fourth day of my hunt, I climbed into my treestand and settled in for the long afternoon vigil. About 6 p.m., I decided to dig into my daypack for a snack and handily dropped the open pack and all its contents on the ground below my stand. I commended myself for the brilliant stunt and descended to gather up my belongings. "Nothing like being subtle and secretive," I mumbled as I crawled around on my hands and knees, looking for my flashlight and various bowhunting sundries. "I'm sure this exercise will really impress the bears. At least they won't think of me as a hunter!"

Eventually, I was reorganized and back in my stand, hoping my little accident had gone unnoticed by the local bear population. I looked back over my left shoulder and there he stood, as black as coal, glistening with a blue sheen in the evening sunlight. He was facing me at a distance of about 200 yards, studying the situation. His thick neck and shoulders and broad head identified him as the bear I was waiting for—the one that had left the huge tracks in the gravel. He finally started walking toward me, making it impossible to turn to prepare for a shot without being noticed. He stopped only 10 yards from my tree, still facing me, cautiously contemplating his next move. After a long pause, he simply turned on his heels and started back in the direction from which he'd come. Something was not to his liking, and he was leaving.

As soon as he turned away from me, I stood up and turned around in the stand. By then, he was walking away through some small pine saplings, making a shot impossible. Just before he emerged in the clear, I drew, anchored and held for what I figured was a 35-yard shot. When the bear stepped clear of the last sapling, offering me a clear quartering-away shot, I touched the trigger on my release and launched 31 inches of Easton Aluminum's finest. The arrow entered behind the last rib on his left side and disappeared. I remember seeing gravel spew from beneath his hind feet as he lurched into high gear in a single bound.

He was out of sight almost instantly, but I monitored his route into the jungle of blow-downs by the sounds of cracking timber. Then all was quiet. Through my binoculars, I could see my crimson-stained arrow lying in the gravel. I was confident that the huge bear was mine—a third record-book bear in as many hunts. Amazingly, my gambler's luck had paid off one more time.

I hung my bow in the tree, climbed out of the stand and walked the mile out to where Arnold was waiting. We quickly organized ourselves to recover the bear. With the additional help of Arnold's right-hand man, Andre (Andy) Chenier, and Harper Turner, we returned to my stand site and picked up the bear's tracks and blood trail. Almost 150 yards into the black timber, among the thick blow-downs, we lost all sign of the bear. It was as if he had simply disappeared. We worked in ever-widening circles trying to find any trace of him as darkness drew near.

Finally I asked myself which way a mortally wounded bear would travel. I had a hunch he would travel the path of least resistance, so I walked back to the last blood sign and started looking for any path that might be less taxing than through the tangles of deadfalls. Eventually I identified a narrow passage through the timber where a bear might walk with relatively little effort. I walked in that direction about 50 yards and found a pool of blood. Immediately I hailed the rest of the crew and, in no time, Arnold spotted the bear lying on his back under a pile of deadfall. Light was fading as Arnold cautiously approached him, trying to determine just where his head was in the dark shadows. The rest of us stood back and waited for Arnold to announce the "all clear."

"Okay, I can see his head now," Arnold finally reported. He took another step toward the bear and stopped suddenly. "Hold it mister," he said nervously. "I saw him blink an eye. This critter is still alive!"

I quickly nocked an arrow and approached the bear cautiously from downwind. After studying the tangle of limbs and branches, I threaded an arrow through them and into the bear's chest. With blinding speed, the huge boar leaped to his feet and dashed 50 yards farther into the timber before suddenly dropping dead in his tracks. Considering the damage of the original arrow, the incident still mystifies me. I can't imagine how he survived the first shot, and I shudder to think what might have happened if Arnold hadn't seen that eye blink when he did.

The bear made the Pope and Young record book with 1½ inches to spare and weighed close to 400 pounds. Each of my last three bowhunts produced record-book bears, which is like winning the lottery three consecutive times. Do I feel lucky? You bet.

EIGHT

Never Trust a Bear

*B*ears are entertaining creatures because you never know for sure what they're intending. They are predictably unpredictable and, therefore, a very entertaining lot. In my career as a professional hunter and guide, I've had my fair, or perhaps I should say unfair, share of strange and sometimes frightening bear experiences. Bear hunting might sometimes be frustrating, but never boring. Just about the time you have them pegged as furry clowns, they pull a sudden change of pace and scare the tar out of you. And in some cases, they're more than just scary.

Once while hunting black bears in northern Saskatchewan, I was advised of a particularly aggressive young bear hanging around the bait over which I intended to bowhunt. My friendly guide gave me a short-barreled shotgun full of buckshot to take with me to my treestand in case that particular bear showed up and wanted to argue over treestand rights. Apparently the hunter the week before me had been paid a visit in this same treestand by the bear in mention. He booted the critter in the nose and fortunately it saw fit to back down the trunk.

A huge boar had been seen in the area, too, one that would make Pope and Young with a pocket full of change. There was even some speculation that his skull might measure as high as 22 inches, which would even exceed the Boone and Crockett minimum. With that in mind, I eased toward my stand with bow in one hand and shotgun in the other.

I tied my pull rope to my bow and climbed the tree. The ultimate plan was to pull my bow up and hang it on a nearby limb, then climb back down and attach the rope to the shotgun and pull it up as well. But first things first. As a matter of safety, I was buckling myself into my safety belt, but before that job was finished I heard jaws popping below me. It didn't take a rocket scientist to figure out the source of the sound. I looked down and there was a very large black bear walking around only 15 yards from my tree. He had apparently heard the noise I made while climbing the tree, and he was displaying an attitude that plainly showed who he thought was boss around the bait. Not wanting to be noticed, I stood stone still until he ambled out of sight.

What a pity! He was a great bear, and I didn't even have my bow in the tree yet. Oh well, perhaps he would return later. It was only 4:30 p.m.

I finished buckling my safety belt, but before I could even turn around, two more bears showed. They were medium-sized blacks—teenagers, I presumed. One went straight to the bait and the other straight to the base of my tree. The latter found the shotgun to his liking and instantly began licking the barrel and action.

Understand, my bow and quiver were still lying on the ground beside the shotgun. I hadn't had time to say "boo," and I had already seen three bears!

After a minute or so of licking and smelling the shotgun, the bear did something totally outrageous. He flopped over on his back and held the shotgun with all four feet, not unlike an infant would hold a baby bottle. Then he stuck the muzzle in his mouth. Fortunately for him, the safety was on, otherwise he might have blown himself into bear heaven.

I couldn't believe my eyes. There below me lay a half-grown bear nursing on the business end of a 12-gauge shotgun. As I said earlier, bears are predictably unpredictable.

The bear finally turned the shotgun around and became fascinated with the walnut stock. He soon abandoned his innocent licking and took a large chomp out of the walnut comb.

My fascination quickly turned to concern, so I yelled, "Quit that, you knothead!" Okay, maybe those weren't the exact words, but it was something along those lines.

The bear looked up at me quizzically and went back to his walnut chewing. I yelled at him a second time, and again he looked up nonchalantly, spitefully continuing to bite chunks out of the stock.

It was time to take action. I imagined the crazy bear somehow slipping the safety off and shooting me out of the tree. Wouldn't that be neat! I could just see the headlines: "Black bear shoots bowhunter out of treestand!"

I grabbed the rope and started pulling up my bow. The goofy bear watched the bow rise above him. I was making no attempt to be subtle now. I untied my bow and hip quiver, grabbed an arrow tipped with a rubber blunt, took aim and popped the bear in the belly. He dropped the shotgun with a bawl and high-tailed it into the timber.

Now don't start in on me about shooting a bear with a rubber blunt. It's not like I was born yesterday. Two rubber blunts occupy my quiver on every bear hunt, and several times they have saved me from having to kill a problem bear that I didn't want to kill. As for those who would condemn me for such actions, I release you to handle such matters your own way. And should you ultimately appear in little heaps of bear scat on the forest floor, I will see to it that the inscription on your headstone reads: "Help Stamp Out Rubber Blunts!"

Now it was time to climb down and bring up the shotgun, or at least what was left of it. I was just about to unfasten my safety belt when bear No. 4 arrived on the scene. As soon as I saw him, I knew he was the problem bear. He was a small male, almost blonde, as described by my guide. As soon as he came into sight, he looked right up at me, popped his jaws, raised his hackles and headed for my tree on the run. If I have learned anything about interpreting bear body language, I'd wager he was coming up for a visit. I nocked rubber blunt number two, and as soon as the bear hit the base of my tree, still looking me right in the eyes, I bounced it off his forehead. He did a 180 and vanished into the timber. As quickly as I could, I dashed down the tree, unloaded the well-chewed shotgun and pulled it up to my stand. I saw a total of eight bears that afternoon, including the monster, which came in nervously but never gave me a shot.

Two days later, my friend and pastor, Dudley Hall, and I went back to that same location with bows in hand. It was early afternoon and we inched cautiously along with the wind in our faces. I was in the lead. When we were close enough to see the bait barrel, I examined the area carefully before advancing farther. Once satisfied there were no bears around, I motioned to Dudley and started slowly toward the treestands. We took more than two steps and Dudley suddenly tapped me on the shoulder. I turned to see what he wanted. With wide-eyed excitement, he whispered: "The bear is right there!" I looked around the tree in front of me to see the black giant of the forest standing right beside the bait barrel, now less than 20 yards away, totally unaware of our presence.

Momentarily forgetting Philippians 4:8, I blurted out the obvious: "That's one big son-ova-bitch!" Without argument or condemnation, Brother Dudley nodded in agreement. The wind was perfect, still right in our faces, so I motioned to Dudley to ease ahead and take a shot at the big bruin on the ground. He inched his way to a 17-yard shot, but somehow, beyond our comprehension, an untimely sapling leaped in front of the arrow. The bad news was that Dudley didn't get the big bear, which loped casually away after the wayward shot. The good news was that he hit the sapling dead center.

Later that same evening, Dudley arrowed another bear on that same bait. It was the third bear he saw from his stand that afternoon!

Years ago, my brother John and I were hiking into a lake in Jasper National Park in Alberta. It was late June I believe, and we had rented a boat from a tackle shop in the town of Jasper. The boat was chained to a tree at the edge of the lake, and we were given the key that would unlock it. We had just finished the 30-minute hike and I was actually unlocking the boat when John screamed, "BEAR!"

I looked up to see a fair-sized black bear coming at us like a black, furry cannon ball. We were standing at the water's edge with no place to go, so I grabbed an oar and prepared to drive the bear in the chops as John and I simultaneously jumped backward into the lake. The bear suddenly skidded to a halt at the water's edge, less than a rowboat's length from us. Then he turned calmly and walked away as if he did this sort of thing for a living. Brother John and I were so choked up we could scarcely speak.

Perhaps the most remarkable part of the story was our subsequent discovery. John and I both clearly remember jumping into the lake at the same instant, as the bear came thundering down on us. Neither of us remembers exactly what we were doing while we were knee-deep in the lake, but as we stood on the shore discussing the incident afterward, I noticed that John didn't have a drop of water on him anywhere. I was drenched up to mid thigh. We got right hysterical trying to figure out how John managed to jump into the lake without getting wet. How it happened is a mystery to this day. Maybe, like the apostle Peter, he walked on water. Whatever he did, he had to have defied some physical laws.

It wasn't funny then, but, in retrospect, as I see the bear waddling away in my memory, I can imagine him saying to himself, "Yup, bet those fellers' arteries are unclogged!"

What caused him to charge at us like he did, I'll never know. And what caused him to call it all off at pointblank range will also remain a mystery. What makes bears do what they do? God only knows.

Back in the early '70s, I used to spend a lot of time with Marion Diesel on his trap line in Alberta. One spring, while trapping beavers, we stopped at a little log cabin on the route only to find that a bear had broken in through a window. We entered cautiously, expecting to find the cabin in shambles. Oddly enough, things were in pretty good shape. There was a large jam can on the table, covered with only a plastic lid. The bear could have feasted on the jam with ease but, for some reason, he chose not to. There were also two large Hershey bars lying there on the table beside the jam can; they, too, had been spared—not typical behavior for a marauding black bear.

After a close inspection, we were amazed to find the only thing the bear had touched was a case of 500 .22 cartridges. He chewed them up and spat the gnarled and twisted cases on the floor. Why .22 cartridges instead of chocolate bars and jam? Who knows?

On the same trap line there was a peculiar bear that had a peculiar habit of eating snowmobile seats. I believe he had a certifiable Naugahyde fetish. As far as we know, that was his only vice, because he did no other damage. But leave a snowmobile or terrain machine unattended, and he'd have the seat chewed off before you could turn around and catch him. He was just nuts for Naugahyde. His fetish finally cost him his own hide. Marion caught him in the act one morning and made a pretty nice rug out of him.

One spring years ago, I was guiding my friend and longtime client, Phillip Harrison of Houston, Texas. After scouting a new area, we located the tracks of a good-sized black bear, and that afternoon I set up a treestand along the bear's travel route. Phillip was to man the stand the following evening. About 3 p.m. the next day, Phillip and I arrived at the appointed tree. To our surprise, the bear had already been in the treestand ahead of us. His fresh claw marks were obvious all the way up the trunk, and his black belly hair was stuck in the pine bark all the way to the stand. The crazy bear had actually climbed up into the stand.

"What does this mean?" Phillip asked with justifiable concern.

"It means you may get a nice close shot," I replied casually.

Phillip shot the bear less than an hour later. It came into view of the stand and instantly looked up at Phillip. He made a fast shot, as the bear was about to bolt for safety. It was an ancient dry sow that squared a full six feet, and she had the best pelt I've ever seen on a black bear.

In truth, the bear knew all about our presence; all about the treestand. I believe in most instances a bear coming to bait knows when there's a hunter in a treestand nearby. Many bears just don't make the full connection between the man in the tree and his ultimate intentions. Their want for the bait might overcome their fear of man. Neither is it uncommon for baited bears to become very possessive of the bait. That's when problems might occur.

My friend, Dave Kelbert, ran a bear and whitetail outfitting business in Saskatchewan for years. In the springtime he was busy baiting sites for his incoming bear hunters. He would haul bait to the sites on his four-wheeler, and the bears soon figured out that the sound of the four-wheeler was synonymous with a dinner bell. When they heard him coming, they would gather around the table—so to speak. Once, after baiting a site, he drove the four-wheeler back to his pick-up truck, only to find it occupied by a black bear. The bear was in the bed of the truck and showed no signs of leaving as Dave arrived. That posed a problem for Dave, since the truck was locked and he couldn't see himself walking up and unlocking it with the bear in the bed. He charged his truck on the four-wheeler and screamed at the bear, which ignored him completely and maintained his occupancy of the truck bed. Since the shotgun Dave used as bear protection was locked conveniently inside the truck (there's a lesson here somewhere), Dave had to apply more inventive tactics. So, he found a dead pine snag that he used like a jousting lance. He charged the bear again, whopping him with the pole as he raced by on the four-wheeler. This was too much for the stubborn bruin. When he got the pine pole upside his noggin, he bounced out of the truck bed and ran up the hill about 50 yards, stopped and watched Dave get in his truck and leave. While this unique tactic worked once, I highly recommend that no one reading this account adopt it as a reliable means of bear removal. If anything, this incident proves just how brazen a bear can become. Dave kept his shotgun a little handier after that. On a couple of occasions, he had to use it to protect himself from aggressive bears.

Grizzlies are another matter. They, too, are predictably unpredictable, but they tend to play by different and often more dangerous rules.

My friend, John Blackwell, carved out a living for himself and his family in the rugged upper Blackwater region of B.C., 120 miles west of Quesnel, back in the late '60s. That was, and still is, grizzly country. Every pioneer in that rugged place has enough hair-raising grizzly stories to burn down a month of campfires.

John guided big game hunters for his livelihood in those days, and many of them came to the Blackwater region to hunt grizzlies in the spring. One exceptionally big bear taken by one of John's hunters showed signs of a previous close encounter with a human being. The great bear was obviously in perfect health when it was killed, but when removing the hide from the skull, a hair-raising discovery was made. Lodged in the gums of the bear's upper jaw structure were three .44-caliber slugs, stacked neatly, one on top of the other. Scar tissue had grown around the old wound, and the bear appeared none the worse for wear. It was apparent that to make three shots like that, the shooter most certainly would have to stick the muzzle of his firearm right in the bear's mouth. Since the bear suffered minimal ill effects from the shooting, one could only imagine how it turned out for the shooter.

Mary Lou, John's wife, recounts an incident when her boys, Justin and Sydney, were still kids. Sydney was riding his little motor bike up and down the runway beside the Blackwell's house. The runway was the only means of summer access, other than a floatplane, to their wilderness home on the shores of Moose Lake. Mary Lou was washing dishes and happened to look out the kitchen window just as Justin rode past the horse corrals, situated alongside the runway. What Justin didn't see (but his mother did) was the grizzly crouched there next to the rails of the corral, watching the motor bike pass within feet of him. In horror, Mary Lou ran screaming from the house and scared the bear before he made a meal of her son.

Bears are crazy, all right. You can't trust 'em. But if you're a bear hunter, or you're just hanging out in bear country, always travel with a partner . . . preferably one who you can outrun. I'm being facetious, of course. In truth, you should never run from a bear. It's very likely to provoke an attack. So what do you do to protect yourself in bear country? Keep a clean camp. Don't store food in or near your tent. Try not to get between a sow and her cubs. Make a little noise when hiking in bear country so you can be heard. Most bears will move away when they hear you coming. Things get tense when you stumble unexpectedly into a bear at close range.

So what about the bear that doesn't flee? Stand your ground or back away slowly while facing the bear. Talk to him in a calm voice. I usually say something respectful like: "Top of the morning, Mr. Bear. Hope you're having a nice day out here in these woods, which are most definitely your very own. If you don't mind, I'll just back up a bit and give you however much room you need and/or want. Nice fuzzy bear—friendly bear—buddy bear—you know that I love every hair on your 27-acre body."

It that fails, prayer is awfully good.

Remember, just because a bear charges doesn't mean he's actually going to attack. Most charges turn out to be false ones.

How can you tell the difference?

It's actually pretty simple. The false charges are the ones we live to recount. I recommend a change of underwear for just such occasions.

Seriously though, while bears might appear cute and entertaining, don't be misled. Even a small black bear can be deadly. I get irate when I see someone who has watched too many Walt Disney and Gentle Ben programs attempting to feed a park bear. This is the kind of thing that gets people killed.

Grizzly bears don't romp through mountain meadows, holding hands with their bearded human brothers, and they don't take raccoons for rides on their heads, either. These critters should be given a wide berth, no matter what you saw on television.

Bears can be crazy, unpredictable critters, but not as crazy as Hollywood script writers. Never trust a bear. In the long run, you'll be glad you didn't.

NINE

Bear Huntin' with a Switch

*A*ctually, it was supposed to be a moose hunt, although I had a black bear tag just in case I saw a straggler before it crawled into its den for the winter. It was Oct. 7, 1999, and I was bowhunting with old friends Ray and Sharon Jackson of Horseshoe Creek Outfitters near Fort St. John, B.C., hoping to nail down a good Canada moose. There is no shortage of them in the Jacksons' area. In fact, the highest population of moose and the greatest bull-cow ratio in western Canada is in their guiding area that ranges from fairly flat woodlands to steep mountains along the eastern slopes of the Canadian Rockies.

I picked the heart of the moose rut for my hunt, but instead of the ideal and more typical cold, frosty weather, we got dry hot weather and high winds. The bulls clammed up and wouldn't talk, so our calling campaign fell on deaf ears. There was nothing to do but "hunt like wolves," as Ray put it, and point our noses into the wind and see what we could find.

On this day, we climbed up the barren side of a long, flattop ridge whose shoulders had been logged a few years earlier. On top, there was still good mature timber, and, in a pinch, it would usually produce a good bull. We alternately walked and called our way along the mile-long length of the ridge, but the winds blew hard and no moose answered. It was frustrating because the bulls were leaving their rubs and fresh scrapes all over the place, but a mature bull wasn't to be found in those hot, dry conditions.

When we reached the end of the ridge, we dropped off the backside and down into the timber, following a seismic line. Eventually we found a well-worn game trail crossing the line, so we followed it up onto a flat timbered bench. Ray spotted some overturned leaves about 50 yards away, so we walked over to get a better look, expecting it to be another moose scrape. It didn't take long to realize that the area, raked completely bare of dead grass and leaves, was not the work of a bull moose, but that of a bear. In the center of the raked area was the large pile of debris the bear had piled up.

"This looks to me like a bear kill," I said to Ray.

"That's exactly what it is," he replied, picking up a 6-foot tree limb and prodding the pile of grass, leaves and twigs. He expected to uncover the carcass of a deer or perhaps an elk. At first, it appeared that nothing was there. Then, surprisingly, when he pushed the stick down, it sank deep into a hole that was covered with leaves and totally invisible to us.

In a split second, the mystery was unraveled when something down in the hole grabbed the other end of the stick Jackson was holding. There was a muffled sound of snapping jaws and woofing down in the ground and a brief wrestling match between man and beast, each gripping their respective ends of the tree limb. Suddenly Ray snatched it out of the hole and jumped backward, uttering a one-syllable expletive that described our situation to a "T."

"There's a bear down there, and he's coming out now!" he yelled with his next breath. With that, the bear erupted out of the ground before our eyes like a 300-pound, furry black genie rising out of a bottle. Somehow I didn't figure this genie was coming to grant us a wish, unless perhaps it was our last!

Drawing my bow must have been totally involuntary because I don't even remember doing it. All I recall is seeing the green and orange fletching being swallowed up by long black hair. I do remember backing up so I'd have room to draw my bow. In retrospect, that seemed a tad closer than ideal.

The bear spun around at the shot and, in a matter of two or three bounds, was out of sight. Ray and I stood there somewhat dumbfounded and at a loss for words until the silence was broken with the bellowing death moan of the bear.

"Guess you got him," Ray said with a grin.

"Yea, I guess so," I replied, "but I have good news and bad news."

"Like what?" Ray asked suspiciously.

"Well, the good news is that all the cholesterol is now blown out of my arteries. The bad news is that I'm in bad need of a change of skivvies!"

We walked down the ridge 50 yards and found the bear as dead as a doorknob. The arrow had passed completely through the animal, as well it should have at pointblank range.

We didn't even have a camera with us. Our plan was, when I shot a moose, to go out and get the pack horses and then we'd bring the camera gear back with us. We skinned the bear and managed to make a sort of carrying device out of our belts. We wouldn't need the horses for this, but we could only take a picture of the rough-skinned bear hide when we got back to camp.

It was the third bear Jackson and I had taken together in as many bowhunts. One hunt is described in the chapter entitled "The Three Bears;" the other appears in the chapter entitled "A British Columbia Bowhunting Odyssey." As Ray Jackson so aptly put it, "Something crazy happens to us every time we get together for a hunt." Truer words were never spoken.

TEN

Blackwater Grizzlies

*C*ivilization ended abruptly a few miles southwest of Prince George, British Columbia. I watched from the window of the small floatplane as the patchwork of small farms gave way to undulating hills, densely covered with fir, spruce and occasional aspens. Lime-green muskegs broke the rolling carpet of forest-green and small, serpentine creeks and rivers formed a network of silver lace through the woodlands and valleys below me. Two black bears fed in a small meadow at the edge of the timber. They would be the only black bears I'd see as the plane droned deeper into grizzly country.

I was en route to my first grizzly hunt, although I had been nose to nose with the great bears on several previous occasions, mostly while fishing. And as I looked down from the plane window, my thoughts raced back to one moonlit night in July of 1972.

After fishing until dark, I was rowing a small boat through the narrows of Amethyst Lake in the Tonquin Valley on the Alberta/B.C. border. I carefully picked my way through the submerged boulders, glancing over my shoulder to pinpoint a large table rock bordering the only clear channel through the narrows. The flat rock rose a couple of inches above the mirror surface of the lake. Two more strokes of the oars, one last shoulder-check for the flat rock, and I could hardly believe my eyes. A huge silver-tipped grizzly was sitting on the rock, not more than 15 feet distant.

I back-paddled frantically, brought the boat to a halt, and sat spellbound as the bear slid off the rock into the water and swam past me, just an oar's length in front of the boat. It climbed onto the bank, still less than 20 feet away and shook himself like a big dog. I was so close that the spray from its silver hair showered me. Then it stretched tall on its hind legs and peered down on me, as if sizing me up for dinner. Our eyes met in a tension-locked stare that seemed to last for an eternity. Finally, the great bear dropped back down on all fours and lumbered off into the night. I never forgot that feeling of helplessness as the bear decided the outcome of our midnight encounter. Even now, years later, a chill runs up my spine as I remember that incident.

The plane tipped suddenly downward, snapping me back to the present and to bears I had yet to meet.

A gangly spring moose appeared below in a willow flat bordering a small, un-named lake, and in the distance, the snow-capped peaks of the Coast Range loomed above the verdant forested hills. Moose Lake, my destination, shimmered like a million golden sequins in the evening sun, as the plane dropped close to the treetops. We were flying very low then, and I realized with amazement how in-credibly thick the maze of timber was below me. It was obvious that even seeing a bear, once we were in that conifer jungle, would mean a close encounter.

John Blackwell was my guide and pilot. He read the concern on my face and addressed it with a grin: "I told you they were going to be close." My close en-counter with the huge Tonquin Valley silvertip came rushing back to me, and I secretly hoped I'd never be that close to a live grizzly again.

Maynard Meadows of Elmira, Ore., was already at Moose Lake when we ar-rived. He is John's brother-in-law. I'd met him on an elk hunt in Alberta several years earlier. Maynard is a serious hunter who has paid his dues in the field, so I was delighted that he was there. But it was his humor as much as his expertise that made hunting with Maynard special.

Over supper that night, I pumped John with endless questions about grizzly bears. The grizzly is sacred to the local Carrier Indians (their name comes from their ritual of burning their dead and carrying their burnt remains in a leather bag on their backs). They believe grizzly bears are gods of sorts—reincarnated an-cestors who can read their minds. Killing the bears is taboo to the Carrier Indi-ans. They believe the bears will retaliate against them if they harbor any ill will against the grizzlies.

It's uncanny, but somehow the grizzlies in this area have come to know the difference between a white man and an Indian. They openly torment the Indian villages while they usually give the white man a wide berth. When a grizzly enters an Indian village, they quake in fright and hide while the bear steals from their meat supply and plunders their camp. Over the years the Indians have paid a high price in lives lost for their superstitions.

We established the game plan for our hunt and John explained that there were several big bears staying close to creeks where sucker spawning runs were still in progress. The bears stay on the streams until the sucker runs subside, then they disappear into the forests. John had seen a big blond male, about eight feet tall (while standing on its hind legs) just a couple of days earlier.

"The bear ran down the creek, herding the suckers ahead of him, forcing them into the shallows or against log jams," John told us. "When the suckers were stranded, the bear flopped down on top of them, pinning them against the bottom with his body. Then he reached down and grabbed them in his teeth and ate them. It was incredible."

The question was whether or not the suckers were still spawning. It was already late in the spring season, but Maynard and I had our fingers crossed. We packed our gear into the floatplane, flew to a neighboring lake and hurried to pitch our spike camp in the waning light. We drifted off to sleep to the patter of raindrops and the whining of mosquitoes. It was not fully dark until 11 p.m. By 4 a.m., there was enough daylight to read my wristwatch.

We rolled out of our sleeping bags and John started a fire while Maynard proudly displayed his telescopic spinning rod. He was going to catch our breakfast. And sure enough, in just 15 minutes, he was back, grinning and chuckling with five gorgeous trout. He had pulled them in right below our camp and had even thrown back some smaller ones.

Rainbows, I thought, when I first saw the fish. But when I looked closer, I noticed they wore the cutthroat's red slash on the underside of their lower jaws. And yet the pink blaze down the side was pure rainbow. Later I discovered that even the biologists couldn't agree on what we ate for breakfast that morning. Some believe that the fish are rainbow-cutthroat hybrids, even though the hybrid is supposedly infertile. Others believe the mystery trout may be an original species from which both rainbows and cutthroat evolved (I don't buy the evolution theory). Nobody can say for sure just what the fish were, but our trio unanimously agreed on one thing: They were delicious! It was a breakfast fit for kings—or grizzly bear hunters.

While we savored our meal and the oncoming light, a bald eagle lifted from its nest below our camp and began its own search for breakfast. The magnificent bird was wary of us at first, but it soon grew accustomed to its new neighbors.

I was contented, sitting there by the fire, sipping coffee, eating trout and soaking in the splendor of my surroundings, when John abruptly backed away from the fire. It was time to get moving. "The bears fish the creeks only early in the morning and again just before dark," he announced. John reached for his bolt-action .300 Winchester Magnum and headed for the small boat tied next to the plane. Maynard and I gathered up our rifles and followed.

In about 20 minutes, we'd crossed the length of the lake and edged into the shallows a half-mile from where we expected to see the blond grizzly. Any closer and the noise of the motor might have spooked him.

On foot now, John led us around the edge of the lake to the outlet of the creek where the bears were fishing. The timber was heavy with deadfalls—every bit as thick as it had looked from the plane. We zigzagged our way as silently as three big hunters can. There was something ghostly about the area, and knowing that we were hunting an animal that could easily turn into the hunter kept me looking over my shoulder.

After a quarter-mile or so, John turned from the lead and nodded to us to chamber our cartridges. We were close to the bear's area, and we didn't have to be reminded that in such dense timber, any shot was likely to be at pointblank range. The sound of ravens croaking and eagles screeching encouraged us. The birds were gathered to feed on suckers, so the bear might still be there, too.

John stopped beside a mangled 12-foot pine tree, bitten in half and battered as part of the territorial marking of the great bear. Other larger trees suffered bites or had big chunks torn out of their trunks—the work of a pair of mighty jaws. The power and strength of the grizzly was apparent all around us, and suspense mounted as we eased closer to the creek bank.

John cautiously led us from a downwind angle toward a small cabin that I could see through the timber. There, against an outer wall, the big bear had dug itself a bed and was obviously using it regularly. Powerful claws had bulldozed the earth, and the size of the depression indicated, as did all other signs, that this animal we were hunting was gigantic. John estimated it at more than 800 pounds.

We edged around the cabin, treading right through the bear's boudoir. The timber was tight, and the alders and willows that shrouded the bank of the creek were higher than my head and so thick that a bear could be in our laps almost before we saw it coming. Then there were the tracks as big as pie plates. I was astounded to see them, not only in the mud along the creek, but also on hard soil.

John explained that in early June, as the mating season draws near, the male bears travel in a circuit, as often as several times a day. Each time they retrace their steps, they carefully set their paws in exactly the same tracks and twist their rumps to and fro, forcing their front claws to grind into the dirt. Eventually, they wear deep gouges in hard soil where a man would leave no tracks at all. Later in the season, the same bear would pass through the country without a trace. The grizzly obviously means for these tracks to be seen, but their reason remains a mystery to me. I suppose it has some territorial connotation.

Whatever purpose the bear had in mind when it left its deep gouges in the ground, they made my size-12 hunting boots look like a child's by comparison. I was beginning to feel like Jack from *Jack and the Beanstalk*. I knew a giant was close at hand.

We surveyed the cabin area carefully before following the creek a mile upstream to a small lake, which was its source. We looped through the timber and emerged periodically at chosen spots where John knew we could command a good view. About 100 yards above the cabin, we edged along in single file from the timber toward the creek bank for another look. That's when the willows suddenly parted with an explosion of golden fur, and the bear came charging straight toward us at pointblank range. The electric charge of adrenaline was still sizzling down my spine when I realized that the bear had plunged into the creek and was busy herding suckers. The grizzly was all charged up over the fish. Thankfully, he didn't even realize we were there.

Once I was sure the bear hadn't noticed me, I looked around for my partners. Both were ahead of me, locked in place by the bear, still dashing back and forth in front of us. A million thoughts raced through my mind at once. Would the bear spot or smell us? Would it give us a chance to shoot? If it did figure us out, would it attack or retreat? As the hungry bear continued its assault on the suckers, I saw John turn his head slowly toward Maynard and heard him whisper, "Shoot!"

Instantly Maynard's .338 came to his shoulder, and he tried with difficulty to get the bear in his scope. The trouble was twofold. For one thing, a spruce tree hid the bear from his view much of the time. And it was so close and moving so fast that when it did appear in his scope, Maynard had precious little time to prepare for a shot. Open sights would have been much better medicine at such close range.

After what seemed like an eternity of waiting, during which I was almost afraid even to breathe, Maynard's rifle bellowed. Then everything fell silent. The bear was down, and just as I was about to breathe, a brief flash of blond fur went streaking through the timber to John's right—grizzly number two, scared off by the shot.

As Maynard chambered a second round, John and I moved up beside him and we all gazed silently at the fallen bear, a mere 17 paces before us. The 250-grain bullet had found the shoulder and lungs, and the bear never moved again.

We stepped into the creek toward the dead bear when a sucker hiding in the shallows splashed suddenly as it fled. We all nearly jumped out of our skins. Only then did we realize just how tense we were. We moved ahead for a closer look at the bear, and discovered yet another shock.

This was not the big blond eight-foot male that John had seen two days earlier. It was blond all right, but at about six feet long and weighing around 400 pounds. It was much smaller than the bear we'd been tracking.

Grizzlies in this part of the country usually range from chocolate brown to nearly black, and we never dreamed that we'd see two blondes so close together. The bear was not young. Its teeth were worn, and its skull was fairly large. The hide was quite blond along the back and head, and the muzzle and lower legs were dark mahogany brown. It was a beautiful animal.

Maynard was initially disappointed that he had not taken the larger grizzly. But his bear had been wet from fishing, so it was impossible to judge its size. Besides, at 17 paces, any grizzly would be hard to pass. If that bear had crossed the creek in one of its sudden bounds, it would have landed on top of us. I was glad that Maynard had taken the shot.

I was also hoping that the shot hadn't spooked the second blond grizzly clear out of the area. It was almost certainly the big male John had seen earlier. We skinned Maynard's bear and returned to the boat, then back to base camp. Seventeen paces kept running through my mind. That was bow-and-arrow range!

We returned to the Blackwell home to care for the hide properly and to escape the mosquitoes for the night. For Maynard and me, the day had been special, but that night, as bear stories unfolded, it became apparent that our day was just one of many in the lives of the Blackwell family.

John recounted his experience with a clever grizzly that had taken to stealing quarters of moose from his meat house one fall. The bear probably could have torn down a wall, but it preferred a more civilized form of breaking and entering. It would reach in through an open window, pull a moose quarter toward it, chew it down to a small enough size to pass through the window, then haul it away with him.

Each evening, John would lie in wait for the bear, but he never did catch it. The sneaky bruin always waited until it was too dark to see before making his raid.

Finally, as the winter moose meat supply was rapidly dwindling, John Blackwell and his Carrier Indian guide, John Jack, decided to try something daring. They would stay in the meat house until the bear arrived, even if it took all night. It was late October, and there was a skiff of snow on the ground, forecasting winter's arrival. Blackwell and Jack sat side by side in the small log building, their backs against the wall, awaiting the arrival of the marauding bear. Hours slowly passed, but no bear. Finally, at 2 a.m., cold and sleepy, the duo gave up and presumed the bear had gone on to parts unknown. They left the meat house and went home to bed.

The next morning, Blackwell was horrified to find that the bear had returned and absconded with yet another moose quarter. The story was written clearly in the snow. There against the cabin wall was the melted snow marking the bear's bed where he had waited for the two men to vacate the premises. Only inches away, against the opposite side of the same log wall, Blackwell and Jack had been waiting for the arrival of the bear that was there all along. It was a true testimony to the bear's cunning and reasoning ability. Those who would claim that bears can't reason obviously haven't spent much time around Ursus horribilis.

After that night, the moose larder was not raided again. That grizzly probably went into hibernation soon thereafter—quite full of moose meat.

John had lots more grizzly stories, but his wife, Mary Lou, told us the most hair-raising of all.

One spring the Blackwells and their two sons, Justin and Sydney, had traveled 50 miles by wagon to collect their horses from their winter pasture. Mary Lou left ahead of the others with four horses tied head-to-tail, and three head-loose, plus the one she was riding in the lead.

She was seven miles from home at the bottom of a long hill and had just managed to herd the horses across a small creek when the brush exploded an arm's length from her. A big blond grizzly came charging out of the timber. Apparently the bear had been in a sound sleep in its bed, dug right at the edge of the trail, and it hadn't awakened until the horses were right on top of it.

The horses whirled in panic, and Mary Lou lost the reins of the horse she was trailing. She knew she had to control the horses and stay in the saddle, but just as she was grabbing for her lost reins, the bear appeared on the trail 30 feet ahead.

Mary Lou talked to the horses, trying to calm them and herself. As frightened and alone as she was, she told us that she couldn't help thinking how beautiful the bear appeared, with its blond back and big brown circles around its eyes. That's the kind of person Mary Lou is. She kept on talking and admiring the bear and praying all at the same time. Then, just as the bear started quartering away, she yelled at it. The noise, however, threw the irritable bear into an instant rage.

"It wheeled around to face me and the horses," Mary Lou said. "With one huge forepaw crossing over the other, the bear lumbered toward the panicky horses, arched its back and cat-danced back and forth across the trail." Mary Lou remembered that she'd been told to look a threatening animal squarely in the eyes. "The bear was fearfully close now," she said, "but I knew that to retreat was to guarantee an attack. So, for a moment that seemed more like a year, we stared into each other's eyes." Finally, the bear moved off the trail into the thick jungle of jack pines.

Mary Lou and the horses hurried toward home. They were starting to relax. But as it turned out, that bear wasn't ready to forgive the rude awakening. It was following the group just out of sight in the thick timber and terrorized Mary Lou and her horses three more times—the last time less than a half-mile from home.

"The horses broke for freedom and ran the last half-mile like their tails were on fire," said Mary Lou. I admired her courage. Few people could have held together so well under such trying circumstances.

Now it was Justin's turn for a grizzly tale. He's the elder of the Blackwells' sons, and his grizzly encounter came when he was just 17. It's the kind of event that makes a man of a boy. Justin had killed a moose and taken some of the meat when he met a grizzly bear with precisely the same intentions. The bear challenged him at pointblank range, and Justin fired 10 shots from his meager .30-30 before the bear finally died. When I asked him about the incident, he just smiled and said, "I bought a .30-06 right after that." He had good reason.

Hours of grizzly stories later, we talked about our strategy for the next hunt. We decided to wait a couple of days to let things settle. Sure, it was a gamble with the sucker run so close to being over, but returning too soon could be a mistake. So we took the gamble and lost.

There wasn't a sucker in sight two days later. They'd all moved back into the lake after spawning. We checked the creek bed for fresh bear tracks. There were none. But when we came to the spot where Maynard had taken his bear, we were in for a shock. The carcass had vanished. The law does not require hunters to take grizzly carcasses out of the field, as the meat is not considered edible. Something must have considered the meat edible, however, and we knew without asking that that something could only be another grizzly.

We studied the spot where the carcass had laid. There were no drag marks, so the bear must have picked up the entire 400-pound carcass and carried it away with him. With what kind of monster were we dealing? John found the awesome answer to my question when he was scouting in the timber. An 18-foot circle had been beaten down where the big bear had wallowed and paced around his cache. In just two days, the great bear had consumed every last ounce of Maynard's bear carcass, leaving nothing but a few polished bones and a putrid smell. Somewhere in the forest roamed an enormous, bloated grizzly with breath that would wilt new spring leaves.

The realization of the nature of big grizzlies was settling in on me, and my .300 Mag. was feeling smaller in my hands all the time. The bear could be within 50 yards of us at that very moment. The timber and undergrowth were so thick that a charging grizzly could be breathing down our necks before we even knew it was there.

"Just 17 paces away" kept creeping back into my memory, and I shuddered. Hunting grizzlies here guaranteed close quarters, and my challenge would be to see the bear before it saw me. I looked up and down the little creek, no more than 10 feet wide. Sturdy 40-foot aspens lined the bank. "If the bear fishes the same spot on the creek next spring," I thought to myself, "I could be 25 feet up in a tree and right on top of him when he started chasing suckers."

The picture was becoming clearer all the time. What I really wanted was to shoot my grizzly bear with a bow and arrow. The more I thought about it, the more sense it made. I'd never have to make a shot of more than 50 feet, so why not with my bow?

I kept my bowhunting secret to myself until we were sure the big blond male had left the area. We really weren't too surprised to find him gone. After all, it was late in the season, and most of the bears leave the creeks and streams for the endless forests by early June.

Back at the Blackwells' home, I decided to pop the question and ask John how he felt about letting me try again next spring with a bow. In fact, John had guided a bowhunter once before for grizzly. They had waited patiently in a tree, 12 feet above the ground, until a big grizzly appeared right under them. The closeness of the bear shook the hunter so bad that he overshot with his first arrow and managed to spook the bear even closer. That's when he really fell apart and missed a shot at pointblank range. What I gleaned from that account was that 12 feet high was about 24 feet short of what I considered a comfortable height!

All this just served to excite me even more. Making a killing shot would not be as much of a problem as keeping my heart from exploding when the bear arrived on the scene. In any case, John was game to try. I spent a couple of leisurely days tossing flies to the ever-willing rainbows of Moose Lake and dreaming of the big blond grizzly bear and how I'd hunt him with my bow the following year. At that time, there were only 17 grizzlies listed in the Pope and Young records. John figured the blond would fall within the top three.

As if I weren't already in enough awe of that bear, I heard one more story about it before I left. Mattie Jack and her husband (also named John, now deceased) were members of the Ulkatcho Indian Band from the Anahim Lake Reserve, and we met them at the Blackwells' when they were en route to their home on a nearby lake. Some of the band members had seen the bear swim out into the lake, kill a full-grown moose and drag it ashore. While we had been looking for the bear at one end of the lake, it had been feeding on a kill only a couple of miles from us.

I forgot all about my bear for awhile when Mary Lou told me one last grizzly bear story. It was about Mattie Jack, and it was the most incredible story yet.

In 1963, Mattie Jack and her husband, John, were camped in a trapping shack on the Mud Lake Ranch, about 15 miles from Anahim Lake. John had been putting in fence posts there. The two of them rode out one evening to round up their straying horses. After they split up, Mattie Jack came to a brushy area, too wet and dense for her saddle horse, so she dismounted, tied up her horse and walked on toward a hillside a little over a mile distant. And there, just 70 yards ahead, she saw a grizzly sow with two cubs—too late.

The sow attacked viciously, biting Mattie Jack's neck, shoulder and leg. She tried to stay calm in hopes that the bear would then leave her alone, but the angry sow just kept biting and shaking her until she fell unconscious.

The next thing she remembered was waking up buried deep in mud and dirt. Grizzlies typically bury their kills that they intend to eat later, so Mattie Jack was entombed and most certainly on the bear's menu.

Somehow she managed to crawl from her would-be grave and drag herself back to camp in blood-filled rubber boots. When she crawled up on the doorstep of her cabin, her husband grabbed his gun and pointed it at her until he realized what he was seeing. He admits not even realizing that his wife was a human being when he first saw her mud- and blood-soaked body.

Mattie Jack paid a high price for the attack, resulting in 200 stitches, a summer in the hospital and four years of follow-up treatments, not to mention an infectious bacteria common to all bears that causes wounds to weep for many years after an attack.

As far as anyone knows, Mattie Jack is the only person to survive a grizzly bear mauling and burial. Surprisingly, her husband guided for grizzlies (The couple had converted to Christianity, so they no longer shared the band's pagan fear of killing grizzlies). Mattie Jack was very proud of him. Perhaps she saw the grizzly hunt as a form of personal revenge.

The grizzly stories continued, and I was planning my second hunt. I pictured John and me perched high off the ground in a treestand and a big blond, humpbacked giant right below us. I draw my bow and . . .

ONE YEAR LATER . . .

John Jack dropped his right hand, signaling us to stop. Kneeling, he inspected the scuffed surface of the dried caribou moss. He looked back at us and silently pointed at the grizzly track, extending his hand in the direction the bear was travelling. By his expression, we knew that he was telling us we were very close to the bear. The rest of our procession fell into single file behind him as he began following the faint tracks. The timber was a thick jungle of pine, spruce and aspen, and everyone was thinking the same thought: "When we finally meet this bear, he's going to be very close."

Behind the 55-year-old native guide was my old friend, Phillip Harrison of Houston, Texas. It was Harrison's first grizzly hunt, as well as his first time in British Columbia. Behind him was John Blackwell, followed by Phillip's wife, Ima Jean, who often accompanies him on his trips. I was bringing up the rear, furnishing moral support and acting as cameraman. It was the 10th hunt Phillip and I had shared. We both wanted grizzlies, and he had won the toss for the first bear.

The ground before us tilted upward and the timber suddenly opened up, offering us greater visibility, which was a relief. Jack pines grew in stunted clumps, and the ground was mostly rock-covered, blanketed by earthen shades of dried moss. It was good to get out of the low lying muskeg and the slushy remains of winter. John Jack looked back at us and signaled for silence with a finger to his lips. He motioned for us to wait where we were while he moved ahead to inspect the situation. Slowly he eased forward to what appeared to be a sheer drop. We scarcely dared to breathe as we waited for his next signal.

As he reached the edge of the bluff, he craned his neck to see what was below him. Suddenly, he jumped away from the edge of the bluff and dropped to his knees. We knew he had seen the bear. Instantly he was motioning for Phillip to come quickly, but quietly. We let Phillip go ahead and then Ima Jean, John Blackwell and I eased up behind them. Phillip was sliding in behind a pine snag to steady himself for the shot as I peeked over the bluff. The bear was there, about 50 yards below us, and he looked like a chocolate brown boxcar. I was stunned at his size, especially his head, which appeared to be the size of a 45-gallon drum. I heard Ima Jean's quiet gasp as she saw the great bear. Phillip's .375 H&H Magnum exploded and a silent world was instantly filled with the terrifying roaring of the bear.

The first shot into the front shoulders was undoubtedly a killing shot, but the bear was still very much alive and on his feet. At first, Phillip seemed stunned that the bear would not fall. Instead, it ripped and tore up trees and put on the most awesome display of savage power I have ever witnessed. I glanced at Ima Jean and she looked as if she were in shock. I grabbed her arm to assure her we were going to be okay. Blackwell ordered another shot, jarring Phillip from his trance. Phillip knew that you don't stop shooting a grizzly until the bear is down for good, but the explosion of fury below had simply mesmerized him. Two more shots flew in rapid succession, then all was quiet. The huge bear lay still.

For the next few moments, we all stood quietly, letting our nerves calm. Then John Blackwell broke the silence as he extended his hand to Phillip. "Congratulations, Phillip, that's one heck of a bear," he said, and we all joined in agreement. With air back in our lungs and legs steady beneath us, we climbed down the face of the bluff to the fallen grizzly. It was indeed one heck of a bear.

The skinning was a monumental job for four men. It was all we could do just to roll the bear from one side to the other. There was no way to actually weigh the bruin but we agreed that it must have been in the neighborhood of 1,000 pounds. Once the hide was removed and laid out on the ground, we estimated it to square 10 feet. The huge head was obviously going to be a contender for the Boone and Crockett book. The big bear smelled like a kelp bed; the smell was so strong, even in the hide, that we were sure it was a coastal bear. Blackwell explained that we were only 50 miles from saltwater and that each May it was common for some of the coastal bears to make the trip over the Coast Range into the Upper Blackwater area in his hunting territory.

The hide was lashed onto a pack frame, and it took two of us to lift it onto John Jack's shoulders. The amazing Indian guide shouldered the load, took a couple of short steps to get his balance, then headed back to camp. Even with the load of the green hide, surely weighing over 150 pounds, John Jack was waiting for us when we arrived at camp.

The next day was spent fleshing the huge hide. The official measurement of the hide was 10 feet in length and 9½ feet across the back, between the tips of the front claws. The green measurement of the skull was slightly larger than the 24-inch minimum necessary to qualify for the Boone and Crockett records. I was amazed to find that 14 of the top 25 B&C grizzlies were taken within a 100-mile radius of Blackwell's base camp. Numerous book bears came from his area, including the No. 17 B&C grizzly. One thing was certain: Phillip Harrison would hunt long and hard to find a better bear than the one he took on his first grizzly hunt.

Phillip and Ima Jean headed back to Houston, and John Blackwell and I got down to the serious business of finding a bear for me.

Justin, Blackwell's eldest son, was my guide when I finally embarked on my dream bowhunt. John flew us into another lake where we unloaded and set up our small fly camp. Early the next morning, we headed up the small creek that emptied into the lake, looking again for bear sign and evidence of the all-important sucker run.

The hair left in the pine bark indicated that its owner's hair was chocolate brown in color with light golden tips. The size of the tracks and the missing chunk of tree trunk, eight feet off the ground, left little doubt that this was a big bear.

As it was nearing dusk, the time that the bears liked to do their fishing, we decided to climb up and follow the ridge above the creek so that we would not meet Mr. Bear face to face. As we tiptoed slowly along the tree line at the top of the ridge, I spotted a large dark object lying beside the creek. We stopped to have a better look through binoculars and discovered the large object was our bear. He was no more than 50 yards below us, very much like Phillip's bear had been, and he was feeding on the suckers. We eased down, flat on the ground to keep the lowest possible profile, and watched the bear feeding until almost dark. What a sight through 10X binoculars! He was obviously the owner of the hair we found in the pine bark. Guesstimating him as a nine-foot bear, I could hardly believe how things were falling into place.

Justin squirmed restlessly beside me. When I looked at him, I could see that he was wishing I was a rifle hunter so we could end the hunt right there.

It was a dream situation for a rifle hunter, but just the beginning for a bowhunter. We both knew that the bears favored specific fishing spots and, if all went according to plan, he would be back there in that same spot again the next day. I picked out a tree a few yards from the creek where I felt I could command a perfect view. Justin nodded a nervous approval. Getting too close was not his idea of fun, a result of his nose-to-nose shootout with the big griz mentioned earlier. I knew he didn't have the same confidence in the bow and arrow that I did, but then only a bowhunter really understands how lethal a well-placed, razor-sharp broadhead can be. On the other hand, only one who has shared the land with grizzlies can fully appreciate how lethal they can be. Suddenly the big bear left the creek bottom and started walking up the hill toward us. We flattened out against the ground, hoping the bear would not discover us. He veered off to our left and topped the ridge 35 yards distant. There he stopped and turned toward us. "Get ready," Justin whispered as he shoved the .375 Magnum toward me. I didn't want to shoot that bear with a rifle, but I was certainly prepared to change my mind if he started for us. For a spine-tingling moment, the bear sniffed the air and thought some very private thoughts while we lay there afraid to breathe. Finally, he lowered his huge head and walked into the timber. To this day, I am not sure whether or not he was aware of our presence. The way he left would indicate that he had not discovered us, but he did walk downwind of us. I believe he smelled us, thought about the situation and walked into the cover. There's that reasoning ability again.

The following morning at 8:30, after the sun was high, we returned to the spot where we had seen the bear feeding. We wanted to wait until he had plenty of morning to feed again and leave the creek before we arrived. In the chosen cottonwood tree, I set up my treestand a full 25 feet above the ground. I climbed into the stand and pulled up my bow and arrows, as well as enough food and water to last the day. The original plan was for Justin to wait on top of the ridge where we had been observing the bear the previous evening. From there, he could see the bear and me and offer a hand in case of unexpected trouble. But since the bear had exited right past his planned post, we were afraid the bear might discover him and blow my opportunity. We agreed that the best bet was for Justin to move farther down the ridge to the west. He could observe my hunt from there, even if not as closely as he had hoped. I could read his mind. He had a gnawing fear that he was going to have to track a wounded grizzly through an alder jungle. But I knew what he could not know: that I would pass on the bear entirely unless I had a perfect shot.

May 20 was a day I shall never forget. It turned unseasonably hot, and I'm sure the temperature reached 90 degrees or more. Leaves were actually popping out all around me in the cottonwood tree. I sat for hours doing what people do while waiting in treestands, such as counting ants as they crawled past me on a limb. I tried not to think in terms of hours. The sun shines from 4 a.m. to 10 p.m. in British Columbia during the month of May, and that can make for a long day in a tree!

I glanced at my watch at 4 p.m. I was getting a headache from the relentless heat. There were not enough leaves yet to provide any shade, and I felt as if I would eventually melt. The headache became more serious with each passing minute. Then, at 4:30, I heard the strange bawling sounds of a bear. I had heard black bears make similar sounds when they were mating. Then two grizzlies appeared on the narrow trail, heading my way. In the lead was a medium-sized blonde female. Right behind her was my big chocolate boar. It was obvious that they were in love. I was amazed at how the bears circumvented every ray of sunlight hitting the ground. They walked only in shadows, avoiding direct light like the plague.

Suddenly the female turned on the boar and snapped at him, and he took off through the timber like a scalded cat. She stood in the trail less than 20 yards from my tree, offering me a perfect shot, but I wanted the boar, so I waited. Soon the giant male came creeping back to his beloved, peeking between bushes and trees like a big bashful schoolboy. One thing was certain in this romance—mama was calling all the shots. For no less than 20 minutes, I had both unsuspecting bears literally right below me. But the boar continued to play his peekaboo game through the thick alders, never giving me a clear shot at his ribs.

The plot thickened as I became aware of my headache once more. I was also getting dizzy and felt like I was going to faint. Then came the nausea. I knew I was suffering from too much sun and I was soon hugging the tree trunk in desperation. I knew that to get out of the tree would likely end the hunt, which I had prepared for and dreamed of for years. It was just ironic that I should be getting sick just when the opportunity of a lifetime was knocking. To complicate matters, I had no assurance the bears would return. Feeding habits play second fiddle to romance in late May, and I realized that the bears might be gone for good. It was 5 p.m. and the moment of decision was at hand. I could see myself fainting and falling out of the tree. Wouldn't that be cute—me lying there unconscious when the bears returned. It might be a little hard to explain. And if I remained in the tree, would I even draw my bow? There were far more questions than answers. I decided to attempt to tough it out, so I used my pull rope to secure myself to the tree trunk. Now if I fainted, I'd simply sit slumped forward in my stand, but I wouldn't fall. Somehow that was comforting.

At 7 p.m., the sun settled behind the ridge and, as the air began to cool, I felt life returning. The dizziness and nausea subsided, but the headache remained. When I felt strong enough, I unlashed myself from the tree trunk and drank the remainder of my water supply. If the bear came now, I would manage.

At 7:30, I heard the bawling sounds again. Knowing the bears were returning, I nocked an arrow and came to red alert. The ground below me was covered entirely by shadows now, so perhaps the big boar would give me the shot I wanted. Then, to my amazement, there was another bear—one that I had not seen. It was smaller than the boar I expected, and it was travelling alone. It came immediately to the creek and made a quarter turn away from me and stopped. It was the perfect shot, and I responded almost involuntarily. I knew the range was 15 yards, so I held my 20-yard pin low, behind his right shoulder, and released my arrow. As the nock slipped from my fingers, I knew the shot was good. The flight of the arrow seemed animated, almost like slow motion, striking the bear low behind his left shoulder, passing through his heart and out the other side. The arrow stopped as the broadhead hit the humerus bone in his offside foreleg, leaving the fletching exposed on his near side. The bear roared as the arrow struck him. Then, to my amazement, he raised up on his hind legs, grabbed the fletching in his teeth, and ripped the arrow back through his heart. Then, with a toss of his head, he slung the arrow end over end 20 yards through the air. Then he dropped back down on all fours and bolted into the timber. Suddenly the forest was totally silent.

I waited 15 minutes before getting out of the tree on shaky knees. Justin was already coming to join me. I walked a few yards back up the ridge as he arrived, and we spotted the bear lying a mere 40 yards from my tree. It was obvious that he died within seconds of the shot, as he barely made it out of my sight. A flood of relief and amazement flooded Justin's face as he offered me his congratulations. "I never believed an arrow would kill a grizzly that quick," he said in amazement. My emotions were torn between jubilation and deep relief. Justin's were the same. Though it was not the big chocolate boar, it was a beautiful bear with mahogany-colored forelegs and a blond back. The dream had come true. I had finally bagged a grizzly with a bow and arrow!

Hurriedly, we began skinning the bear with less than an hour of daylight remaining. It was not a job we wanted to do in the dark with so many other bears in the neighborhood. When the skinning was complete, we rolled the hide into a bundle. As I was tying it, I heard a cracking sound coming from the black timber. My mind was cloudy from the ordeal of the day and, at first, I gave it little thought. Then it was closer and louder. Suddenly I could hear the popping of jaws and the chugging, woofing sound of the charging bear. Justin and I instinctively jumped to our feet. I was closest to his rifle leaning against a nearby tree, so I grabbed it and cranked a round into the chamber. I couldn't see the bear, but I knew he was closing in on us quickly. The timber downwind of us was a wall of small jack pines and by the time the bear broke into the open, he would be in our laps. The surge of adrenaline brought back the strength I had lost as I shouldered the .375 and prepared for the shot. The bear was right in front of us, coming like a bolt of furry lightning at 30 yards. It was obvious that one shot would have to do it all since there would be no time for a second. The huge chocolate boar suddenly broke his charge and made a hard right turn, dissolving into the dense forest just as I was squeezing the trigger. Somehow I held my shot and the last rays of daylight faded into black night and all was still once again. Justin and I stood back to back for a long moment, shaken to our cores. "Guess we ought to leave," he said—an understatement if ever I heard one!

I climbed back up into my treestand and hauled my bear hide up and tied it into the tree, where it would be safe. When we arrived at our spike camp, we built a huge campfire, enough to light up the surrounding timber. As we recounted the awesome events of the evening, I realized one important fact that had not yet registered with me. Just before the bear I shot arrived, I heard the bawling sounds of mating bears. That meant the two original bears were returning to the area. They must have pushed my bear out ahead of them, and in my stupor, I failed to realize that the other bears were returning. Had I waited and passed up the blonde bear, I might have had a chance at the big chocolate boar after all. Oh well, that's the way hunting goes. I felt lucky to have survived the day in the tree, lasting nearly 12 hours from beginning to end. And after all, I had taken a beautiful grizzly with my bow.

Then there was the fact that the big boar had enough manners to call off his charge at the last possible second. There was plenty about which to be happy. The experience was one I will never forget. We piled more logs on the fire, laid back and watched the shadows flicker in the treetops. I realized how totally exhausted I was. The heat, the headache, the nausea, and then the charging bear, had taken their toll on me. I remember thinking as I drifted off: "All the grizzlies in British Columbia couldn't keep me awake tonight."

The next morning, when we returned to get my bear hide, we found that the carcass has been picked up and carried off without even a trace or drag mark. I was glad I had decided to skin my bear the night before, rather than leaving the job for the next morning. Had I waited, I would have had nothing for my effort but some remarkable memories.

POSTSCRIPT

The following year, in May of 1987, the late Derril Lamb of Brunswick, Maine, bowhunted grizzlies with Blackwell. Lamb had been scheduled to hunt with Blackwell in the spring of 1986, but he suffered a heart attack that sidelined him for a year. His hunt with Blackwell, his first hunt since his heart attack, rewarded him handsomely for his one-year delay. On May 17, he arrowed a giant grizzly with a skull measurement of $25^{13}/_{16}$, establishing the bear as Pope and Young's No. 1 grizzly and also ranking high in the Boone and Crockett Club records.

Lamb shot his bear from a treestand at 7:45 p.m., and as instructed, he remained in his stand until Blackwell called him down at dark. Wisely, Blackwell decided to leave the bear until morning light rather than risk tracking him in the dark through the thick jungle of spruce, pine and alders. I was one of six men who accompanied Lamb and Blackwell to recover the bear the following morning. Lamb's grizzly only traveled 60 yards before turning to face his back trail and slumping down on his belly. We found him easily in the light of morning, lying there on his belly as if asleep. I don't know how much the bear weighed, but seven grown men couldn't budge the huge animal to move him out of the shadows into better light for pictures.

My friend, Derril Lamb, passed away in 1999. I miss him.

SECTION III

Hunting in Thin Air

ELEVEN

Backpacking for Dall's

*T*he turbo-powered Porter lifted powerfully from the float plane base at Norman Wells, NWT, and began climbing above the vast Mackenzie River and to the northwest. On the horizon was the distant blue, saw-toothed skyline of the Mackenzie Mountains. The landscape below was thick aspen and mixed conifer forests dotted with muskegs and myriad tiny lakes. Serpentine rivers twisted their way from the base of the Mackenzies toward the mother river, more than a mile wide, flowing to the Arctic Ocean and dividing the Mackenzie Mountains from the Franklin Range.

This was my first hunt for Dall's sheep. The Arctic Red River area of the Mackenzie Mountains was my destination. This is the northernmost range for Dall's sheep in the Northwest Territories. My outfitter was Ray Woodward, owner of Arctic Red River Outfitters. Jackie Brittingham of Dallas, Texas, was my hunting partner, and we burned up several rolls of film from the plane windows while Ray conferred with the pilot.

The mountains were under us at last, and we strained for any sight of white sheep amid the grays and browns of the autumn mountain. Finally in the distance ahead, there was an emerald dot shining in the center of a high alpine pass. That little jewel was the lake where our hunt would begin.

The Porter's floats streaked the mirror of the little lake's surface as it settled on the water. Once upon shore, the plane was secured and our hunting party, consisting of Jackie, Ray, one stout pack dog named Terry, and me, piled our gear on the shore and watched the Porter return to the sky and disappear into the clouds. The feeling of being alone with nothing more than what we could do for ourselves was overwhelming. No horses, no telephones, no nothing—just an eternity of mountains waiting to be hunted. It was 5 p.m., Aug. 30, 1981.

By the evening of Aug. 31, we were 12 miles down an unnamed river valley from where we deplaned. The first afternoon, we had hiked eight miles. The following morning, we awoke in a dense fog, which resulted in a late start. As we pitched the small Gore-Tex sleeping tent and prepared a fire, the magic hour of sunset poured down like golden honey on snow-covered mountaintops and set the world aglow. It was in that last hour of daylight that we spotted two respectable rams across the valley in a high saddle. In the fading light, it was impossible to determine just how good the rams were, but they were already bedded down and we felt confident that the following day would tell us what we wanted to know.

We awoke the next morning to a blanket of fresh snow, which is part and parcel of late-season mountain hunts. Seeing a white sheep in snow at a distance of four miles might be the most difficult endeavor in the world. We felt sure the sheep were there, but spotting them was another matter. It was 2 p.m. when Jackie found them, no more than 200 yards from where they had been bedded the previous day. They had been there all along, but were simply invisible against the snow. One ram appeared to have one tremendous horn, which we judged to be in excess of 40 inches, and one broomed-off horn, perhaps four inches shorter. The other ram had a tighter curl, but was perfectly even on both sides and not broomed at all. They were certainly worth a closer look, so we packed light and left our spike camp at 2:30 p.m.

Jackie and I alternated first option on the rams each day, and it was my day for first right of refusal. I was naturally excited at the proposition of getting my first Dall's sheep. Jackie had taken an excellent Dall's ram in Alaska several years earlier.

The first three hours of the stalk were pure labor. The spongy muskeg and lichen-covered slope robbed us of our efforts as we sank deep with every step. The face of the mountain was flat and steep, and we traversed our way upward, stopping periodically to relieve burning calves and thighs. The east face of the mountain was shaped like a huge triangle. The tip formed a rocky saddle that bridged westward into steeper rock formations and shale slides. The rams were feeding in the saddle when last seen. Three hours of steady climbing put us behind a ragged outcropping of reddish-brown rock above where the rams had been. We slipped out of our packs, caught our breath, then crept forward a step at a time. Ray suddenly stopped and flattened out against the ground and motioned for Jackie and me to do the same. He was right above the rams. I edged slowly forward. When I reached Ray, he whispered that the rams had just bedded down directly below us. I could just see their heads as they laid with their backs to us at no more than 150 yards. This was going to be a simple matter. Now we could use the spotting scope to properly evaluate the rams.

I laid my rifle aside and was setting up the spotting scope when all hell broke loose. Ewes and lambs from across the canyon caught our scent, and they began a hasty climb for the mountaintop. This signal was picked up immediately by the two rams and suddenly they were on their feet and running out across the shale mountainside. My perfect shot was quickly dissolving into a memory. Our vertical view of the rams in their beds was deceiving and made accurate judging of their horns difficult, even with binoculars. I didn't want to shoot just any ram. I asked Ray how good he thought they were as they rambled farther from reality. He didn't want to make a hasty decision without a better look, and all he could say was that they were both good rams. The question of just how good was yet to be established.

The rams finally stopped running below a steep, snow-covered rock wall, at least a half-mile distant. They stood with their backs to the wall and faced us. We couldn't move without being seen. At least we were finally able to get a good look at the rams through the spotting scope. Our first evaluation appeared to have been pretty close. The larger-horned ram would be very close to 41 inches on the right side and broomed back to about 38 on the left. The other ram would go about 37 to the side, with even horns and no brooming. Both animals were impressive. I was intrigued by the larger of the two in spite of his broomed horn.

I was certain that approaching the rams was now impossible, but Jackie optimistically suggested it could still be done. He asked me if I really wanted the ram with the broomed horn, and I quickly admitted that I would gladly take him, but I couldn't see how it could be done. He told me to slip back down behind the saddle to the backpacks. In his pack there was a pair of white snow goose hunting coveralls he had brought along for just such an occasion. He figured I could put on the suit, climb out over the saddle from another location, and move in on the rams in plain open sight of them. It sounded crazy, but we had come a long way for this opportunity, so I agreed to try it. Jackie and Ray stayed there in sight of the rams to keep their attention while I tried the white snow goose suit trick. I climbed down to the packs and found the suit and slid into it. Slowly I climbed out over the saddle, several hundred yards up the mountain from Ray and Jackie. I felt ridiculous. The rams could see me, but somehow they didn't seem to mind this hunkering, white creature.

As I reached the shale slide, I lost sight of the rams, but Jackie and Ray directed me with hand signals. I stepped into the shale and was suddenly swept off my feet and plunging downward in a mass of flowing rock. The snow had melted and drained into the shale and frozen all but the surface layer, which was as slippery as ball bearings. Desperately I scrambled toward a piece of solid rock where I anchored myself amidst the moving mountainside. I had only begun and still had several hundred yards to go. On hands and knees, I crept and stumbled through the slippery shale in constant fear of falling right off the side of the world. I had long since lost sight of the rams and could not believe they would stand still for such a fiasco. I looked back at Jackie and Ray through binoculars time after time, and to my amazement they directed me onward. After 40 terrifying minutes of plowing my way across the shale face, I reached a vantage point that allowed me a view of the place where the rams had been the last time I saw them. My heart sank. They were gone. The draw below me was empty white. I searched for any trace of them, but could find none. I glassed back to my comrades for any clue, and they were both pointing straight up. It could only mean that the rams were somewhere above me. After 10 minutes of searching, the rams came into view 400 yards above me and across the steep draw. They were feeding casually and obviously unconcerned about my presence. They had watched me the whole time and neither my clumsy progress nor the noise of rockslide after rockslide had disturbed them at all. Yet any movement my partners made from their position a half-mile away brought both sheep to full alert. They must have believed that I was just another sheep. The white suit was nothing less than magic.

I had worked out a method of judging distance through the duplex crosshairs of my scope by viewing the broadside length of the ram at 6X. A ram at 400 yards would fit perfectly between the ends of the heavy, horizontal, plex crosshairs. At less than 400 yards, the ram would extend past the ends of the plex portions of my crosshairs, and at more than 400 yards there would be some daylight between the ram and the plex crosshairs. Sheep hunting seems to constantly demand range judgements with absolutely nothing to use for gauging relative distance. The system worked perfectly, and the rams were in fact very close to 400 yards distant. I'm sure I wouldn't have been able to make that judgement without the use of the system I've described.

Now that distance was established, I faced a whole new problem. I was going to have to shoot right-handed, if at all. Being a southpaw shooter, this was to my disadvantage. The mountain was extremely steep where I was standing (or lying, depending upon one's choice of words). In any case, my toes were dug into the face of the mountain in order to keep me from sliding away, and I remained in a standing position even as I leaned in to the mountain to steady myself.

I laid the ultra-light .270 across the shale in front of me and tried to lean into the mountain and find the ram I wanted. When I allowed my weight to rest on my elbows, my footing would begin to slip and I would slide out of my position. Three times I tried to get behind the rifle and as many times I slid out of my position. On the fourth attempt I was able to see a half-moon image through the scope. I couldn't get directly behind the rifle because of my awkward position on the steep mountainside. I raised the crosshairs a foot above the shoulder of the big ram and touched the trigger and simultaneously slipped out of my footing.

The shot went too high and now the sheep were standing at full alert. I tried desperately to reposition myself for another shot. Twice more I lost my footing before I could make the shot. Finally, in desperation, I climbed 50 feet higher and laid down across a sheep trail that was worn into the mountainside. The thin, flat surface helped. The big ram was walking by then and was rounding the base of the little knob where he had been feeding. I held high, led him slightly, and was reaching for the trigger when I lost my hold on the mountain. I lurched forward and repositioned myself. The ram was still in sight, but only for another step or two. I hung on to the shale slide with desperation and fired. The ram buckled in the scope a split second before the recoil dislodged me from my perch.

Soon Jackie was beside me. He told me that the sheep was still alive and lying directly below the spot where I had last seen him. The snow swallowed the white sheep. Sometimes I had to look right at the sheep for a long while before I could see them. I glassed the snow-covered knob below the point where I had shot. To my amazement, the ram was standing directly on top of the knob looking down at me. "He's still standing," I whispered to Jackie.

"That's not the ram you shot," Jackie said. I was totally confused by his statement.

"That's the ram I thought I shot!"

Jackie explained that the big ram had been walking around the knob, and I had been aiming at him when I slipped. During the time it had taken me to get repositioned, the larger ram had walked out of sight; the second ram followed him around the knob, right in his footsteps. When I looked through my scope again, I had seen the second ram, and since he was walking away at 400 yards, I never suspected he was any other than the ram I had been watching.

After the shock of realizing that I had shot the wrong ram, I still had to find him. Jackie directed me to the spot, and the ram was lying in the snow facing me. The larger ram stood there waiting for the other one, which indicated that my sheep must have been the boss ram. Now Ray topped the ridge above me. There were some large boulders up higher, so I climbed into them in hopes of getting to shoot left-handed. No sooner had I reached the boulders than my ram was on his feet and slowly climbing. I found a perfect rest and was catching my breath when Ray told me to wait until he stopped before I shot. The ram was on top of the knob and showing no sign of stopping. I held a foot high once more and touched the set trigger. I felt steady for the first time. The .270 roared across the canyon, and the sheep faltered, then rolled backward. He slid nearly 1,000 feet down the mountain and came to rest in the steep rock draw.

After the fatal shot, I realized how incredibly exhausted I was. There had been no rest since we left camp. All the while I was stalking sheep, the tension and strain of staying on the mountain had sapped my energy. The ram, in spite of mistaken identity, was a beautiful ram of 37 inches to the horn. The confusion of the day had me spinning, but I was still proud of my ram.

We rough-caped him and packed the cape, horns and meat down the mountain, making it back to camp as darkness fell. I was exhausted.

The next day was spent fleshing the cape and resting around the fire. That was fine with me. I was in my mid-30s then and in relatively good condition, but Jackie, 10 years my junior, had prepared for this hunt like an Olympian. I knew keeping up with him was going to be tough. But as we sat around the campfire that day, he told me of his dilemma—a sheep hunter's worst nightmare. His new boots, which he thought were broken in before the trip, had worn deep blisters the size of silver dollars on both his heels. I looked at the wounds and the sight turned my stomach. Jackie was in for a long painful hunt. I dug through my first aid kit and found some Merthiolate. The pain of the application brought tears to his eyes. He sat around the fire barefooted for the rest of the day, letting his wounds dry. Thankfully, I had brought enough Moleskin with me to pad the open sores so that he could continue the hunt without debilitating pain. "Look at it this way," I teased, "at least I'll be able to keep up with you now!"

While dressing Jackie's wounds, I failed to notice the wind change. My own boots were sitting on a rock upwind of the fire, drying after wading across the river twice the previous day. By the time I noticed the wind change, my left boot was charred on one side. What a deal! It was only day three of a 10-day hunt and already one hunter was crippled and the other had burned up one boot.

I was wearing LL Bean's Bulldozer boots, and to their credit, they are remarkably tough. The fire had torched one side of my wet boot and had shrunk it considerably. In order to get my foot into it, I had to cut several slices through the charred leather. Then I tied the boot on my foot by winding the laces all the way around the boot, under the sole and back over the top. It was a makeshift arrangement at best, but in the wilderness, necessity is truly the mother of invention. Amazingly, the charred boot held together for another seven days of hard hiking and climbing.

The next day, we hiked another 10 miles down the valley, glassing rams as we went. The summer before our hunt, Woodward had used a helicopter to fly in 45-gallon metal barrels with bear-proof lids and deposited them in 10-mile intervals along the valley. He then filled each barrel with freeze-dried foods. That enabled backpacking hunters to travel a little lighter and be assured of plenty of food. The freeze-dried rations combined with sheep steaks made pretty good eating.

Early on the sixth day, we spotted a band of rams from a distance of about three miles. They were on the opposite side of the valley, close to the top. The weather was clear and sunny, promising good conditions, so we packed up and headed toward the rams for a closer look. After several arduous hours of climbing, we were close enough to tell that one ram was better than a full curl on both horns. Jackie and Ray both thought he would go 40 inches. The gorgeous ram was all alone, lying on a shale slide above us. Jackie and Ray estimated the distance at 300 yards. I scoped him, using my crosshairs as a range-finder, and calculated the ram to be right on the 400-yard mark. Ray and Jackie disagreed with my findings. Jackie took a prone rest and held for 300 yards. When he fired, I saw the bullet hit the shale 50 yards in front of the ram. At the shot, the ram jumped to his feet and bolted out of our sight into a nearby canyon. We ran to the mouth of the canyon to see if we could see him, and to our amazement we found the ram in his death throes. Unbelievably, Jackie's 130-grain .270 bullet ricocheted off the shale in front of the ram and hit him in the chest. How's that for luck? In the end, my calculations were correct. The ram, in fact, had been 400 yards distant. It had 41-inch horns on both sides—a lifetime trophy for any sheep hunter.

There is something deeply satisfying about hunting in a vast wilderness mountain range and knowing that you have done everything under your own steam. Walking and climbing 100 miles under full pack might not appeal to all sheep hunters, but those who really want to hunt, unencumbered by horses, will love it.

We named the locations where Jackie killed his ram "Ricochet Mountain," and the canyon where my ram fell, "Wrong Ram Canyon." After all, these places needed names, even if they were at our expense.

TWELVE

Cats and Dogs and a Man Named Simpson

"**S**o you want to hunt cats!" Jim snapped wryly, through an almost sinister grin. A month later, I would understand the meaning behind his tone of voice and the expression on his face that had left me feeling a bit uneasy.

Jim Simpson is a name that rang a lot of bells in the world of bighorn sheep hunting. He was certainly one of Alberta, Canada's great bighorn outfitters. In addition to sheep hunting, he was noted for his grizzly and elk hunts, and he was as good a still-hunter for whitetails as I ever saw. And back in the woodwork, among that select few who have the fortitude and stubbornness it takes to follow him through the Rockies of southern Alberta on foot in the dead of winter, he was known as the best cougar hunter in the country.

I had heard many intriguing Simpson stories, so in January of 1978, while I was covering the Alberta Outfitters Convention for the press, I decided to pop the question. Arrangements were made for a hunt in February of that year, and I was advised to appear with snowshoes and as much "TRY" as I could muster. "TRY" was a word that would hold new meaning before my first cougar scooted up a tree.

On Feb. 12, I arrived in Pincher Creek, Alberta, where the Rockies start to rise from the "flap jack" flatness of the southern Alberta prairie. Jim, his son, Dayle, and two innocent-looking hounds greeted me. Sam, the elder of the pair, was a black-and-tan/golden Lab cross. The junior was a purebred red bone hound appropriately named "Red." I don't known what I expected a cougar dog to look like, but I still remember wondering how two such lazy-looking characters were going to muster the necessary pizzazz to tree a cougar.

It was suppertime and I kept picking subtly away at Jim until he loosened up and started to talk cougar hunting. I learned that in the southern Alberta Rockies, the Chinook winds blow in from the Pacific, which keeps the cold weather in check due to periods of warm weather, well above freezing. The warm spells created by the Chinook winds eat away deep snow and create a natural winter harbor for game animals in the region. The deer, elk, moose and bighorn sheep find the winters in this area very favorable, and since they survive well, they exist in great numbers. These game animals serve as prey for a thriving cougar population. I only had to wait for the next rising sun to begin my formal indoctrination, but I wanted to hear about previous hunts. I had a thousand questions to which there were 10,000 answers, but by 1 a.m., though I was anything but sleepy, Jim decided it was time to retire. I dreamed of cougars that night and bolted from my bed at the sound of the alarm clock the next morning.

After a hearty breakfast, we piled the dogs in the back of the Bronco and edged into the mountains, which looked larger than I'd hoped. Simpson quickly explained his philosophy about cougar hunting. For openers, he only hunted them on foot. He was seriously opposed to the use of snowmobiles because it gave the hunter an unfair advantage, allowing him to cover too much ground too quickly. He said there would always be a good population of cats as long as man hunted them on foot. It took longer to get a cougar that way, and that was precisely the point. Almost anyone could hunt them with the luxury of modern machinery. Only a few would bother if they had to do it the hard way. Even though I had no experience one way or the other, I was inclined to agree with him.

The first step, I learned, was to find a track—not just any cougar track, but a big one. That was not always an easy task. We surveyed the haunts known to Simpson where cougars had crossed ridges for thousands of years. For reasons known only to cougars, they were not on the move. After finding no tracks the first morning, the guide decided that it was time to explore the situation on foot. The lesson was about to begin.

Jim and Dayle pounced into their snowshoes and I was still fiddling with my harnesses when both Simpsons and the two dogs vanished over the bluff above me. I could see that there would be no lollygagging about on this trip, so I attacked the snow-covered bluff expecting to scamper along behind my hunting party. I made about 10 vertical feet before gravity realized what I was up to and the problems began. I slid backward down the incline. The snowshoes wouldn't grip the hard packed snow at the foot of the bluff. I could see the faint impression in the snow where the two dogs and two sets of snowshoes had already passed ahead of me, so I knew it was possible. I thought about it for a moment, then decided I was simply not making a proud enough effort.

I psyched myself up mentally as I remembered doing just before the kick-off during my distant years as a football player. My streamlined 205-pound fullback body was now a robust 220, but it still possessed the heart of a lion, so I took two steps back and attacked the bluff with a victorious scream. The scream was muffled with a mouthful of snow as I plunged headlong into the drift. The crust had broken under the weight of my attack, and I floundered in three feet of rotten snow. When I finally righted myself, I peeked sheepishly around in hopes no one else had seen the net result of one attack by "Russell the Lion-Hearted."

The Chinook winds had crusted the snow hard on the surface and had rotted it away underneath. The result was that you either walked lightly or you broke through. When you break through a three-inch crust on snowshoes, the holes are the exact shape of the snowshoes. The crust is hard enough to demand that you step out of the hole exactly as you went in or the snowshoes will hang up underneath the crust and trap you indefinitely. In three or more feet of snow, that precise stepping up and out of the broken crust has a tendency to grind old football heroes down to sniveling wimps in about 15 minutes. It became obvious that this hunt was designed for featherweights.

Both Dayle and Jim were built of lean sinew, bailing wire and outrageous mental toughness. I remembered Jim's words: " . . . as much 'TRY' as you can muster." I was starting to understand the word "TRY." By now the Simpsons and the dogs were 15 minutes ahead of me. I was afraid to estimate how their 15-minute lead might translate into distance. With sheer determination, I reattacked the bluff and thereby gave birth to a whole new means of snowshoe travel. It is a kind of combination of running, slithering, kicking, cursing and praying, all rolled into one sequence of ungainly thrashing, otherwise known as "main strength and awkwardness."

When I reached the first ridge on the side of the bluff, I felt as if my lungs were the size of BBs. I was light-headed and rubber-kneed. I thanked the Almighty that I had never taken up smoking. Upon realizing that I was going to survive that first encounter, I began to feel a real sense of pride for having made it that far. That sense of pride, I was to learn, is what keeps a cougar hunter going.

I was the only one carrying a rifle, so I felt sure that my friends would not let me get too far behind. After all, who would shoot the cougar if I weren't there? That little misconception proved just how wrong a man can be. Jim and Dayle loved chasing those cats and could have cared less about rifles and such. They just wanted to chase cougars for the pure love of the cruel and outrageous infliction upon the human body.

I followed the scant snowshoe tracks climbing ever upward amidst the rocky ridges that rose, one above the other, into the horizon. Three hours later, I reached the top of the first mountain. I shinnied up to the edge of the dwarfed spruce timber that lined the tip of the ridge like bristles on a wild hog's back. I was standing, or should I say kneeling there, gasping for breath and wondering what in the world

I had gotten myself into when Dayle poked his head out of the trees and yelled "Boo." I nearly flipped over backward. "Thought we'd lost you," he grinned.

"So did I," I said with relief. "Any tracks yet?" I inquired.

"Some old ones," he replied. "But that's better than no tracks." Dayle and I caught up with Jim within a few minutes, which made me feel like I was still in the race. Jim was circling the ridge where the snow had blown away and the tracks were lost. Eventually, he picked them up again farther down in the snow and the dogs were put back on the trail. Both hounds stuffed their muzzles eyeball deep into the old tracks and came up with a mournful bawling and resumed the search. I watched the Simpsons, who I am sure have a deal worked out with Sir Isaac Newton, dance lightly over the snow drifts that swallowed me whole, and I cursed every pound of my faltering hulk. Late that evening, I stumbled back onto the little road where the day had begun, only to find the Bronco loaded with men and dogs, waiting patiently for my return. I tried to fake a determined comment about tomorrow, but I didn't fool anyone. They knew I was wasted. There's no place for mercy among cougar hunters. The chase belongs to the one who gets there first, and those who don't make it have no one to blame but themselves.

As we drove back to Jim's house on Pincher Creek Ranch, I began to come back to life. After a hot bath, I felt like I just might survive.

The next day was definitely the toughest that I will ever experience. I was sore and stiff, which did little for my faltering uphill snowshoe speed. Jim was convinced that there were several cougars working in the area we had explored the day before, and he was going to play a hunch and approach the mountain from the other side. The Bronco was parked and the game was underway. Soon I was alone in my distinguished place as anchorman. I crossed the ice lying on the Westcastle River on the faint snowshoe tracks left for me to follow. I held my breath and tried to weigh as little as possible. If the ice was as unforgiving as the snow had been about my weight, I might have to develop a new stroke for underwater snowshoeing. The ice held, and I stepped gratefully onto the bank. Clamoring up the bank to the high water bench, I followed the snowshoe tracks for about 300 yards before hitting the end of the trail.

The tracks suddenly circled a ragged old pine tree that stood alone on the riverbank, then vanished. I followed them once, made another circle and was flabbergasted. It was one thing to be a little slow, but to lose the tracks of two men and two dogs in good tracking snow was unforgivable. It was not my first hunting trip in the snow by any means, but this one had me stumped. Several circles later, a silly feeling came over me. I began to suspect that I was the victim of a cruel prank. Somehow they must have climbed up into the top of the pine tree and were still up there fighting laughter. Should I look up and let the joke be over? I stood there debating my position in the matter and slowly let my eyes lift to the treetop, expecting to see the whole hilarious crew. To my further amazement, the tree was empty. I couldn't figure it. Had they flown away?

I sat down and studied the situation. Finally, I walked over to the sharp drop of the riverbank. There, 15 feet below were the faint tracks for which I had been looking. The men and dogs had made a circle around the tree and then just broad-jumped over the bank without even ruffling the snow until they hit the bottom. With glee, I picked up the chase but never saw my companions again until dark. Eventually their tracks directed me back to the Bronco. I felt bad because I knew I was even farther behind than yesterday. If this trend continued, I would be hunting my first cougar for the rest of my life, which was a bit uncertain on the steeper slopes. Jim announced they had finally cut the fresh track of a big tom. I imagined them waiting for me and then giving up the chase. Fortunately, that was not the case. As the track became fresher, darkness and a threatening sky called off the hunt. "Thank goodness," I thought. At least I hadn't blown it.

Day three was the turning point. My poor aching body accepted the inevitable and began responding to hitherto ignored impulses from the brain. I was keeping within hearing distance of the baying hounds and even caught a glimpse of the foursome from time to time. My endurance was building, and it was a glorious feeling.

Jim must have noticed I was starting to come around because he began to let me catch up from time to time to show me interesting and important signs left by the cougar. This spurred me on, and I was soon at heel except on the steepest upward efforts where my weight alone slowed me.

As we crossed a small ridge, the dogs dipped down below us into the timber and began howling with obvious excitement. We plowed our way down to them in waist-deep snow and found the remains of a mule deer. The cat had made a kill. It was a few days old, but a good sign nevertheless. Jim explained that when a cougar makes a kill, it stays close until the carcass is eaten or freezes hard. The cougar's short jaw structure makes it impossible for him to rip at frozen flesh as a dog or wolf would do. If the weather is extremely cold, the kills freeze quickly and the cougar might have to kill two or three times a week to survive. We found another mule deer kill within a quarter of a mile. This one was fresher, but completely eaten.

There was more than one cat track there, according to Jim. He figured there were three. The dogs became more excited by the minute, and that made the adrenaline flow in my veins. Soon we were standing over an elk kill. It was a large animal and very little of it had been eaten. The 20-below temperature had frozen the carcass solid, and it would remain there where the cat abandoned it until scavengers such as coyotes and ravens picked it clean. Simpson showed me how the cougar had dragged the animal down into the shelter of the trees and buried the carcass. He explained that the process helped insulate the carcass, making it edible for a longer period before it froze. I was snapping a photo of the elk kill when the dogs ahead of us really hit high gear. We clamored ahead to find the remains of a yearling cougar. I could hardly believe my eyes. "What the heck is this?" I gasped.

Simpson gazed thoughtfully at the half-eaten kitten. "Most people don't know this," he said, "but a big tom cougar will eat every young one he can find. After the mating is done, the toms have no regard for their own." I photographed the hair-raising scene, and Jim packed the remains in his backpack. "The Fish and Wildlife Department will want to see this," he said.

Darkness fell while we were still on the hottest trail of the hunt, but Jim called in his dogs and leashed them. We headed back down the mountain. I learned later that Simpson's dogs were rare in that they could be turned loose and still be controlled. Most dogs are kept on leashes until the track is red hot and the cougar is sure to be close. Then they are turned loose to tree the cat and quickly tied up again. The reason being that most hounds are beyond control when they hit a good track. If darkness falls and hunters must stop, most dogs will continue and are often lost. But that was not the case with Red and Sam. They would range ahead, covering more ground in less time than a man could, and yet would respond to commands even in the heat of the chase. Sam's mother, a purebred black-and-tan, had been retired on her 50th cougar. Jim had already lost track of how many Sam had treed, and while Red was only a youngster, he was showing the nose of a champion. I didn't know it then, but that was Sam's last cougar hunt. He was getting on in years. He died later that spring.

On day four, we were determined that this would be the day. The 20-below weather had suddenly turned to 30 above, thanks to a Chinook wind. The heavy clouds began to drizzle on the snow-covered mountains. The rain made it difficult to tell a fresh track from an old one, but the dogs were not fooled. They raced ahead, offering occasional howls that echoed through the timber and down the mountainside. We crossed a ridge lined with large fir trees, and Simpson showed me where the cougars had clawed them. They stood up on their hind legs and hooked their claws into the bark and raked long gashes down the tree trunks. I had seen common house cats do the same thing on trees and furniture. By careful observation, we could determine the size of the cougar by the width of the claw marks.

Simpson explained that the cats followed the timbered ridges because the limbs of the conifers sheltered the ground beneath them from the deep snow. Deer and elk also traveled the ridges for the same reason. The cougars knew they would find game there, and if they had to make a quick exit from danger, they too would also benefit from the sheltered path below the trees.

The drizzle kept loosening the snow from the treetops and puffs of the soggy stuff fell at random, occasionally plopping on my head and soaking me. The heat of the chase and my woolen clothing, however, kept me warm in spite of it. The monotone bawling of the dogs ahead suddenly quickened, and their pitch rose a full octave. The chopping rhythm of their barking was so fast it sounded like the dogs were trying to catch one choking gasp with another. Jim and Dayle broke into a dead run straight toward the hysterical hounds. I fell in behind them. The extra pressure beneath my feet soon had me bogged down in snow. Men and dogs covered the ground quickly, and I could hear them crossing the little draw a couple of hundred yards ahead. The dogs shifted into a frenzied wailing that spelled "Treed!" even to a novice. I could hear Jim and Dayle howling as if they were purebreds, too. I decided to take the short cut through the bottom of the draw in an effort to gain time. Big mistake! Little did I know that the snow was five feet deep in places. I kicked and swam my way forward toward the finale. "Hurry up Russ!" they screamed as I floundered ahead, burning oxygen no longer in my lungs. The nearer I got, the harder I tried, and although the body had given its all, the mind drove me ahead and dropped me flatly beneath the tree where men and dogs howled furiously.

Burning for a breath that I thought would never come, I gazed up into the huge pine and saw the tawny form of the big tom cougar. This was the reward for the physical torture of the past four days. It was truly the most spectacular sight my eyes had ever beheld in the wilds. The big cat began to move his feet restlessly. Jim told me to shoot quickly because the lion was getting ready to jump. He instructed me to aim at the dark crescent-shaped mark on the cat's chest, as I leaned against a neighboring tree trunk to steady my trembling body. I fired, and the cougar leaped out of the tree and vanished over a snow-covered embankment with two screaming dogs at his heels. "Did you miss him?" Simpson snapped over his shoulder as he vanished behind his hounds. I was too breathless to even answer. I knew the shot was good. After a good deep breath, I followed him. Below me were the men, the dogs and one cougar.

That night we raised our glasses to an incredible hunt and my first cougar. I drank a silent toast to the fact that I had survived the whole event. Jim reminisced about the years when he hunted cougars for 30 and 40 straight days without even a rifle. He did it just for the chase. I asked him how many cougars he had treed in his career. He couldn't remember exactly, but he figured somewhere around 100. I asked him what his success rate was when guiding hunters. He said that in his career he had never failed to tree a cat for his hunter, but over the years, two hunters had given up the chase even though the cat was treed. Somehow that didn't surprise me. Fortunately, Jim told his hunters that it was going to be tough, and most of them did what they could to prepare themselves. I gazed in amazement at this man, over 10 years my senior, who did not even know the meaning of the word "quit." I asked him why he kept on cougar hunting, considering it had to be hard on him too, although obviously not as hard as for some I could mention.

He pondered the question over a swallow of rum, then replied flatly, "Because it's tough!" That summed it up, alright. It was darn sure tough! Every line in his stony face was tough, and I tried to imagine what struggles, what degree of "TRY" had carved them into his determined features. He was a man to be taken seriously, and his expression was a testimony to a lifetime of severity, relieved only occasionally with an unexpected smile, which always caught a stranger off guard.

When I returned to Edmonton, I was the envy of all the hunters I knew. It was a good tom, just a fraction out of the record book. In my book, it was No. 1.

I had learned a lot about the mysterious cats that are seldom seen, even by woodsmen who share their habitat. But equally as important, I learned about "TRY." I have hunted sheep in the Alberta Rockies, the Mackenzie Mountains of the NWT, and even in the High Altai of western Mongolia, but this was, without a doubt, the toughest physical challenge of my life. Cougar hunting, Jim Simpson style, makes sheep hunting look like child's play. If a trophy were to be measured by the difficulty in obtaining it, surely this cougar would remain my best forever.

For two years, the thought of hunting cougars again was quickly abandoned in my mind. I still remembered the torturous, lung-bursting climbs above timberline and wondered what possessed men to demand such extremes of themselves.

The phone rang in January of 1980, two years after that first cougar hunt, and Jim Simpson's voice cracked in my ear. "Cut a big track today," he said. "Ya coming down?"

Would I be crazy enough to do that again, I wondered? I swore I never would. I paused. "Sunday afternoon," rolled off my tongue as if someone else were in control of my speech.

"Good 'nuff. See ya then," he said, and the receiver clicked in my ear.

As I walked from the den, I looked at my retired snowshoes hanging on the wall beside my cougar. "There are the snowshoes," I thought to myself. "Now if I can just find my 'Try.'"

THIRTEEN

Hunting Siberian Ibex of the Mongolian High Altai

The old saying, "Getting there is half the fun," couldn't be truer than when traveling from my former home in central Alberta, Canada, to the wilds of Outer Mongolia. Mongolia is a football-shaped country sandwiched between China, to the south, and what used to be the Soviet Union, to the north. My hunting companion, Gary Sitton, and I met in San Francisco and flew nonstop to Tokyo, where we refueled and continued on to Beijing, China, in September of 1989. It was only months after the slaughter at Tianenmen Square, and the oppression in the air was thick enough to slice. We spent several days doing the tourist thing in and around Beijing, and we were always aware of the fact that we were the only tourists there. Next we caught the "Iron Rooster" (the Trans Siberian Railway) that took us up through northern China and into Mongolia, finally arriving at the capital city of Ulan Bator.

The 34-hour train ride was a unique cultural experience, to say the least, the highlight being at the Chinese/Mongolian border. There, the train was pulled into a long hanger where, for the next five hours, every wheel and axle was changed. Why? Because the gauge of the rails changed at the border. I guess the Chinese still haven't quite gotten over the licking Genghis Kahn hung on them all those years ago. In any case, the Chinese weren't going to be invaded again by Kahn's descendants, at least not by rail.

The next leg of the journey was via a four-engine, Russian-built, turbo-prop passenger plane to the little town of Hovd (pronounced Hov-da) tucked between the north end of the Gobi Desert and the south end of the famous Altai Mountains on Mongolia's western border. Hovd looked like a broken-down Mexican border town, right out of a spaghetti western. Clint Eastwood would have felt right at home there.

From Hovd, we were transported to our base camp via small Russian jeeps that bounced over rocks and mountain passes for nearly six hours before rolling into a little village of yurts (Mongolian portable dwellings pronounced "gers" by the Mongols). En route, our jeep procession stopped high in the saddle of a mountain pass. The Mongolians dutifully picked up stones and added them to a large pile already in place. According to my interpreter, this was a Mongolian custom. Adding a new stone to the pile each time you passed by would supposedly entitle you to safe passage on your journey. With that in mind, I added a stone of my own.

The absence of trees was obvious. The landscape was barren, devoid of anything but rock and grass, so when I spotted a clump of green trees in the distance, I sat up and took notice. As we drove closer to the trees, I realized they were growing along the banks of a gorgeous blue river. I'm not sure of their exact genus and species, but I could readily identify them as some type of willows.

The rocky jeep trail paralleled the river for several hundred yards. As I watched the water with interest, I saw something wonderful: the rise forms of feeding fish dimpling the surface. I told my interpreter to tell the driver to stop immediately. As a matter of principle, Gary and I never go anywhere far from home without stuffing our backpacker fly rods in our duffels and enough terminal tackle to torment any members of the trout family that we might encounter. Both jeeps stopped. I went back to Gary's jeep and told him what I had seen. As he stepped out, several more forms appeared on the river's surface. We quickly dug out our fly rods and started assembling them. Gary got rigged up first and tossed a Goofus Bug on the water. He was instantly rewarded with a delicious slurp. I looked over just in time to see him set the hook, and a wonderful arc appeared in his rod as he fought the mystery fish. Minutes later, he landed a lovely grayling of about 15 inches. He then removed his fly from its tiny mouth and flipped it back into the river.

What happened next was hilarious. The moment Gary threw the grayling back into the water, as if on cue, all eight of the Mongolians in our entourage rushed into a huddle, as if they were in the Super Bowl. Then my interpreter and huddle spokesperson, Altan, broke from the group and walked casually up to me and asked: "Is it the American custom to throw the first fish back in order to please the gods, so that they will allow you to catch many more fish?" he asked politely.

"Heck, no," I replied. "It's our custom to keep from wiping out an entire species when fish are this dumb!"

About then, Gary set the hook on his second grayling. Before he could even begin to play the fish, a Mongolian streaked in front of him and dove forward, snatching the rod out of his hands while in midair. His moves reminded me of a

Mongolian Deion Sanders going up for an interception. The mad Mongolian was clutching the line tightly against the rod with both hands so that no line could escape as he continued to run full-tilt away from the river. When he managed to drag the poor grayling out over the bank, the balance of his team pounced on the hapless fish like so many cats. It was at that point that Altan politely announced that catch-and-release was not a Mongolian custom. Gary and I caught grayling up to 18 inches on nearly every cast, and finally even taught a couple of the Mongolians to fly fish, which was really a hoot. We finally quit before the grayling did in fact become an endangered species, which would have been inevitable given the dictates of our somewhat utilitarian comrades.

We were on the other side of the world now, in a country where little had changed in terms of lifestyle in the last 2,000 years. The people, then under Communist rule, were primarily still nomadic herdsmen, traveling by camel caravans and moving their herds of sheep, goats, yaks, camels and Mongolian ponies across the barren mountainsides, far above timberline to new grazing areas.

Our base camp was situated at an elevation of about 10,000 feet. The terrain was constant, containing only rock and the protein-charged mountain grass that reminded me of the "prairie wool" of southern Alberta and Saskatchewan. Also, like Canadian prairie days of old, yak chips were the fuel for all fires instead of wood (The Canadian prairie settlers used buffalo chips). Wood simply didn't exist at that altitude. The landscape was somewhat bleak on overcast days, a world of browns and grays. But under a clear blue sky, those same rocks came alive with color, especially on the snow-capped peaks.

The visibility in that timeless landscape is incredible. One can see for 20 miles. The obvious question perplexed me. If I could see forever, how much farther could the keen-eyed ibex see me? I couldn't imagine how I was going to approach these critters without so much as a bush to hide my advance.

Fortunately, after reading everything I could get my hands on about hunting in the Altai Mountains, I was prepared in advance for the rule of long-range shooting. I had cut a life-sized silhouette of a Siberian ibex out of a sheet of ¼-inch plywood. Then I practiced shooting at the wooden ibex out to 500 yards with my .300 Winchester Magnum. Shooting 180-grain Nosler Ballistic Tip bullets in front of 80 grains of IMR 4350, zeroed at 250 yards, I could drop a bullet into the kill zone every shot with relative ease. The Nosler Ballistic Tip bullets produced excellent accuracy, and they also tended to be somewhat explosive upon impact. They are actually hollow point bullets with carbonate wedges in the tips to hasten expansion. I had shot plenty of North American game with Ballistic Tip bullets and never had a bullet pass through an animal. Since I was hunting herd animals in Mongolia, I wanted to know that my bullet would stop in the animal I shot, and not pass through and possibly hit another.

Naturally, I was shooting with a bipod rest. At 400 yards, I had to aim at the hairline on the top of the animal's shoulders. At 500 yards, I had to hold level with the top of its head. I used the heavy portion of the horizontal duplex crosshairs as range-finders, as noted in the previous chapter on hunting Dall's sheep. That practice would serve me well before the hunt was finished. I passed the concept along to my friend, Gary, who was also prepared with the same range-finding ability. This was before the invention of the modern laser range-finders, but it gave us a respectable reference gauge for range.

On the first day of the hunt, Gary and I went separate ways with separate hunting parties. Each of us was assigned an interpreter, a horseman (in case we decided to hunt from horseback), a jeep driver (in case we didn't), and a guide. So, including the hunter, each hunting party consisted of five men.

Gary left camp on horseback, but I opted for the alternate choice, whatever that might be. I took one look at those Mongolian saddles and knew my posterior would never touch one. The primitive little saddles looked like small cushions with steel saddle horns both fore and aft. I had been abused by plenty of North American ponies, so I decided not to accept the equestrian challenge on the other side of the world. I didn't figure they'd accept my Alberta Health Care card at the Hovd General Hospital, even if such a place existed. And even if the saddles had been designed for a man my size, the squatty little horses were built so low to the ground that I'm sure I'd have worn the soles off my boots even while sitting astride one of the wretched little creatures.

On that first morning of my hunt, we drove off into the darkness, headed for who knows where. After crossing a river and bouncing across rocks and boulders, the driver stopped the jeep and announced something in Mongolian. Altan, my interpreter, politely advised me that we would now begin the hunt on foot.

I could see the foot of the mountain beginning to materialize in the faint morning light. It was huge. No, it was colossal!

My crew began glassing for game. I was advised in advance to bring an extra spotting scope and extra binoculars for my guide, as he would have none of his own. This proved true. In the haze, he spotted a huge ibex and, by the time I found him in my spotting scope, he was almost out of sight. He was the same color as the rocks around him, brown and gray, but even to my uneducated eye, I could tell he was a monster with his long, corrugated horns sweeping over his back, nearly touching his rump. And there was that very distinct goatee, typical of wild goats throughout the world. After a little collaboration with the guide, Altan told me the ibex was very big. I assumed that was an understatement.

My four Mongol hunting partners worked out a strategy of approach among themselves. Then Altan turned politely to me and said, "We must climb the mountain now." And climb we did. I had no idea at the time, but my body had not yet acclimated to the extreme altitude. My feet felt like lead, and my lungs like BBs. It was all I could do to climb five steps at a time before stopping to gasp for air. I was 45 years old at the time, and I felt like I had made a grave mistake by coming to the Altai. "I must be over the hill," I thought. "I'm just not man enough for these mountains!"

My legs burned as they tried to climb. I thought that I would collapse at any moment. I kept thinking the return portion of my plane ticket back to North America had been an unnecessary expenditure.

Somehow, after hours of grinding out the death climb, we stood knee-deep in snow at the pinnacle of Blue Ibex Mountain, elevation 14,500 feet. It was an exhilarating experience, even if at the brink of death. If nothing else, I made it to the top.

By now I was wondering if the plan was really to kill me off the first day so my crew could lay around camp for the next two weeks. However, since I still had a little life in me, the hunt proceeded.

The guide walked out on a rocky outcropping and glassed the rocks below us. Soon he eased back and whispered something to Altan, who relayed the message to me. The guide had found the big ibex bedded down with several other trophy-class billies on a rocky spire sharply below us.

We climbed down a rock trough until the guide motioned for us to stop. Then he lay down on his belly and slithered out to a narrow ledge between two huge boulders. He peeked over the edge and pulled back quickly. Obviously he saw the ibex. He motioned for me to come out onto the ledge beside him, so I crawled on my belly as cautiously as I could.

There was a problem with the available space on the rocky ledge. The guide, who erroneously assumed that I would be shooting right-handed, rolled to the left side of the ledge to make room for me. Since I didn't speak his language and since my interpreter wasn't there, I had trouble explaining to him that he was in my way and on the wrong side of the ledge. When I finally grabbed him with one hand and shoved him to the right, he got the idea. In the meantime, while we carried on like two bear cubs in a telephone booth, the ibex must have become suspicious. When I first peeked over the ledge, they were all standing at red alert. One of them must have seen me at that very instant because they exploded from their lofty perch and were suddenly running down the mountain at break-neck speed.

I got a flashing glance at what I thought was the largest billy as he disappeared behind a boxcar-sized boulder. I squared the rifle on the far side of the boulder and, when the ibex dashed into my crosshairs, followed and squeezed the trigger. Since I was not shooting from any sort of stable position, the recoil knocked me onto my side, and I instantly lost sight of the ibex. I was still lying there in a bit of a daze when I realized that the rest of the troops were whooping and hollering with glee. I assumed that meant that either I had killed the ibex, or they thought I had expired while trying.

I raised myself up to my knees and looked at my guide. He was grinning and giving me the universal "thumbs up," which I knew meant I had scored.

Together we moved down the mountain about 300 yards and found my ibex lying dead, shot through the center of the lungs. I was impressed. So were the Mongolians.

We took pictures and, as the crew began to cape the animal, I realized that somehow I still had to get off the mountain. I politely informed my interpreter that if I were going to go back to camp with the rest of the crew, I would have to start down the mountain right then. He agreed, and I started my descent. To my further agony, I found that downhill was just as exhausting as uphill. My knees felt like rubber, and it seemed as if my mind could not dictate where my next step would land. After an hour of easing my tortured body down the slope, I sat down to rest my aching legs. All the training I had done back in Alberta seemed to no avail. I was really whipped.

I heard something above me and turned to see my guide walking casually down the mountain with the head and cape of my ibex cradled by the horns across his shoulders. To my further amazement, there was my horseman carrying the rest of the animal on his back—guts, feathers and all!

This was the most amazing feat I had ever witnessed. This little man was barely five feet tall and weighed no more than 130 pounds, soaking wet. And he was carrying the whole ibex, minus its head and cape, which must have weighed at least half again as much as he did. But down the mountain he went with his incredible load. If I felt wimpy before, I felt truly useless now. I was the last one off the mountain that night and slithered into the little jeep like a whipped dog. Yes, I had shot a real trophy ibex, but I felt something less than triumphant. I was too weary to care.

On the way back to our hunting camp, the driver took us to a remote mountain valley that was inhabited by a Mongolian family and their livestock. As we bounced across the rocky valley floor toward their yurts, I asked Altan where we were going. "To see the family," he replied nonchalantly.

"Why?" I asked.

"They milk the mares," he retorted.

That threw me. We're going to see a family that milks mares? Obviously there was more to it than I was capable of understanding. I just decided to go along for the ride and see what would happen.

Upon arrival, we were greeted by the man of the yurt, and soon we were all squatting around a low wooden table in the middle of the floor of the small, dome-shaped dwelling. Mongolians don't bother with chairs. They're short people anyway, as are their tables, so squatting seemed appropriate enough. The mood was festive as the Mongolians jabbered at one another with animated and joyful gestures. I flashed back to a Steve Martin line in one of his crazy movies: "These people have a different word for everything!"

Next, the man of the yurt unveiled a large wooden bowl covered with a white cloth. When he lifted the bowl, all the other Mongolians chortled with animated glee. The bowl was set on the table before us and the cloth removed, revealing the white liquid within. Now the Mongols were cheering. Ceramic bowls the size of large cereal bowls were passed to each of us. Then our host produced a wooden ladle and began dipping up the white liquid, lifting the ladle high above the bowl and slowly dribbling it back inside. Whatever this strange foreplay meant, it served to set the Mongols into a fever pitch. Finally, the host came around and filled our bowls with the white elixir. The Mongols waited with bated breath for his next signal. When he lifted his bowl toward his lips and uttered the magic words, the Mongols tipped up their bowls and completely drained them in one long gulp. I sniffed at the white stuff and was repulsed. It smelled like ammonia with a horse standing in it. Well, I was close—it was fermented mare's milk. The Mongolians call it "Irik," and it's the official national drink of Mongolia.

After a sniff, I was horrified to think that I was actually going to have to consume the nasty liquid. But not wanting to insult my hosts, I took a deep breath and sipped some into my mouth. My body shuddered involuntarily as the taste registered on my tongue. It was the nastiest thing I'd ever tasted. My throat closed off and refused my attempt to swallow. All the others had emptied their bowls and were staring quietly at me. With great determination, I forced the sip of Irik down my throat and fought valiantly not to woof my cookies all over the table. It was embarrassing to say the least, but embarrassing or not, one thing was abundantly clear: I wasn't going to drink any more.

I turned to Altan and looked him squarely in the eyes so that he would get the full impact of my words. "Tell the people the American has a weak stomach, or whatever you need to tell them, but I am NOT going to drink this stuff. It'll kill me."

Altan explained that I had a weak stomach, which brought a roar of laughter from the rest of the men. But humiliation was a small price to pay for abstinence. For the first time, I understood why the Chinese were so afraid of Genghis Kahn. It wasn't so much that they feared dying at the hands of the murderous Mongol. It was that the survivors might have to accept Irik as their national drink. For that reason, any rational man would fall gleefully upon his own sword to avoid such a fate.

When we arrived back at camp, Gary greeted me with the news that he had also taken his first ibex. I congratulated him weakly and announced that he could visit me in intensive care. Between the strain of the hunt and my humiliating introduction to Irik, I doubted that I'd be able to walk the next day.

Unfortunately, the next day I was still alive, so I mustered all my remaining strength to try for my second ibex. It was as tough as the first, and again that night I doubted that I would live until morning. I truly believed I was no longer man enough for such hunting.

The camp menu added to the stress of the situation. We were assured by the booking agency back in the States that there would be a cook in camp who cooked western cuisine for us. We quickly learned, however, that we were relegated to a steady diet of the Mongolian Blue Plate Special: "sphincter stew." It was a loose meat soup (my assumption, though I can't prove it) garnished with small blighted potatoes. It appeared that whatever creature furnished the meat for the stew was butchered with machetes while he was still lying on the ground. The gritty texture in the tiny knots of meat was undoubtedly dirt. On one occasion, I was walking around our camp looking for my interpreter, when I happened to poke my head in the cooking yurt. The cook was frying a small mountain of chicken. I quickly abandoned my search for Altan and ran back to our yurt with the good news. "Gary," I yelled with unbridled exuberance. "Don't send out for pizza! You're never going to believe what's for dinner . . . fried chicken!"

We sat in our yurt, kindling the fires beneath our culinary expectations as we waited for dinner to be served. The Mongolians always brought the meal to us in our yurt. Presently the delivery service appeared at our door. We enthusiastically beckoned him to come in and were overcome by the sight of more sphincter stew.

"What about the fried chicken?" Gary gasped in disappointment. I had no answers. Suddenly it was all too clear. The Mongols were eating the stuff that was sent out for us high-paying Americans, and we were eating sphincter stew. We considered a mutiny, but thought better of it when we considered how far we were from home and how badly we were outnumbered. On top of all the other obstacles we faced, we didn't fancy ending up buried under a remote pile of rocks somewhere in Outer Mongolia by the great, great grandsons of Genghis Khan. Worse yet, if we were taken captive, they might sentence us to life in prison, with a diet of Irik and sphincter stew. Perish the thought! We have since discovered that our experience was typical for Americans hunting in Communist countries. Honesty is a truly foreign concept to Communists. It's every man for himself, and whatever he can steal or scam is considered quite normal, if not honorable.

On the morning of day three, I awoke and felt strangely wonderful and energetic. My body had finally adapted to the altitude, and I had a whole new lease on life. For the first time since the hunt began I could honestly say it felt good to be alive. We continued to hunt for our second ibexes, and it was becoming a joy.

I was so relieved to realize that I wasn't really washed up after all. What I had experienced was the three-day adjustment period required for my body to adapt to the extreme altitude.

Late one evening, we spotted a band of billies feeding on the low shoulder of a mountain. There wasn't time for a stalk because they were several miles away, so we watched them bed down before we returned to camp. We were back the following morning well before daylight. As we watched the ibex rise and begin to feed, it appeared that one of them had a bluish-looking coloration around his neck, like a collar. I asked Altan what that indicated and he conferred with the guide who explained that the oldest males get that bluish-looking collar around their necks with age, and that ibex was the oldest billy in the bunch. His horns didn't appear to be noticeably longer than the others, but they were very heavy. I decided he was the one I wanted — the old "blue ibex."

I explained to Altan that I did not want to shoot another ibex on the run at some great distance, but rather wanted to make a classic stalk and shoot him before he knew I was in the country. All agreed that's how we would do it. After the animals ate their fill, they began to climb the mountain, presumably to bed. We followed them for two hours before they vanished into the rocks. Gingerly we edged along, glassing every nook and cranny for a trace of them, but there was none. We eventually came to a sharp, hog-backed ridge. The guide said he would climb it alone to peek over the top and see what was on the other side. As soon as he looked over the top, he slid down a few feet and motioned for me to come up. Soon I was at his side and he motioned with his hands that my ibex was below us on the other side of a steep shale draw, bedded down with the other billies. Together, we crawled quietly to the top and looked. At a distance I guessed to be 250 yards, I saw the old ibex lying in his bed in the shale slide sharply below us. He didn't know we were there.

I nodded to the guide that I saw him, cranked my scope up to 9X and settled into the ridgetop for a steady rest. When I put the crosshairs behind the ibex's shoulder, I could see that his left horn was curled down into the path of the bullet. I didn't want to hit a horn, so I waited. Eventually, the old ibex tipped his nose down and closed his eyes. As his nose went down, the horn raised up and out of the way. I took a deep breath, steadied myself and squeezed the trigger. When the rifle cracked, the old ibex's head slumped. Other than that, he never moved. The rest of his band, which were hidden farther below us, suddenly emerged in single file and climbed right over the top of the mountain before us. It was a grand sight to see. Since they never saw us, they left at a casual pace.

That hunt will certainly rank as one of the most memorable experiences of my life. When I arrived back at camp, I found that Gary had also collected his second billy, so the hunt was a total success. The long-horned Siberian ibex of the Mongolian High Altai are regal trophies, inhabiting the top of the world in a country where only the tough survive. It was a fitting backdrop for the fierce Mongolian hero of old, the legendary Genghis Kahn.

POSTSCRIPT

The rear saddle horn on Gary's Mongolian saddle rubbed a spot raw on his backside that became infected. By the time he got back to his home in Chico, Calif., he was a very sick man. Doctors operated on him immediately upon his return home and advised him that he would have died in another 24 hours. This substantiates my position that mountain ponies are deadly creatures with a vendetta against hunters.

The Life and Times of an Alberta Whitetail Guide

FOURTEEN

The Right Place at the Right Time

My life and professional connection to the great outdoors certainly gives credence to the old adage: "Timing is everything." Through no planning on my part, I was in the right place at the right time. For instance, I am a native Texan who ended up in Alberta, Canada, in the late 1960s. I thought I was going to Canada for a week's vacation, but I ended up marrying, settling and living there until 1990, when my family and I moved back to the U.S. Contrary to the rumors started by a couple of notable (if not quotable) outdoors writers, I did not go to Canada to escape the draft. I finished my stint in Uncle Sam's Army and was discharged in the summer of 1965. The truth is that while I was always an outdoors enthusiast, I was neither a guide nor a writer when I went to Canada. That came later as the result of my first moose hunting experience chronicled in the chapter entitled: "A Moose for the Tenderfoot." By the mid-1970s, I had discovered the gargantuan whitetails of eastern Alberta and decided to offer trophy whitetail hunts and leave the moose struggle to someone else. Why? Try a regular diet of packing moose quarters out of the muskeg on your back and you'll get the picture.

About that same time, I was teaching an eight-week trout fly-tying course on Thursday nights in Edmonton, Alberta. One of my students, Dave Reidie, was the head photographer for the *Edmonton Journal*, the province's largest newspaper at that time. He came into class one night and asked (in jest, I'm sure) if anyone there would like to be the new outdoors columnist for the *Journal*. The former columnist, Gary Cooper, had quit. As has been typical of my life, I volunteered. The next day, I had an interview with the sports editor and, bingo, I was suddenly the new outdoors columnist. At that time, I had written only one outdoors article that I submitted to *Field and Stream*. They rejected it. Before giving up, I sent it to *The American Hunter*, and they bought it. It was a story about my first moose hunt whereupon I met Marion Diesel. That was it. I was one for one as an outdoors writer. As the saying goes, "Yesterday I couldn't spell outdoors columnist . . . Today, I are one!"

Writing for the newspaper trained me to think and write upon command. My experiences in Alberta's fledgling whitetail outfitting business were sometimes inspiring enough for me to put on paper. I began selling Alberta whitetail stories to U.S. hunting magazines that were really salivating over the giant whitetails of western Canada. I was the only one writing about those big Canadian bucks back then, and, as far as I know, the only one guiding for them, too. If I'd been anywhere but Alberta at that time, I would probably not have received the attention from the magazine world that I did. Subsequently, I might not have been thrust into the world of outdoors writing. Like I said, timing is everything. I was definitely in the right place at the right time.

Oddly enough, most Canadians thought all the big whitetails were in Texas. Other western Canadian outfitters concentrated their efforts on the more exclusive game such as elk, moose, bighorn sheep and grizzly bears, and they couldn't imagine why anyone would come all the way to Canada from the U.S. to hunt the lowly white-tailed deer. Obviously, the whitetail had not yet reached its coveted status with western Canadians. In fact, anywhere in rural Alberta you could find record book racks nailed to barns or fence posts, or lying in gardens, rotting away and being eaten by rodents. Since I was from Texas, I knew those Canadian bucks were far superior to what most Americans had at home. It was upon that premise that I set out to be a trophy whitetail guide and outfitter in Alberta. In those early years, I was the laughing stock of the Alberta outfitting industry. They're not laughing anymore.

FIFTEEN

Growing Pains

$\mathcal{A}$t first I was cautiously optimistic about offering trophy whitetail hunts in Alberta. Back then, according to statistics, one Alberta whitetail buck in 600 harvested would qualify for B&C. While that didn't guarantee my hunters that 1-in-600 buck, it did mean they would be hunting where the odds were as good as they get. In the late '70s, the trophy whitetail industry exploded virtually overnight in western Canada, and most especially in Alberta. Hunters came knocking, and thanks to my exposure in American hunting magazines and the word of mouth of my hunters, I turned down business. The downside was that American hunters prospecting for "BOOK" whitetails were victims of bad propaganda and often believed that if they could just plunk themselves on Alberta soil, record book bucks would come squirting out of every hedgerow and thicket. Some less than scrupulous outfitters created that myth, but it just wasn't that way. And when one of those "Sho-Nuff" book bucks did appear, they usually made monkeys of the hunters and left them with egg plastered all over their embarrassed faces.

I want to make a necessary distinction at this point. Most non-resident hunter opportunities at record book white-tailed bucks resulted in something less than success for one of several reasons. Most western Canadian whitetail guides of that era grew up driving the country roads and shooting whitetails from their truck windows. That might appall some readers, but in reality, back in the 1960s and earlier, there were few whitetail hunters in western Canada. In fact, at that time there were relatively few whitetails when compared with today's populations. And much of the privately owned farmland was unoccupied. It still is. Killing a whitetail was a casual pursuit that might render a little meat for the freezer, but the trophy bucks were not killed so much by design as by simple luck. Most resident meat hunters favored moose. The truth was, a few good ol' boys driving around the nearly empty farmlands of western Canada didn't create much of a problem. But when that mentality and style of hunting turned professional, it soon got out of control, and some guides took liberties on lands that were forbidden. Soon, those evil American hunters were held in contempt by resident hunters, despite the millions of dollars they were pouring into the Canadian economy. Somehow the local folks who got so anti-American chose to overlook the fact that there was a Canadian guiding every one of those "evil Americans." I say all this to make this point: Since many Canadian whitetail guides of that era had never actually hunted whitetails on foot, a truck ride through the back roads was what they offered their American clientele. That practice became so rampant by the end of the 1970s that an entire industry of road-hunting outfitters and guides proliferated in eastern Alberta, rightfully aggravating the residents who were largely hunting from the same roads. Hunters were expected to take shots at running bucks a quarter or more mile away, from pick-up trucks that were sometimes still rolling. Then guides told stories about hunters who had muffed their "chances" at record book deer. To add insult to injury, they condemned their hunters for missing those ridiculous shots that should never have been considered in the first place. Incoming hunters would be told about the "book" deer that last week's hunters missed, fueling the fires of anticipation, only to face more running bucks out on the horizon. The road hunt raged onward.

It became very ugly and, eventually, a runaway whitetail industry had to be tamed and government regulations were implemented. The transition period was volatile, but today it is under reasonable control. Happily, in the meantime, many Canadian guides have honed some real whitetail hunting skills, well away from roads and pick-up trucks. They have learned to respect big whitetails for what they are: the greatest hunting challenge on earth.

Back in those hectic days, I would get calls from hunters who wanted to come to Alberta to shoot a B&C buck. "How many book bucks did your hunters kill last season?" they would ask. I found myself trying to explain that though (in many cases) we had killed no record book bucks, we had seen five or six and the hunters just couldn't make it work. Even though my outfit didn't subscribe to the road hunting approach, hunters still muffed opportunities at huge deer for a multitude of reasons. A missed deer is a missed deer, but at least I can look back and say that the bucks my hunters missed were not due to stupid truck hunting tactics. Record book whitetails have a way of foiling even the best laid plans.

I suppose if I retraced my steps through the 18 years that I guided whitetail hunters in Alberta, I encountered between 50 and 60 bucks that I believe would have qualified for any record book in the world. Some of them were too big to believe. Of those 50 or 60 bucks, a dozen or so were caught completely flat-footed with no way to escape, and yet somehow they did. For the first five years of my Alberta whitetail outfitting career, I awoke many a night in a cold sweat, dreaming and reliving the anxiety I experienced in trying to get a hunter to shoot the deer of his dreams. I erroneously believed that justice was only done if that deer's head was hanging in my hunter's trophy room. But time changed my perspective as I came to grips with reality. I finally made peace with the fact that I was in the opportunity business. If I presented my hunter with a quality opportunity to shoot a book deer (or any trophy deer) and he blew it, that didn't make me a failure. In fact, I was a success. I couldn't take responsibility for what my hunters could or couldn't do.

I also learned something interesting about dedicated trophy whitetail hunters. Unlike moose, elk or bear hunters, true trophy whitetail hunters are forever. A hunter might book an elk hunt this year and then go for a bear next year, as he adds more species to his hunting repertoire. But if he's hooked on whitetails, regardless of what other game he pursues, he will hunt whitetails as long as he can hold a weapon. Another curious fact about hard-core trophy whitetail hunters is that they might know more about their quarry than does their guide. After all, they probably hunt them every year in their own backyards, as well as numerous other places. I guided hunters who had been hunting whitetails longer than I had been alive. The snag is this: The dream of a record book whitetail burns so passionately in their minds that when they actually come face to face with the object of their obsession, it is often simply overwhelming. A hunter might have to ask his guide if the bear or the moose he's looking at is a trophy animal. Initially, he might have very limited experience in judging those other species. But not whitetails! When a trophy whitetail fanatic finally lays eyes on the deer he's been dreaming about all his life, his electrical system sometimes seems to short-circuit. The results can be devastating to both hunter and guide.

After coming to grips with this fact of life, I quit trying to explain about the missed opportunities to hard-breathing idealists. In truth, it got to the point that when I was guiding a hunter and spotted a buck that I felt sure would make the record book, the first thought that entered my mind was: "Well, let's see how this one gets screwed up." I wasn't necessarily being pessimistic. It was a conditioned response. In the end, I saw it as a contest and simply felt like the best man would win. He usually did, and he was usually the deer.

Many hunters have asked me, "How many of those 50 or 60 book bucks could you have killed if you'd been hunting instead of guiding?" There's no way to know. One of the advantages of being the guide is that you don't have to make the shot. I believe I could have taken quite a number of them, but then again, I know I could never have hunted as hard for my own amusement as I had to hunt as a professional guide. Therefore, I might have been home in bed instead of hunting on many of those magical mornings.

SIXTEEN

Panic Attacks

I have a catalog of nightmares, indelibly etched in my brain, of giant white-tailed bucks that managed to perform their amazing Houdini acts and escape the clutches of my panting hunters. Now that the pressure is off and I am blissfully retired from the guiding and outfitting business, I can remember them with only mildly debilitating pain and trauma. Some of those incidents are amusing, if not downright funny now. I'll share some of the classic cases, but in each mishap the name of the hunter will be fictitious (unless otherwise noted), just in case his memories are not yet fully healed.

During the first week of November in the late '70s, Bill and I were en route to the property we intended to hunt. I stopped the truck and he opened the gate and jumped back inside. We'd gone no more than 100 yards on the narrow dirt trail when I looked out Bill's window and saw a buck standing there broadside, only 75 yards from the truck. The buck was immense. His 10-point rack towered above him in a cluster of saber-like tines—several of which were over 12 inches long. The width of the rack was well past the buck's ears—I estimated his inside spread at 24 inches. At a glance, I knew I was looking at a 190-inch typical buck. The best part was that he was standing in the open, a full 200 yards from the nearest bush!

I took my foot off the accelerator and let the truck slow to a crawl. In the calmest voice I could muster, I said: "Bill, there's a real nice buck (intentional understatement) standing off to your right about 75 yards. We've got him flat-footed, so I'm going to slow down, let you step out with your rifle, and I'll just crawl away from you with the truck (It was illegal to shoot from a vehicle). As soon as you step out, crank a round into the chamber and shoot him. Just move slowly and deliberately. He's an easy shot, and you've got him dead to rights."

As I was talking to him, Bill looked out his side window and saw the buck. What happened next was unbelievable. Bill gasped and jumped out of the truck with his rifle and started frantically trying to find his ammunition. Meanwhile, to my amazement, the buck just stood there while Bill literally tore the pockets out of his hunting jacket. Finally he located his ammo and tried to stuff cartridges into the magazine of his bolt-action rifle. By then, the buck was becoming less and less interested in Bill's antics. He turned and started walking toward the timber. Bill was having a fit of pure panic as he managed to jam two .30-06 cartridges into the throat of his chamber at once. In fact, he jammed them in so tight we had to finally use a hammer to get them out of there.

Meanwhile, the buck was 150 yards away, still walking casually. He finally stopped for one last look at Bill, who was still wrapped around his rifle and sputtering some choice New Jersey, four-letter friend-getters. I was sitting in the truck 50 yards away, praying for more grace and alternately watching Bill and the buck through my binoculars. I still remember when Bill looked up from all his rifle troubles and our eyes met for a split second. The look on his face seemed to say: "I'm really screwing up, aren't I?" To which my eyes replied: "Yes, Bill, you're really screwing up!"

The buck vanished, and to this day I doubt that Bill realizes the magnitude of his blunder. I do though. I've scored that buck a thousand times in my memory.

Many of my hunters were from Texas. In fact, in the beginning of my whitetail career, all my promotional efforts were directed at Texans. I was one, so I knew how they thought. If there were bigger or better deer anywhere on earth, a Texan would be the first to sign on for the hunt. I knew that if Texans went for the Alberta whitetails, the rest of the world would follow. I was right.

A long-suffering Texas hunter (to whom I'll refer as Fred) was as intense about his trophy whitetails as any hunter I've ever known. He lived, breathed and dreamed book whitetails. In truth, I think they were his reason for living. He coveted book whitetails with a white-knuckled passion, although he had never seen one on the hoof.

Fred and I came around a red willow thicket at dawn in mid-November and there, less than 30 yards in front of us, stood Ol' Moses. The buck's gnarly nontypical rack looked so huge that it made the animal look front-heavy, as if his head were too big for his torso. Fred gasped, dropped down on one knee and shouldered his rifle as the buck stood statue-still. I was waiting for the crack of his .300 Mag. when I heard him whisper in panic: "Where did he go?"

"He didn't go anywhere," I hissed. "He's still standing right there in front of you!"

"I can't see him!" Fred choked.

I assumed he'd breathed on his scope and fogged it up in the cold morning air. He pulled the scope away from his eye to locate the buck again, and seemed shocked to realize that the buck was still where he'd seen him last. Again he shouldered the rifle and again he could see nothing. Fred was on the brink of coming completely unhinged when the buck turned and started into the willows, but his rack was so big it got entangled in the rubbery limbs, causing him to pause momentarily.

"You'd better hurry!" I urged, as Fred scoured the earth for the buck through his scope.

Finally, the buck backed up a step, lowered his massive head, and lifted all the limbs that were blocking him, tossing them over his back as he walked into the willow thicket and disappeared. Fred, in the meantime, realized that he had his scope cranked up to 10x in preparation for one of those barrel-stretching long shots for which Alberta was famous. By the time he realized what was wrong and cranked the scope down to 3x, his opportunity had passed. It was a long quiet walk back to the truck. Few hunters will ever stand within 30 yards of a buck like that with a loaded gun in their hands and a tag in their pocket. My mental etching of the buck's rack puts him somewhere in the 230s non-typical.

A closer look at Fred's mishap illustrates a common trend among American hunters coming to Alberta to hunt whitetails. They were encouraged to be ready for long shots in wide-open spaces. Just like Fred, they typically showed up with the biggest magnum they could stand behind and a high-powered variable scope.

Such was the case with Jim, who hailed from Dallas. He was an able young man, eager to do whatever was necessary to up his odds on an Alberta braggin' buck. That included long-range rifle target practice, which he had done at home in preparation for his Alberta hunt. A buck at 400 yards was in serious trouble if he walked out in front of Jim. The problem was that a 200-class typical buck walked out in front of him at about 80 yards.

I remember the sight of that buck like it was yesterday. It walked broadside out into a stand of sparse, 8-foot wolf willows as Jim and I were bouncing across a pasture in a pick-up truck with Gordon Hollinger, the farmer who owned the land. Gordon was giving us a guided tour of his property before turning us loose to go hunting. Gordon and I spotted the buck at the same time, and he stopped the truck instantly. Simultaneously, the buck noticed us and froze in his tracks, still broadside but with his head turned toward us. Two things struck me about the buck the second I saw him: (1) he had the longest body I had ever seen on any kind of deer, and (2) his rack was extremely high and narrow. Still unsure of whether it was a whitetail or a mule deer, I snapped by binoculars to my eyes. What I saw nearly stopped my heart. It was, in fact, a whitetail—a monstrous whitetail. Binoculars revealed that his rack was not actually narrow at all. It just appeared to be narrow because of the height of the rack. I could see four inches of daylight between his main beams and the top of his ears, putting him solidly at 25 inches between the beams. His tines were the longest I have ever seen—so tall they that they made his 25-inch wide rack appear narrow! I believe I am still conservative at estimating several of his tines at 16 inches. In any case, the number 200 popped into my mind as I struggled to believe what my binoculars revealed.

Jim was sitting by the passenger side door, and I was sitting in the middle between him and Gordon. As soon as the truck stopped, I commanded him to jump out and take a rest over the front of the truck. The buck was on the driver's side.

Jim was out like a flash and took a solid rest on the hood with the short bipod attached to his stock. The buck was so close that I never considered point of aim as being worthy of discussion, so the instant I knew it was a whitetail, I told Jim to take him. Moments later, the .300 Winchester Magnum thundered. I was watching the buck with bated breath through my binoculars, and what I saw confused me at first. At the report of the rifle, the buck snapped his nose high up into the air. He held that odd pose for a few seconds before looking back at us. Upon realizing that he wasn't hit, I told Jim to fire again. He did, and again the buck snapped his nose high in the air. That time, I saw the tip of one wolf willow branch topple from above the buck's head. Only then did I realize that Jim was shooting way over the buck. "Where are you aiming?" I begged. I could see the light dawning in Jim's eyes. He was so geared for those 400-yard shots that he had forgotten how to shoot a buck at pointblank range. "He's less than 100 yards," I instructed. "Pull it down!"

Jim nodded and snuggled in behind his rifle just as the amazing buck made a slow, animated turn away from us. When Jim's rifle spoke again, the buck bolted into the thicket and out of sight. When we went over to examine the area for sign, we found enough deer hair to fill a Safeway bag. Jim's last shot was finally down where it should have been, but it only grazed the moving buck's left flank. We found one tiny piece of flesh smaller than a pencil eraser, but we never saw the buck again. Of all the bucks I've encountered in my guiding career, the memory of that one haunted me the longest. I have never seen another typical deer to compare with it. I can say, with the utmost confidence, that Milo Hansen's No. 1 B&C Saskatchewan rack would look anemic beside the one Jim missed, regardless of its net score.

I suppose the moral of that story is that while it's good to prepare for the long shots, it's best not to get so programmed that you can't make the chip shots when they present themselves.

For the three previous years, Randy, who hails from just outside Dallas, Texas, had bagged trophy white-tailed bucks in my camp. Now he was back to try for his fourth. He was a pleasure to guide. Not only did he do what he was told, but he was also lucky! What more could a guide ask for in a hunter? However, the longer you hunt big whitetails, the greater the odds are that one will eventually undo you. This is the story of Randy's undoing.

My guide, Shane Hansen, was guiding Randy, and I was simultaneously guiding Jackie Bushman and Alan Brewer (their real names). Brewer and Bushman were both from the head office of the then fledgling Buckmasters organization. Bushman had taken his great 12-point Alberta trophy the previous day, and now I had placed Alan in a stand where I thought he could score. Well before dawn, after putting Alan on stand, Jackie and I drove off to watch the sun rise over the Battle River valley. We were driving across a barley stubble field toward the lip of the valley when we noticed a buck and a doe standing off to our left between two small patches of willows, right in the middle of the field. I stopped the truck and glassed them and was staggered by the size of the buck's rack. His 10-point typical frame would have put him in the 180s, not to mention all the trash and kickers growing from around his antler bases. Jackie and I stared in stunned silence.

"Gawwwd, what a buck," Jackie finally groaned.

"Where is Alan when we really need him?" I groaned back.

The buck was preoccupied with the hot doe, standing there not more than 60 yards from us. I had a tag in my pocket and a .264 Magnum right beside me, but I couldn't bring myself to shoot the buck. As long as I had a hunter in camp with an unfilled tag, it was my policy that my guides and I would never shoot a buck. As bad as I wanted to shoot that huge deer, I knew that bringing him back to camp would raise doubts as to why I shot it, rather than one of my hunters. I sighed and watched in awe as the buck trotted along behind the doe as if he were on a string. The doe finally led the buck to the edge of the river brakes and down into a clump of brush on a hogback ridge in front of us. By that time, Jackie and I were out of the truck, standing at the lip of the valley and watching the spectacle.

"I've got to find Shane!" I finally concluded. "Randy and Shane are hunting somewhere close by!" We turned and started walking back toward the truck only to discover that the doe and buck had circled back around us and were now standing between us and the truck less than 80 yards distant.

"Now he's tempting fate!" I whispered to Jackie.

"Gawwwd, what a buck!" Jackie repeated.

By the time we reached the truck, the doe and the buck had trotted back down the ridge. We watched them bed down in the brush. We backed out of the field and, within minutes, I found Shane sitting in his truck, watching Randy through his spotting scope. Meanwhile, Randy was in a treestand, a quarter-mile down in the bottom of the river valley.

I explained where the buck was bedded and told Shane to position Randy in the river bottom below that spot. Once Randy was in position, we'd jump the buck out of his bed and he'd run for the cover of the river bottom and right into Randy's lap. Jackie and I drove back to the lip of the valley and waited for Shane to join us. While waiting, we watched to make sure the buck didn't leave his bed unnoticed. Fifteen minutes later, Shane drove up and announced that the trap was set. I pointed out the spot where the buck and doe were bedded and told Shane to walk casually down the ridge and into the brush. He agreed and took off on foot. Jackie and I sat there with a ringside seat to watch our wonderful plan produce Randy's fourth, and undoubtedly his best, Alberta trophy whitetail.

Shane walked down the ridge about 300 yards. As he entered the brush, we saw the buck stand up and face him. The buck then whirled and dove off the ridge, heading down the terraced river brakes toward Randy. Then something very strange happened. Shane fell face-first into the snow, as if he'd suddenly died on his feet. In shock, we watched in suspended horror, wondering what had happened. Then we saw Shane move. At first, he got up on his knees, then stood up, dusted the snow off himself and started walking back toward Jackie and me. I hurried down to meet him to see what was wrong. Shane anticipated my question. When I drew close, he said, "You ain't gonna believe this!"

"Believe what?" I inquired anxiously.

Shane explained that when the buck stood up and headed down into the valley toward Randy, he yelled to signal the waiting hunter. "Get ready Randy, here he comes!" Shane yelled.

To his disbelief, after shouting the "get ready" signal, he heard Randy shouting back at the top of his lungs: "Okay, I'm ready!"

Unfortunately, the buck heard Randy's reply and headed west instead of down into the valley where he would have presented Randy with a chip shot.

The excitement of the chase sometimes inspires hunters to do some pretty stupid things. Right at the top of the stupid list was Randy's unthinking response. It cost him the opportunity to read his name on a page in the record book. Unfortunately, that incident seemed to break Randy's lucky streak. He botched opportunities at no less than three more bucks on that same hunt, and he went home empty-handed for the first time in four years.

Yet another Texas hunter had a chance at a true record book typical buck. It was one of those mornings when everything happened according to plan. Well, almost everything!

Mac was a well-traveled big game hunter, and very much into the wild sheep and African safari scene. He had taken animals with names I'd never heard of, and others I couldn't pronounce. Mac was "Mr. Trophy." I don't think he had much whitetail experience behind him, but he was about to have plenty. I had heard of Mac's heroics in Africa on a Cape buffalo hunt. The animal charged him and his guide, impaling the guide on his horns. While wearing the white hunter on his head, the buffalo turned and charged Mac. Under great duress, Mac shot the charging beast and killed it, saving his guide's life. Knowing that about Mac made me confident of his ability to stand up to the stress of shooting a record book whitetail. Of course I'm not referring to the stress of a whitetail threatening a hunter's life as the Cape buffalo had done, but rather the stress that hits the brain when that elusive, once-in-a-lifetime buck appears.

My guides had spotted a giant typical buck working a rub line around a stubble field just days before the season opened. There was plenty of evidence that the buck was still working that rub line and fresh new scrapes the size of pickup truck beds were appearing daily.

Before dawn, Mac and I were situated in the edge of the timber overlooking the stubble field. A blind draw fed up into the middle of the field that made it possible for a deer to suddenly pop into view, as if from out of nowhere. Minutes after dawn, a doe did just that. She popped up in the middle of the field almost magically as she stepped out of the head of the draw. She stopped, looked behind her down the draw, twitched her tail from side to side and walked on across the field. Mac had a bipod attached to his rifle. I told him to get steady and ready. Then the buck stepped up out of the draw, appearing suddenly in the middle of the stubble field about 400 yards in front of us. He was walking with his head held high and erect, perfectly broadside. I heard Mac slip off his safety, take a deep breath and fire. Through my binoculars, I saw dust fly right behind the buck's heels. The buck stopped and looked our way for a brief second, then resumed his journey as if nothing had happened.

"You're behind him and low!" I whispered. "You're going to have to raise it up and lead him a little when he's walking."

My words barely left my lips before the second shot thundered, landing just as the first, right at the great buck's heels. Again the buck stopped and looked in our direction, then continued on his way, still without alarm.

Now I could hear Mac's breath coming in short, choppy gasps. He knew he was messing up, but he couldn't connect with my instructions. He was starting to panic.

I knew I had to get him under control, so I made a quick point-of-aim calculation and grabbed him by the shoulder and shook him. "Listen to me, Mac!" I commanded. "Aim right at the buck's head while he's walking and you'll drill him right in the boiler room. If he stops, hold a foot over his shoulder. Do you hear me?" Mac drew a deep breath and got himself under control and chambered another round. We both knew this would be the one. His breathing was quiet and steady once more. The buck was still walking at the same pace, and at about the same distance. I glued my eyes into my binoculars and waited for a climax to the spellbinding episode. The world stood still as Mac squeezed the trigger, now fully under control. The silence of the moment was split with a hollow click as his firing pin fell on an empty chamber. The buck walked into the timber at the left end of the field, never to be seen again. In Mac's panic, when he ejected his last spent cartridge, he failed to pull the bolt back far enough to pick up another live round. He then closed his bolt on an empty chamber. Who says those giant bucks don't live charmed lives?

I'm not picking on Texans, but they represented over 50 percent of my business, so it's natural that they get their share of trips down my memory lane. In their defense, Texans were more willing to pass up good bucks in lieu of great bucks than most other hunters, so they subjected themselves to greater pressures in the process.

Richard was a wealthy young Texan who was keen on putting a book deer on his trophy room wall. Money was no object to him, but somehow record book whitetails have a way of leveling the playing field between the "haves" and the "have-nots." Before the high fence craze and genetically engineered whitetails came along, they were considered to be the only trophy that money couldn't buy. In wild, free-roaming populations, that's still true. I had offers from several well-heeled individuals who would have sent my kids to college if I could have pulled a rabbit out of the hat and magically produced a book buck for them upon command. The money was appealing, but my conscience wouldn't let me play that game.

I placed Richard in a 14-foot tripod in a funnel between two major bedding areas. The tripod was snuggled into the willows just off the banks of the Battle River, and any deer that passed through the funnel would be a stone's throw from him.

There was a foot of snow on the ground that first morning. I told Richard to stay in the stand until at least 10 a.m. because the bucks were not moving through that area much before 8:30 or 9 o'clock. By 8:30, he had seen only one doe and was getting bored. He was a smoker, so he decided to light up during this supposed lull. It was the most expensive cigarette he would ever light.

He laid his rifle upside down across the round metal framework of the top of the tripod, pulled out a cigarette and lit it. In the middle of his first puff, out walked the buck we eventually called Tyrone (so named by another of my Texas hunters named Phillip Harrison). Since we eventually killed Tyrone, I can say for a fact that he was a 17-point buck that scored 197⅝. Suffice to say that Richard wanted to shoot this deer.

At first sight, Tyrone was 60 yards away and walking broadside. Richard was stunned to see him and immediately panicked at being caught with his pants down, so to speak. His brain simply hung up on what to do with his cigarette. With a foot of snow on the ground, all he had to do was drop it, but under the great stress of the moment, that wasn't as clear as it should have been. Finally, after waiting far too long to react, he dropped the cigarette and grabbed his rifle, righting it as he swung it to his shoulder. Tyrone hadn't actually seen Richard, but that sixth sense possessed by all giant bucks told him that something was amiss. He picked up his pace slightly and started looking for trouble. In the process of turning his rifle upright, the sling wound around the front of the scope, blinding Richard. When he realized he couldn't see, he dropped the rifle from his shoulder, lifted the sling free of the scope, shouldered the rifle again and led his walking target, which was now only 75 yards distant. Then he blew a hole in the ground a foot in front of the buck. Why did he lead a walking deer at only 75 yards? Panic—of course— the reason hunters always miss easy shots at giant bucks. There's an old saying that applies here: "Luck always favors the prepared mind."

The odd tendencies of panicked hunters to lead and over-shoot great bucks eventually inspired what I believe is the most profound and helpful hypothesis I ever offered a visiting deer hunter. After enduring experiences like these, I decided to make this fact a part of my indoctrination spiel to my incoming hunters. The official Russell Thornberry "Point of Aim Hypothesis" states: "On your first shot, aim at the deer. If that doesn't work, then aim somewhere else!"

Nuff said?

Top: This is my "tenderfoot" bull moose—completing the saga of my first great Canadian hunting adventure.

Left: Alberta 1973: Marion Diesel's moose-calling lessons paid off with this, the first bull I ever called in for a hunter.

Right: Alberta 1973: Marion Diesel (far left) poses with four of our moose hunting clients and two of their racks.

Top: Yukon Territory 1986: Glassing for moose from horseback on Two Pete Mountain.

Bottom: Outfitter Dave Coleman (left) and I pose with my Hess River, Yukon, bull I arrowed on Sept. 18, 1987. At the time it ranked No. 69 in the Pope and Young records.

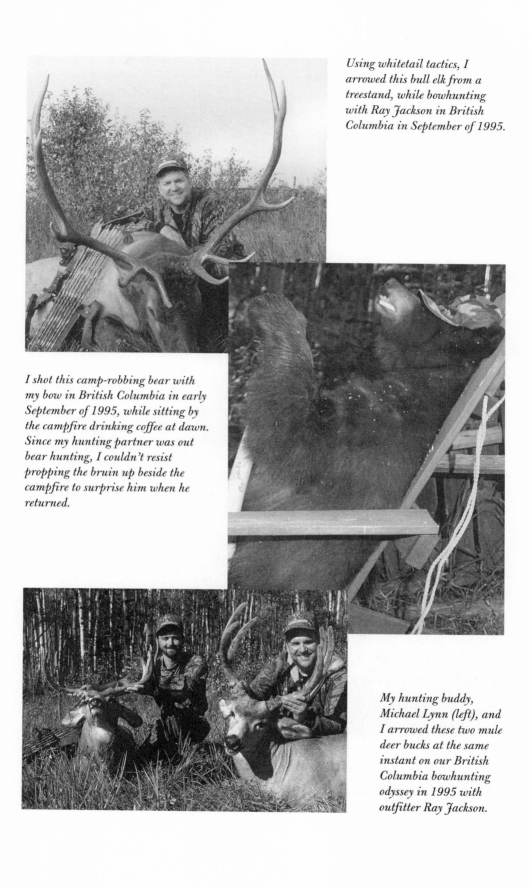

Using whitetail tactics, I arrowed this bull elk from a treestand, while bowhunting with Ray Jackson in British Columbia in September of 1995.

I shot this camp-robbing bear with my bow in British Columbia in early September of 1995, while sitting by the campfire drinking coffee at dawn. Since my hunting partner was out bear hunting, I couldn't resist propping the bruin up beside the campfire to surprise him when he returned.

My hunting buddy, Michael Lynn (left), and I arrowed these two mule deer bucks at the same instant on our British Columbia bowhunting odyssey in 1995 with outfitter Ray Jackson.

Left: Native guide Bobby Migwi and I approach my first Canadian barren ground caribou at War-burton Bay, NWT, in late September of 1994.

Top Right: In the traditional native fashion, Bobby Migwi straps the caribou hide bundle, con-taining all the edible meat, across his forehead for the trek back to the boat.

Top: Dave Reidie pilots our boat on northern Alberta's Peace River in the mid-1970s, shortly after taking his first trophy black bear.

Left: After dodging a night of bad weather in this cabin on the Peace River, Dave Reidie and I enjoy one last cup of coffee before our unexpected adventure began.

Right: This is the bear that cost us our boat and a long wilderness trek out of the Peace River valley.

Top: This was No. 1 of the three bears, a provincial bow-and-arrow record for British Columbia.

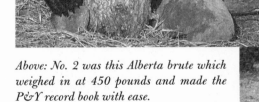

Above: No. 2 was this Alberta brute which weighed in at 450 pounds and made the P&Y record book with ease.

Right: This Saskatchewan boar was the third of the three bears, also qualifying for the P&Y record book.

The late Derril Lamb poses with his world record P&Y grizzly.

Above: Phillip Harrison of Houston, Texas, shot this giant grizzly in the Upper Blackwater region of British Columbia in the spring of 1985.

Harrison's huge grizzly measured over 10 feet from nose to tail.

Outfitter John Blackwell displays the skull of a Boone and Crockett grizzly bear taken in his hunting area in the Upper Blackwater region of British Columbia.

Above: Here are the two amazing cougar hounds, Sam and Red, that led me to my first cougar.

Right: Cougar hunter extraordinaire Jim Simpson with his red bone cougar hound, appropriately named "Red."

My first Dall's sheep ram, after a trying hunt.

Left to right: Outfitter Ray Woodward, Jackie Brittingham and I proudly display our sheep horns after a tough backpack hunt in the Arctic Red River region of the Northwest Territories.

Putting on these white overalls worked like magic. The white sheep obviously thought I was one of them.

Top: My Mongolian hunting party and I pose with my High Altai Siberian ibex. My guide, immediately to my left, honored me with a Mongolian dress hat embroidered by his mother, which I'm wearing in this photo. Any resemblance between Porky Pig and me is purely coincidental.

Bottom: My hunting partner, Gary Sitton, and his Mongolian guide pose with his first Siberian ibex.

My hunter, Joe Aiello of Longview, Texas, poses with the elusive buck we named "Tyrone."

His huge Alberta white-tailed buck dwarfs Joe Sedutto of New York.

Top: *Phillip Harrison and I pose with the 8-pointer I rattled in. Initially he turned it down, but when the buck turned and ran, the "bad" Phillip took control.*

Left: *James Robison of Fort Worth, Texas, shot this old Alberta buck, only to watch an even greater buck attack his fallen quarry.*

Right: *Jackie Bushman with the Alberta buck that cost him his shirttail.*

Top Right and Left: I arrowed these two P&Y Saskatchewan bucks from the same treestand, using the same arrow, just one day apart.

Bottom Left: This Montana buck is my best with bow and arrow. I managed to bag him in spite of "Deer TV."

Bottom Right: This is the slippery Iowa buck I took on the 10th day of my seven-day bowhunt in 1997.

A spellbinding bowhunt in South Carolina, with my friends Rusty and Billy Shannon, produced this gnarly, heavy-beamed trophy.

My son, Darren, bagged this great South Carolina 11-pointer—his first buck with a bow and arrow!

Approaching a trophy Coues' whitetail, taken only a quarter mile from camp near Sonora, Mexico.

Ted Keaton of Greenville, N.C., poses with his first Coues' whitetail. Also shown are tracking dog "Pirata" and Mexican guide Brigitta.

I was with my son, Darren, when he shot his first whitetail in Alabama when he was 15 years old. It's a memory we both cherish.

SEVENTEEN

A Couple of "Me and Joe" Stories

Joe Aiello (his real name) of Longview, Texas, came to hunt with me in Alberta in November of 1986. I had donated a hunt to the Houston Safari Club for their annual fundraising auction. The man who bought the hunt had to cancel at the last minute due to business complications, so he asked me if he could resell the hunt to recoup his money. I agreed, so he advertised it in a Texas hunting magazine. Joe Aiello purchased the hunt for about half what the original hunter had paid. Joe had little "away from home" hunting experience and showed up at my camp in jeans and sneakers—hardly adequate for hunting in snow and 20-below temperatures. I loaned him some of my clothes to equip him for his Alberta hunting adventure.

Joe was among the nicest hunters I have ever guided. He was a quiet, God-fearing man who was refreshingly unpretentious. He never mentioned the term "book deer," nor would he have to shoot one to be happy. He was also a very laid back individual—so much so that I believe his resting pulse rate wouldn't register more than about 10 beats per minute. His natural state of calm would eventually serve him well in a somewhat pressured situation.

By that time, no less than four hunters had missed opportunities at Tyrone. Other than Richard's failed attempt (noted in the previous chapter), all three others failed due to frozen firing pins. I always advised my hunters to remove all oil and grease from the inner workings of their firing pins and bolts before they brought their rifles to the cold Alberta clime. Some paid heed; others didn't bother. I'm sure the three that had Tyrone in their crosshairs, only to discover their firing pins frozen, will listen more attentively to their outfitter's advice in the future.

I saw Tyrone cross the same ridge on the Battle River brakes three mornings in a row, so I told my guide, Gordon Kitchen, to take a tripod stand up on the ridge and hide it in a little clump of stunted aspens. That afternoon, he arranged to put Joe in that stand. The plan was to drive around to the south side of the river valley and let Joe walk down the hogback ridge to his stand. Then Gordon was going to drive back to the north side of the valley and watch Joe through binoculars. If Joe scored, Gordon would then drive back around and retrieve him. If he didn't score, Gordon agreed to meet Joe back at the top of the ridge just after dark.

No sooner had Gordon driven back to his vantage point on the north side of the river than a full-blown blizzard hit. Snowflakes the size of silver dollars instantly reduced visibility to almost zero as they sailed along on a screaming west wind. Joe realized that he couldn't see, but reasoned that there was no sense in climbing back up the ridge since Gordon wouldn't be there until dark. Thus, he decided to remain in the tripod until the appointed hour.

The blizzard hit without warning, and Joe was sitting there in a virtual whiteout when motion caught his eye. A doe emerged from out of the flurry, walking right between the legs of his tripod stand, only a few feet beneath him. Then the second and third does appeared. The fourth figure to emerge was a buck, and a darn good one. The buck followed dutifully in the does' tracks, also passing between the tripod legs. Joe let the buck pass and was about to lift his rifle when the buck stopped in his tracks and looked back at the odd structure. It was obvious that Tyrone hadn't noticed it there before when he crossed that ridge. After pondering the structure for a few seconds, the buck turned back toward the does and resumed his pursuit.

Joe got the rifle almost to his shoulder when the buck stopped again, turning back once more to ponder this strange new object in his world. Joe froze and waited. The buck finally turned away again and Joe got the rifle all the way to his shoulder. As he peered anxiously through his scope, he could see only white. He scanned back and forth in the whiteout and suddenly saw a vague dark object almost obliterated in the swirling world of white. He could see just enough to know it was the buck, so he centered his crosshairs on the heavy end of the deer and fired. The buck crumpled in his tracks.

Gordon picked Joe up at dark as planned, and due to the complications of ever-deepening snow, decided to come back to camp and get help to drag the heavy buck out of the steep river valley. After dinner, our whole crew went back and dragged Tyrone out of the valley and to glory.

Joe's modesty still amazes me. When Gordon asked him how it felt to have taken the best buck of the season in our camp, he said: "I'm just happy because Russell is so happy."

I replied: "Partner, I believe this buck is big enough to make us both happy."

The whitetail gods had spoken and Joe Aiello, on perhaps his only hunt away from home, bagged a whitetail of a lifetime. I'm glad he did!

In November of 1980, I guided another Joe. Joe Sedutto was from Staten Island, N.Y., and was a certifiable, card-carrying whitetail fanatic. He had hunted the Adirondacks religiously, as well as New Jersey and Pennsylvania, and had taken some good bucks for those areas. But he wanted to try his hand at a monster-class whitetail, just once.

Joe was on my first hunt of the season during the first week of November. That hunt could be very good, depending upon the weather. If it were cold, we were in business. If not, we might not see a single mature buck. We had hunted hard and seen some medium-sized bucks, but certainly not what Joe had come 2,500 miles to shoot. At the end of the fifth day of his six-day hunt, the guide was feeling the pressure. A sensible man realizes he cannot govern the weather, women, taxes and big whitetails (not necessarily in that order), but be that as it may, there is still a certain amount of pressure on the guide to produce. The pressure was self-inflicted in this case because Joe remained a perfect gentleman throughout the dry spell. He maintained undying confidence, which was gratifying in one sense, but it only served to make me all the more anxious for his success. I pondered a plan for the last day of the hunt in my sleep that night, but woke up with all the same questions that I had taken to bed.

After breakfast, we headed east to an area where we had not yet hunted. We arrived in pitch-black darkness and parked the truck. There was a large summer fallow field in front of us, and I knew that many deer, both mulies and whitetails, fed there in early November. We walked quietly along the edge, keeping ourselves concealed in the edge of the stunted aspen timber that bordered the field. I picked a spot that would offer us a good vantage point when the sun rose. Then we sat quietly and waited for dawn. The field tailed off into a low marshy area, full of red willows, where the deer bedded during the daylight hours. The usual routine was for the deer to come into the summer fallow under the cover of darkness, then slip back into the draw at sunrise.

As a matter of routine, I scanned the field through binoculars. I could make out the vague silhouette of a feeding deer. Although I could not be sure, I assumed, by the way the animal carried itself, that it was a white-tailed doe. I whispered the discovery to Joe. A few minutes later, I began scanning the field again. This time I saw something that confused me. There was a large deery-looking object in the field, but it seemed too large for a whitetail. It happened to be right in line with the only sapling in the whole field. The 8-foot sapling was about 50 feet in front of us, standing in the middle of my field of view of the suspicious object, which I guessed to be 200 yards distant. Perhaps it was two deer standing close together. I finally decided that must be the case.

As the faintest trace of first light made my straining eyes water, I was still having trouble making out the mystery deer. Small limbs from the sapling made it impossible to see if there were antlers. Joe knew I was on to something, but I did not want to sound a false alarm. Degree by degree, the sky lightened and, at last, I could see what appeared to be antlers—one on each side of the sapling. Whatever I was looking at was deathly still. I was about to doubt myself when the antlers slowly turned. Now there was no doubt! It was a buck. I still thought we were looking at two animals standing together, and I wasn't sure whether they were mule deer or whitetails. Both species occupied the area, and Joe was licensed for each.

Seconds dragged like hours as we sat there playing a waiting game with the teasing sunrise. The animal moved his head occasionally, but other than that, remained stone still. I eventually concluded that it was not two deer, but one huge animal. At this point, it was time to get Joe involved. I tried to contain my excitement so as not to rattle him. I whispered to him in my finest imitation of calm control: "I don't know whether it's a muley or a whitetail yet, but whatever it is, it looks pretty good." I told him to take a careful rest and to take all the time he needed. The buck had no idea we were in the same county. Joe had a long-legged bipod attached to the fore end of his .257 Weatherby. He eased down behind the rifle and began trying to locate the deer. In the next few seconds, the sky began to lighten quickly and I could see the magnificent buck that I remember thinking looked like a cartoonist's conception of the world's largest deer. The buck was barrel-chested and shaped more like a fat quarter horse than a deer. I was now sure that it was a whitetail, and this excited me even more.

"Do you see him yet?" I whispered.

"Not yet," Joe replied. He had a high powered variable scope, and unbeknown to me, his magnification was set on 16x. I was popping rivets internally as I waited for him to locate the deer, but I faked a calm assurance. Joe was softly mumbling something about seeing the doe but not the buck.

"To the right," I whispered. "You'll know him when you see him."

Joe was mumbling again. "How far to the right are you looking," he said. "I can't see anything but a . . . Oh my god!" With that, I knew he had seen the buck. I could hear his breathing hasten sharply, so I quietly assured him that he had all the time he needed and not to rush. I glued my eyes to my binoculars and found myself holding my breath as if I were doing the shooting. An eternity passed in what must have been 10 or 15 seconds. The Weatherby exploded just before my lungs did. The big deer dropped his head for a split second, trotted about 50 yards and dropped.

"You did it," I yelled, as I took off on a dead run for the downed deer. We arrived together and were astounded at what lay before us. This buck was to whitetails what Hulk Hogan is to the average high school librarian. I had never seen such an animal. His antlers were wide with long saber-like tines. He had five points on one side and four on the other. His net B&C score was 164. He would have been a shoe-in for the book if he had grown that fourth point on both sides. The fact was that this deer was some kind of record even without antlers. We measured the distance around the base of the big buck's neck. It measured 49 inches. The measurement around his throat, just below his jaws, was an unbelievable 30 inches. The chest measurement was 57 inches and the horizontal distance straight through the center of his rib cage was 22 inches. The deer was officially weighed, field-dressed, at 290 pounds. We estimated that he must have weighed at least 375 pounds on the hoof.

EIGHTEEN

Doozies and Ding-a-Lings

My whitetail guiding and outfitting memories are not relegated merely to big bucks won and lost. More than anything, I remember the characters I met and guided. Some were great hunters, some were real doozies, and some were pure ding-a-lings. For the most part, my hunters were smart enough to know that they were hunting on unfamiliar turf and that their best odds for success were in doing what their guides told them. But there were those hunters whose missions were to ignore every instruction we gave them and prove how much more they knew about what we were doing than we did. Interestingly, statistics showed that success typically favored those who did what they were told. Conversely, those who were determined to prove the guide wrong went home empty-handed. There's a lesson in there somewhere.

One lovable cuss from south Texas devoted his entire hunting week doing just the opposite of what he was told. And he wasn't subtle about it. At the dinner table the night before the hunt began, I casually gave my hunters the breakdown of how we would approach the upcoming hunting week. As soon as I finished explaining my game plan, the hunter (whom I shall refer to as Butch), slammed his fist down on the table and said flatly: "Aw B—S—!" Things got quiet for a minute and I asked him what his problem was. Oddly enough, he had no problem. "Aw B—S—," was simply his standard reply to everything. He was a hilarious, but impossible man to guide. In truth, he was his own worst enemy.

Once we placed him on point and stressed the importance of staying in that exact spot while we guides made a drive through a strip of timber we knew to harbor a huge typical buck. For years, we had made drives through that strip of timber and the deer always came out at that exact spot. We started the drive, and Butch immediately decided he would find a better position. The buck walked right through his tracks in the snow where we'd told him to stand, but of course he was elsewhere and never saw a hair. We brought him back to his intended position and showed him where the buck had walked right over his boot tracks in the snow. "Might be a good idea to start doing what you're told," I said. "You've spent quite a bit of money to come up here and ignore what you've paid for."

He just grinned, spit his wad of chewing tobacco in the snow and said, "Aw B—S—!"

On another occasion, Butch and his guide drove to their chosen hunting area where they were going to attempt to rattle in a good buck. They arrived a good 30 minutes before first shooting light, so the guide suggested that they just sit tight in the truck until they could see where they were going. Then they would continue on foot. They sat there quietly in the truck for a couple of minutes, then Butch rolled his window down, held his rattling horns out the truck window and started knocking them together. Instantly a huge buck was standing directly in front of the truck, ready for the fight. The guide elbowed Butch in the ribs to get him to be still. Guide and hunter stared at the impressive black silhouette against the moonlit snow until the buck bounded out of sight. Back at camp that evening, I told Butch that it might be worth saving the rattling until he could at least see to shoot. He grinned and offered his standard reply.

At the end of the week, Butch was empty-handed, as could be expected. But he went away as happy as a clam. I think he got his money's worth in tormenting his guide and being uncooperative. I used to console my frustrated guides by reminding them that guiding was a job, but the hunter was on vacation. If he chose to spend his leisure time screwing up his chances to succeed, then we would help him every way we could.

Brad was another case study. He was a spoiled, 35-year-old mama's boy who'd somehow survived 35 years of choking on silver spoons. That, unto itself, wasn't a particular detriment to his hunting success, but it seemed to weigh heavily on his patience, which was a factor. Brad couldn't sit still to save his life. We would put him on a strategic stand and make him promise to stay put, but no sooner would the guide be out of sight than Brad would be down tramping through the woods, scaring every deer away for miles. Then he'd have the audacity to complain about not seeing anything.

I told Brad's guide to place him on his stand and then get up on the Battle River brakes and watch him through binoculars to see what was happening. The report came back that night. Brad was out of his stand within five minutes and walking all over the country he was supposed to be quietly watching. Then, after his morning stroll, Brad returned to his tripod stand, dropped his drawers and had his morning constitutional right below it. Once his mission was accomplished, Brad climbed up into the stand and fidgeted for about 15 minutes before climbing back down and disturbing more terrain. That night, he announced that he wanted to move to a new location because he had seen nothing all day. We politely announced that he was going to stay in that stand for at least one more day, and that if deer viewing was as slow as he described, he could spend at least part of the day burying the trophy he dropped between the legs of the tripod. Brad didn't see a buck on his hunt. I don't think he even saw a doe. After his last day of unsuccessful fidgeting, he complained about his hunt and the fact that he hadn't seen a buck all week—"not at all what we advertised," he complained.

I explained the problem as I saw it: "Brad, have you noticed anything suspect about your lack of success—like, for instance, the fact that the other five hunters in camp who did exactly what we said, all have nice trophies? Have you noticed that we have only one hunter in camp that refused to do as he was told, and coincidentally, we only have one unsuccessful hunter in camp? And Brad, have you noticed that the unsuccessful hunter and the uncooperative hunter are one and the same? And finally, Brad, have you noticed that both of those hunters are you?"

"I guess you're right," he shrugged.

All costs considered, he paid well over $4,000 to ignore our instructions all week, and, believe me, he got his money's worth! Happily, it cost not a penny more to adhere to the game plan and take a nice Alberta buck home for posterity.

NINETEEN

Good Phillip—Bad Phillip

No account of my career as a trophy whitetail guide in Alberta would be complete without mention of Phillip Harrison (his real name) of Houston, Texas. Phillip loved coming to hunt Alberta whitetails, and he was clearly my longest suffering client. And while Phillip desired one of those true monster-class bucks, he made it clear from the beginning that there was a limit to the amount of suffering he was prepared to do to get one.

Early in our hunter/guide relationship, I found it very frustrating to guide Phillip because I would often go to great lengths to set up a trap for a good buck on his behalf. As likely as not, he would abandon my plan just because it was too much work. I hasten to point out that in my mind in those days, no sacrifice was too great when it came to trophy whitetails. In particular, I remember the little point that jutted out of the timber on a narrow little eastern Alberta river. It was a half-mile downstream of a standing barley field that was being invaded nightly by whitetails. The buck sign around the perimeter of the field was tremendous. It was obvious to me that the bucks were leaving the barley just before dawn and following the steep little river valley to a sanctuary of timber just beyond the point. I showed it to Phillip and he agreed it was a natural place to intercept bucks at first light. So, we carried a tripod stand a half-mile to the little point and set it up in the edge of the timber where Phillip could sit and enjoy a perfect ambush. The next morning, an hour ahead of dawn, Phillip and I parked the truck beside the fence line that cut through the timber and led right to the tripod. "Okay Phillip," I said, "get on your warm clothes and go get 'em!"

"Naw, I don't want to go down there this morning," he said, to my disbelief.

"What do you mean, you don't want to go?" I asked.

"It's too much work and it's too cold. I'll just sit here in the truck. This is a good spot."

"C'mon Phillip," I pleaded. "You know that spot is going to pay off! What the heck did we carry that tripod all the way down to the river for if you're not going to use it?"

"I know it's a good spot, but so is this. Let's just sit here."

"If we just sit here and talk, we won't see anything," I urged.

"Then you go down there and sit in the tripod," he argued.

"You're the one who's paid for my service," I reminded him. "What good does it do you if I shoot the buck?"

"Go on down there," he continued. "I hope you get a big one."

By then, I was as frustrated as I could be. All that scouting and all that work had been for nothing. The rut was on and the weather was perfect, and now my hunter didn't want to cooperate with my best plan. I thought for a minute and decided that I'd better take a walk and cool off a bit. It was Phillip's vacation, I reminded myself. I stepped out of the truck, put on my parka, grabbed my rifle and walked off in the dark. I followed the fence line toward the tripod. The time spent arguing with Phillip was going to mean shooting light would arrive before I reached the stand. I could already see the timber taking shape on the ridge across the river. Finally, I could see the tripod sticking out of the edge of the brush. As I approached it, I thought, "What in the heck am I doing? What am I going to do if I see a good buck?"

My question was answered in less than a heartbeat. I was about to step up on the first rung of the tripod ladder when I looked upriver and saw the buck walking right to me, on the opposite bank. Without even thinking, I shouldered my rifle and dropped him in his tracks.

Now what? I have a beautiful 12-point buck on the ground—the one Phillip would have had if he weren't so darn stubborn—and he's sitting back in the truck drinking coffee! "Well," I thought, "maybe this will convince him to go along with the plan in the future."

Nothing could have been farther from the truth. In fact, Phillip couldn't have been happier that I had shot the buck. I don't think I taught Phillip Harrison anything by shooting that buck, and, in retrospect, I wish I hadn't done it. But I did learn something important from Phillip. He came to Alberta to hunt or just goof around, whichever struck him as most important at any given time. He had all the pressure he wanted in his business life back in Texas, and he was simply not going to do anything that added up to "more pressure" in his mind. That included walking down to the tripod that morning. When I learned to guide Phillip according to what he wanted, rather than what I wanted, we began to have a blast together, and we are dear friends to this day. He just liked to do things differently than most.

Phillip was a crack shot and a good judge of a trophy whitetail on the hoof. On more than one occasion, Phillip and I would encounter a fair buck that he would turn down flatly, until the buck turned to run. Then what he described as the "Bad Phillip" would take over. There was just something about a fleeing buck that tempted Phillip beyond his control.

On one such occasion down in the bowels of the Battle River valley, I rattled a pretty buck in at first light. We could see that it was a 140-class 8-pointer—a pretty buck, but no trophy by Alberta standards. It was a glorious sight as the buck walked out of the timber to the river's edge in the first golden rays of dawn. He looked like a bronze statue standing there at full alert in a foot of snow, looking for the fight. Phillip and I watched quietly, soaking up the moment in the silent stillness of that cold November morning. The buck stood stone still for several minutes, then caught wind of something that he didn't like—perhaps a wayward breeze carrying our scent across the river ice. It was obvious that he was startled by the way he jerked himself backward, turned on a dime and bolted for the timber. That sight was more than the "Good Phillip" could take. Instantly, as if by pure reflex, his .300 Mag. flew to his shoulder and he dumped the fleeing buck in his tracks.

I turned to him in speechless surprise, convinced that we had both agreed it wasn't the buck for him. "Can't help it," he groaned, as he spit a double helping of Red Man in the snow. "I'm okay 'til they turn to run, then the Bad Phillip takes over." It was by no means the last of the Bad Phillip that I would come to know.

On another November morning a year or two later, at first possible light, Phillip and I spotted a buck in the edge of the timber along an oat stubble field, with just his head visible, looking right at us. In the dim gray light, all I could tell about the buck was that he had pretty heavy looking main beams and some long brow tines. I whispered my appraisal to Phillip just in time to hear his .300 thunder. When we got to the buck, we were amazed to find that he had heavy main beams, good brow tines, and not another point on his odd-looking head. It was a true "what you see is what you get" buck. Other than a pretty funky looking rack, the buck, which we referred to as "Old Ugly," had extremely heavy eyebrows, reminiscent of a retired prizefighter.

"Look's like Rocky Marciano with a screwed-up rack," Phillip grunted. I couldn't argue. Was it a buck to retire on? Hardly. Phillip just felt like drilling him, so he did. "I'll add him to my ugly collection," Phillip mumbled as we loaded the buck into the back of the truck. Seems Phillip had an affinity for shooting the ugliest critters of the species. I doubt if he'd been any happier if "Old Ugly" had made the record book.

Phillip's motto was: "Let's don't make work out of this." And he meant it. He proved it one morning when we spotted a tremendous buck crossing a ridge near the top of the Battle River brakes. "That's the third morning I've seen that same buck cross that ridge," I announced enthusiastically. "We need to get you up there tomorrow morning for an ambush. I think that's a book buck, and I really believe it will work!"

"Put somebody else up there," he groaned. "That's too far to climb. I believe I'll wait for an easy one."

Eventually I did, and Joe Aiello of Longview, Texas, shot the buck we called Tyrone (mentioned in a previous chapter) from that very stand.

Was Phillip unhappy when the buck that was first offered to him was taken by someone else? Not in the least. He was as happy for Joe as the rest of us. For Phillip, shooting a retirement buck wasn't the issue. Having a good time and relaxing was. Once I learned to adopt his priorities as my own, I had as much fun as he did. It was his leisure time, and while I was on the job, if relaxing was what made the customer happy, then relaxing it would be.

Perhaps the classic of all my Phillip Harrison experiences was with the "Mile-or-More" gun. I had a 1,000-yard rifle built—a wildcat in 7mm x .300 Weatherby. I borrowed a World War I Bausch and Lomb infantry range-finder (sold into surplus after World War II) from a friend, and calibrated my long-range rifle in 100-yard increments, all the way out to 1,000 yards. With an adequate rest and the aid of the range-finder, it was a truly lethal weapon. Being a rifle builder and tinkerer, I knew Phillip would find my "Mile-or-More" rifle appealing.

When he arrived in my camp, I showed it to him and asked him if he'd like to try it. Naturally, he was game. We drove up to the top of the north side of the Battle River brakes and set up my shooting bench and the range-finder. Then we propped up the 16-pound rifle on the bench. All was ready. Now we would just sit and drink coffee and wait until we spotted one of those real chokers on the opposite of the valley. In those days it was fairly common to spot book-class bucks popping out in small openings in the timber on the other side of the valley, too far to consider with conventional deer rifles. This was going to be an interesting experiment.

About 3 p.m., a coyote stepped out on a snow-covered knob on the opposite side of the river. It was a long way. I found the coyote in the range-finder, sitting there observing his domain. He was right on the 1,000-yard mark. I cranked up the external elevation adjustment on the 24x target scope the prescribed number of clicks and asked Phillip if he'd like to give it a try. When he touched off the shot, the coyote left his serene perch as if hit by a truck. The "Mile-or-More" experiment was working!

Just before dark, two bucks came walking together into an opening on the other side of the river valley. I dialed them up in the range-finder. They were at 650 yards. I adjusted the scope elevation, Phillip picked the best one and touched off his shot. The buck hit the ground like he was pole axed. The other buck just stood there, trying to figure out why his companion had suddenly decided to bed. We were so far away that the sound of the shot didn't even register as trouble in his ears. Phillip finally got an easy one. He has probably killed more whitetails in his life than most hunters have seen—and some whoppers, too. He was well past the go-go-go stage of hunting. I never heard him complain about a hunt. The way he looked at it, he was going to have a good time, regardless of what the deer did. Whether we were hunting whitetails, black bears or grizzlies, he made hunting fun. I can't say that about every hunter I've guided.

TWENTY

Best Buck Ever

One of the most difficult problems I faced as a whitetail guide in Alberta was trying to keep Pennsylvania and New York hunters from shooting the first buck they saw. I understood their dilemma. They so seldom saw bucks over 1½ years old in their own stomping grounds, that just about any Alberta buck they saw would be the biggest they ever laid eyes on—even the immature 2½-year-old 8-pointers that they routinely shot on sight.

In particular, I remember a Pennsylvania hunter named Marty. It was his first hunt with me. After he arrived at my camp and got his gear situated, Marty asked if he could speak to me privately. I led him into a vacant room and closed the door and asked him what was on his mind. "What do you think the odds are of me taking my best-ever buck on this hunt?" he asked.

"Guess I'd need to know what kind of bucks you've already taken before I can answer that," I replied.

He reached into his shirt pocket and pulled out a tiny little skull cap with one spike about an inch long and held it in the palm of his hand. I remember thinking when I first saw it that it was one of those little sets of vampire fangs like kids used to buy in the variety store at Halloween. Then I realized that it was actually a whitetail rack!

"Are you serious?" I asked.

"Yep, this is my best buck ever," he answered flatly.

"Well then, I'd say your odds of bettering that buck are about 100 percent if you live 'til tomorrow morning," I said. Marty wasn't kidding. That was his career-best buck in Pennsylvania. Two days later, I rattled in a gorgeous 8-pointer, about 150 times as large as his "pocket buck." He was thrilled, and I was thrilled for him.

TWENTY-ONE

Gunslinger

One of the most unusual and memorable events ever to take place in my camp occurred when young Mike Sutton came up from Lakeland, Fla., to shoot his first Alberta whitetail. I believe Mike's father bought the hunt for him as a high school graduation present. The next afternoon, while walking down the frozen river ice of the Battle River, Mike's guide, Shane, spotted several does up on the side of the river brakes, about a half-mile distant. After studying them through his spotting scope, he was suspicious that there was a buck hanging near them. The does acted edgy and kept their attention focused on the timber below them. Shane suggested that they follow the river ice and come out below the does for a closer look.

They shuffled quickly along the ice to a place where the steep river valley made a sharp bend to the east. Then they climbed back up on the bank to secure a higher vantage point. Soon they spotted the does at 300 yards, on the opposite side of the river and above them. The does were still concentrating on something in the timber. No sooner had Mike and Shane settled on the bank than the buck emerged from the thicket and headed straight uphill toward the does. It was a spectacular sight. The bull-necked Alberta buck had high, white tines and moved effortlessly through the deep snow. It was a post card scene depicting the essence of the great northern whitetail in his winter wonderland habitat.

Quickly Shane shed his pack and jammed it into the snow in front of Mike. "Here, rest on this and take your shot!" he whispered.

Immediately, Mike laid his .300 Win. Mag. over the pack and rested the crosshairs on the buck, which was still climbing with his back to the hunters.

Shane whispered, "He's 300 yards."

Mike nodded his agreement and squeezed the trigger. The stillness of the afternoon quaked as the roar of the magnum rolled down the valley. The buck flinched at the shot, but he kept climbing. Mike jammed another shell into the chamber and fired again. The buck seemed to ignore the second shot. With a third shot, the buck rolled down the hill into the timber. Shane ordered Mike to stay put and to keep watch on the hillside while he climbed up to make sure the buck was down for good. In case the buck got up again, Shane would dive off into a log pile so Mike could shoot. With that established, Shane streaked across the river ice and up the river brakes toward the place the buck was last seen. As he closed the distance between him and the buck to less than 20 yards, it suddenly jumped to its feet and started walking again. Shane, who was unarmed, ordered Mike to shoot again as he dove under the shelter of some deadfall, out of the line of fire. The magnum roared repeatedly from below until the magazine was empty.

"I can't see him anymore," Mike yelled from below.

"Did ya get him?" Shane echoed in return.

"I don't know!" Mike yelled back.

Shane crawled out from his hiding place and took off like a greyhound on the buck's tracks. In a matter of seconds, he spotted the buck lying in the thick timber ahead of him. At first he thought the buck was dead, but as he drew near, the buck jumped to his feet and took off through the timber. Shane instinctively gave chase. Quickly he gained on the wounded buck and, with a valiant leap, landed astride the buck's back, hanging onto the antlers with both hands. The buck bulled his way through the jungle of willows and rose briars with Shane hanging on for dear life and screaming at the top of his lungs for Mike to get there with the gun.

Eventually, Shane bulldogged the buck and together they toppled over in the deep snow with Shane wrapped around the buck's head in an effort to control the long, sharp tines. Meanwhile, 17-year-old Mike, a Florida flatlander, was bursting his lungs trying to negotiate the vertical, snowbound terrain. Shane continued yelling for Mike to hurry, and the poor exhausted lad was propelled by adrenaline alone as he floundered upon the scene.

"Get your gun ready!" Shane commanded. "When I let go of this buck and get out of the way, you shoot him!"

Mike, still gasping for air, nodded in stunned amazement as Shane jumped free of the frantic buck. Like a bolt of lightning, the buck was on his feet. But instead of running away, he whirled and charged headlong at Mike. This was much more than Mike had bargained for, so he jumped back as the buck lunged at him, narrowly avoiding a belly full of long, white tines. The buck reared his head up after his initial charge, just in time to catch the sling of Mike's rifle in his antlers. Mike was still falling over backward when the buck literally snatched the rifle out of his hands.

It was the buck's move as Shane and Mike waited in horror. The .300 Magnum was loaded, off safety and tangled in the antlers of an enraged animal. Hunter and guide scrambled on their bellies trying to stay out of the line of fire in case the rifle went off as the buck shook his head.

Suddenly the buck turned on his heels and dove off into the thicket once more, clanging and banging the rifle against the timber as he went, finally entangling the rifle and sling in the underbrush and forcing himself to a standstill. Shane jumped to his feet and gave chase once more, approaching the buck from the butt side of the gun. Within 30 yards, he was on the buck's back again, bulldogging him for the second time.

A stunned Mike Sutton sat in the snow with eyes as big as saucers, wondering what to do next. Abandoning ship was starting to sound like a great idea. If the buck wanted the gun that bad, he could just have it, and Mike was willing to call it even. But there was Shane, lying in the snow once more, wrapped around the buck's head and yelling for Mike in no uncertain terms.

Reluctantly, Mike slugged his way through the deep snow toward Shane, and the buck that had attacked him. He was visibly shaken as he arrived at the scene for the second time. Shane freed one hand long enough to throw Mike his rifle.

"You gotta shoot him this time!" he frantically commanded the bewildered young hunter.

The warning was unnecessary. Mike knew full well what he had to do. As Shane jumped free of the buck, Mike fired before it could regain its footing. The buck lay quiet at last. Both guide and hunter stood solemnly still, gathering their wits and waiting for their shattered nerves to calm.

The buck was an 8-pointer—a wonderful symmetrical trophy. It would be a stunning wallhanger, but the memory of the bizarre incidents surrounding the hunt would be a trophy in its own right.

Several of Mike's shots had connected. It was a complete mystery how the buck could have even moved, much less carried Shane on his back the way he did. At camp that night, over dinner, Mike and Shane recounted their incredible experience to the other hunters. Some laughed until tears streamed down their faces. Others were too astonished to speak. It was truly the most outrageous deer story any of them had ever heard.

"Well, when you get back to Florida," one of the guides teased, "you can tell your friends that these Alberta bucks are tough!"

"Tough!" Mike jeered. "You shoot 'em three or four times with a .300 Magnum and then they take it away from you!"

Someone asked Shane why on earth he jumped on the buck's back.

"Tired of seein' 'em get away," he grunted.

TWENTY-TWO

"Monday Mike" Szydlik

When a hunter arrives in your camp on a Sunday afternoon, shoots a buck scoring in the high 160s on Monday morning and heads home on Tuesday, you would probably consider him lucky. When he does exactly the same thing the second year, you just shake your head in amazement. When he does it three years in a row, you begin to suspect that it's more than just luck. But when it happens the fourth time in as many years, you start to wonder what magic he possesses. Perhaps you should follow him to Las Vegas or to the racetrack! No matter what else he is, Mike Szydlik of Houston, Texas, is the luckiest hunter I have ever guided, or, for that matter, ever known. Every hunter who knows him would agree, "Monday Mike" was born with a built-in horseshoe. No one can guarantee who will get a crack at a huge white-tailed buck, or when, but this I know: If he shows himself to Mike Szydlik on a Monday, he's "D.R.T.," as they say in Texas ("Dead Right There").

Aside from the phenomenon of luck, in terms of big deer that never fail to present themselves to Mike on the first day of his hunt, Szydlik prepares himself to be lucky. He can't explain why big whitetails follow him around, but I can vouch for the fact that the man can shoot! For every great deer Mike has bagged, a crack shot has been made. Shots have ranged from pointblank range to 300-yard, offhand shots at bucks running full tilt. Each time he connected. That's not luck, dear reader, that's skill. That is the skill a guide prays his hunter will possess. Showing a man a great buck is a heart wrenching experience if he can't shoot. There is only so much a guide can do. In Mike's case, my guides were all eager to guide him. They knew he was charmed.

On Mike's first hunt with my operation, he was guided by Cliff Hanna and bagged a very large 10-point buck scoring in the mid-160s. The buck's rack wasn't very wide, but it was massive, as was its body.

When he arrived at my camp for his second Alberta whitetail hunt, I told him that I'd be guiding him. As we drove off into the pre-dawn darkness, en route to the Battle River valley, Mike made this amazing statement: "Russ, remember the big gray buck I shot last year?"

"Yea, I remember," I replied.

"Remember it had a tall, heavy rack, but it wasn't all that wide?"

"Yea, I remember that, too," I said.

"Well, this year I want to shoot a really wide-racked buck. And you know how some of the bucks up here are real reddish in color—well, I'd really like to shoot one of those red ones—with a really wide rack."

"Oh well, no problem," I retorted sarcastically. "Just browse through my catalog and pick out exactly what you want! You know—trophy whitetails are just like new cars—no sense in settling for anything less than your absolute heart's desire!"

We laughed.

"I know, I know," Mike sighed. "I'm just daydreaming out loud, but if I had a choice, that's the kind of buck I'd pick."

At first light, we were sitting on the lip of the Battle River valley, scouring the valley with binoculars. On a ridge a half-mile away, I saw the black silhouette of a buck walking the skyline. I showed it to Mike and he watched it through his field glasses as I set up my spotting scope for a better look. At 20x, I watched the buck stop abruptly and begin stamping his right foot as he concentrated his attention on the draw beyond him. "I don't think that buck's a shooter," I announced, "but there's something down in that draw he doesn't like. Just in case it's another buck, let's go have a look."

When we finally reached the opposite side of the draw where we'd seen the buck, we crawled forward on our hands and knees in the snow, trying to keep as low as possible. As I peeked into the draw, right below us, no more than 60 yards away was a tremendous, wide-racked buck, rubbing his antlers on a clump of willows.

"He's a keeper!" I hissed at Mike. "Take a rest and let him have it!"

We were lying side by side in the snow at that point, but the problem was that Mike couldn't see the buck clearly from his position. He kept scooting forward trying to get a clear shot at the buck, which was partially obscured by willows. I was afraid the buck was going to hear or see him moving. He squirmed there in the snow for what seemed like forever, finally telling me that he just couldn't get a shot from where he was. I simply reached over and grabbed his jacket and dragged him across my body and rolled to my left, planting Mike on the opposite side of me. Quickly he propped himself up on his elbows, just as the buck was losing interest in the willows. His shot split the cold morning stillness and the buck slumped into his tracks, just as the first rays of golden sun poured down like honey from the heavens. The buck that had been a monotone creature, standing in dark morning shadows, was suddenly illuminated by sunlight. As Mike raced down the bluff to his fallen prize, I heard him scream at the top of his very excited lungs: "Oh Russ, it's just the color I wanted. Look how red he is!"

There was no denying it. The buck was red, his rack was 24 inches wide, and he scored in the mid-160s, just like Mike had daydreamed. It was 30 minutes into legal shooting light on Monday morning, the first day of Mike Szydlik's second Alberta deer hunt. The next day, he flew back to Houston—mission accomplished.

The third year when Mike arrived, he asked me if I had decided where we would hunt on Monday morning. I told him that Shane Hansen was going to be his guide that year, and that he should confer with Shane about where they'd be hunting. Mike paused momentarily and looked a little dejected. "I'm sure Shane is a great guide," he stammered, "but why aren't you going to be my guide?" It was a legitimate question.

"Well Mike," I explained, "Shane has been down on his luck this season. The truth is, I need you to hunt with Shane to bring up his average."

Mike looked at me in disbelief, then we both started laughing. It sounded ridiculous, but that was the truth. The next morning at daybreak, it was 50 degrees below zero, and there was a 35-mile per hour wind blowing, creating a wind chill factor of 85-below (F). It was the most brutal weather I had ever endured for any purpose. Deer disappeared from the face of the earth. There wasn't a fresh track to be seen anywhere. But an hour into his hunt, Monday Mike shot another 24-inch wide 10-pointer that scored in the low 160s. He was thrilled, as usual, and Shane's average came up dramatically. The truth was that my guides would probably have fought one another to the death for the opportunity to guide Monday Mike. Not only would the winner be assured of bringing a nice buck in first thing Monday morning, but the lucky guide could then sit on his hands for the rest of the week!

The unseasonably bitter cold temperatures continued through Thursday of that week and not another buck was seen. Finally, on Friday it warmed up over 50 degrees, and the deer suddenly popped out everywhere. The other five hunters in my camp were tagged out by sunset on that Saturday. Mike had been back in nice warm Houston since Tuesday afternoon.

The fourth year Mike hunted with me, he shot another heavy-beamed 8-pointer before lunch on Monday. In my opinion, that buck was the finest trophy of his "Alberta, Monday Morning Collection." The following year I retired from my guiding business to pursue other things. I have little doubt that Monday Mike would have kept coming back, hunting on Monday, and returning home on Tuesday, had I not retired.

Mike shot four wonderful bucks with me in Alberta during the late 1980s. Four bucks in four years: that's impressive. But what's more impressive is the fact that he hunted and shot all four bucks in less time than it took to drive him back to the Edmonton International Airport from my camp in eastern Alberta. Now that's impressive!

TWENTY-THREE

Buckmasters, Porch Monsters and Other Bull

The Characters:
Jackie "Horseshoes" Bushman of Montgomery, Ala.—founding father of Buck-masters—who hates cold weather, field-dressing elk, green vegetables and other healthy foods. Trophy bucks follow him around like he was the pied piper of white-tail hunting.

Jody Davis of Gainesville, Ga.—all pro catcher formerly with the Chicago Cubs and Atlanta Braves. He's a crack shot, whitetail hunting fanatic, Buckmasters member and the president and only member of Bullmasters Inc.

Russell Thornberry—humble servant, steely-eyed guide, step-n-fetch it, resident treestand placement guru and nervous wreck.

Place: Caroline, Alberta, Canada
Date: November 15, 1988
Time: Dawn

I, the humble servant, positioned Jackie and Jody on either side of me at the intersection of several cut lines in the mixed spruce, pine and aspen timber. Once settled in our positions at the proper vantage points, I smacked the rattling antlers together. The sound echoed through the crisp morning air, and, within minutes, I heard the eager response of an aggressive whitetail buck to the north of us. He thrashed the willows and cracked timber as he approached. Jackie and Jody both nodded toward the buck, indicating that they too knew he was com-ing. Everything was perfect. The slight breeze was blowing in our faces, and the buck was oblivious to our presence. As he came closer, perhaps now only 40 yards away, it appeared that Jackie would be the first to see him. I quietly hoped it would be the huge 10-pointer I had seen in the same area earlier in the fall. He was a monster, easily a book-class buck. We could hear him walking in the corn flake carpet of aspen leaves. Then suddenly he stopped. For a moment, there was no sound at all. While I strained my ears to listen, I felt the breeze hit the back of my neck. It had changed direction 180 degrees. I knew it was over before I heard the buck explode in retreat. Jody was now directly upwind of the buck, and his scent ended what was almost a successful morning hunt.

It was the first morning of our hunt together, so it was not the end of the world. But I decided that it would be the end of hunting that buck from the ground. It was time to get treestands in place. The following morning, we would try again from treestands, well above the buck's nose. Hopefully, our opening morning mishap would not spoil him completely. A buck like that doesn't give you many chances. Once the stands were in place, we vacated the area and didn't return until the following morning, giving the area a little time to settle.

THE SECOND MORNING

Well before daylight, Jackie was in a tall pine at the edge of a dark evergreen thicket. Jody, 150 yards to the west, was perched in an ancient poplar tree at the edge of a small slough, which formed an oval opening in the timber. To eliminate the amount of commotion in the area, I gave Jackie the rattling antlers and headed south to give the operation plenty of room. I agreed to meet Jackie at his stand at 9:30 a.m.

At 9:30, as promised, I was standing under Jackie's stand. He climbed down and told me the story. He rattled at dawn and immediately the buck responded.

"The second time I rattled, I could hear him coming," he said. "He came marching through the evergreen thicket and walked right out behind that spruce tree over there, not 25 yards from me. I could see a glimpse of antler as he passed through the spruce boughs. His rack looked really high, though I could never see it clearly. Then he stopped behind that spruce tree, and thought things over. Only two more steps and I would have had a clear shot. Something spooked him, but I know he couldn't smell me. I don't know what went wrong."

My heart sank. That was strike two for the hunters, and I seriously doubted if the buck would cooperate further. We examined the circumstances of Jackie's close call. The only thing we could figure out was that the buck might have smelled some of the freshly cut pine boughs that were removed while setting up the treestand. It was a new smell in the area and obviously just enough to put the buck ill at ease. I normally set up stands well ahead of the season, just for this reason. I made an exception in this case, and it came back to haunt me. Hindsight is 20/20.

We were discussing the near miss as we walked toward Jody's stand. When we were less than 40 yards from him, we looked up and saw him waving his arms for us to stop and be quiet. It was too late! As we were approaching, he was watching a buck working its way around the red willows bordering the slough. The buck was only 20 yards from an opening that would have given Jody a clear shot. Another 15 seconds and Jody could have nailed him, but the buck heard us approaching and simply vanished. Ill-fated timing, to say the least! Jackie and I kicked ourselves for not being more observant, but what was done was done. Morning two and the score was bucks three, hunters nothing.

On the way back to the truck I mentioned seeing fresh elk tracks earlier that morning as I was scouting to the south. Jody's ears perked up, and immediately he wanted to talk elk hunting. I explained that non-residents could only harvest 6-point bulls or larger (at least six points on one antler). The odds were so slim of his even seeing a bull elk, much less a 6-pointer, that I felt it was a waste of time buying an elk license. But nothing would do but to go into town and get Jody an elk tag. That accomplished, he felt much better.

LATER THAT EVENING

"Leave those rattling antlers with me this time," Jody said. "Where I hunt in Georgia there are so many does that the bucks won't respond to antlers. I'd just love to rattle up one white-tailed buck while I'm in Alberta, just so I could say I've done it."

I handed him the antlers and watched him climb back up the big poplar at the edge of the slough. Jackie headed back to his pine tree stand, and I headed south again to clear out of the area. I found more elk tracks, but I decided not to mention them to Jody. If he got sidetracked any farther on elk, I knew he'd never get the trophy whitetail he also wanted.

A half-hour before dark, I sat down and rested against a poplar tree at the edge of a grassy meadow. I would wait here until dark, then go back and collect my hunters.

With barely 15 minutes of daylight left, movement caught my eye at the edge of the meadow. A cow moose and her calf of the season emerged from the dark shadows of the timber and immediately began feeding on the meadow grass. They looked comical as they rested on their front knees while their hind legs were still standing upright: a common practice for moose when feeding on grass or clover or anything growing close to the ground. Their forelegs are so long that kneeling on them makes eating grass much easier.

I was enjoying the moose show when I heard a shot. My heart jumped with excitement. Someone connected! I waited a few minutes. There were no more shots, so I headed back to my hunters with high anticipation.

It was completely dark when I arrived under Jody's stand. "Did you shoot?" I asked.

"Yea, Buddy!" came the excited response from high in the poplar tree.

"Well, didja get him?"

"Yea, Buddy!" he repeated in his slow Georgia drawl.

"Well, where is he?" I asked.

"Right behind you," Jody chortled.

I turned around and saw a huge dark lump lying on the snow 20 yards behind me. Either my eyes were deceiving me or this was the largest white-tailed buck in the history of deer hunting. As I started toward the mystery lump, the smell hit my nostrils. This was no whitetail. It was the unmistakable, musky smell of a rutting bull elk.

"Jody, that's an elk!" I croaked as I grabbed the antlers and nervously started counting.

"Yea, Buddy!" came the standard reply.

A quick count revealed no less than six points per side. Then from above, the story came forth.

"Man, I rattled that baby right in under this tree," he began. "I rattled every half hour, just like you told me, but nothin' happened. Then, just before dark, I decided to give it one last try. I hit the horns together and I heard him coming. I got my gun ready and pretty soon I saw him moving through the willows, coming right to me. At first I thought it was a huge whitetail, then I realized it was an elk. I thought since it was alone that it was probably a cow. But when it walked up into the snow, I could see horns. I was getting real excited then. When it stepped out into the open, I could see that it was a 6-pointer, and I let him have it. He walked over here and piled up, just like that!"

I was utterly amazed. The odds of seeing a 6-point elk in that zone were next to none, but what were the odds of rattling one up, especially in November? It was a full 60 days past the elk rut.

"Didja get one?" Jackie yelled as he approached us in the timber.

Jody answered teasingly, "Sure did! It's the biggest buck you'll ever see in your life!"

As Jackie got closer, he saw the huge lump on the snow.

"Gooolllyyy," he said. "That must be the biggest deer in the world!"

Jackie was totally dumbfounded until he got close enough to see that it was an elk.

"I knew we shouldn't have let him buy that elk tag," he mumbled as he extended a weak congratulations to Jody. "Guess you're the Bullmaster now."

"Cheer up," Jody quipped, "Me and Russ'll dress this critter out, won't we Russ?"

Jackie's spirits rose immediately.

The next day was spent tending to the elk. After that, we moved operations to southeastern Alberta, along the Red Deer River.

THE MORNING OF NOVEMBER 18, 1988

Jackie and Jody left the ranch house in the dark, en route to their treestands. I peeked through the patio doors that open to the back porch of Simon Schonhofer's home on the sprawling 30,000-acre Majestic Ranch. There were two yearlings feeding on the lawn, 10 yards from the house. Simon told me that he had seen a fine trophy 10-pointer from the back porch two days earlier. The rut was going strong, and the bucks were on the move. I poured myself a cup of coffee and pulled a chair out on the porch. From there, with my binoculars, I could watch the movement of the deer as dawn broke over the river valley.

It was pretty still for the first hour. Only a few does could be seen moving across the flats between the house and the river. Then, at 8 a.m., deer suddenly appeared everywhere. Bucks, both mule deer and whitetails, were following does in every direction. It was a grand sight to behold. My hunters were in place, and the deer were coming out of the woodwork. "What a touch," I thought, as I sat on the back porch watching a great morning unfold. "If this were all there was to guiding, it would be a snap. This is as good as it gets."

But how well I remembered, from 15 years of experience guiding whitetail hunters, that moments like these are the exception rather than the rule.

Four does emerged from a willow hedge, 300 yards to the north. They were moving from west to east. Then a larger-bodied deer trailed them out of the willows. A quick peek through the binoculars revealed heavy dark antlers. He was a great buck. I called Simon to the porch, and he looked at the buck through his binoculars.

"Yep, that's the one I saw just 80 yards from the porch morning before last," he said. "He's a real dandy isn't he?" I agreed. With that, Simon left to check on his cows.

The buck and the four does were heading toward the sprawling, ancient cottonwood where Jackie was waiting in a treestand. It was tremendous to be able to watch the whole event unfold. I couldn't have been more excited if I was the one doing the hunting.

The lead doe changed course to the south. My heart sank. This would take them out of Jackie's visibility. At the last minute, however, one doe broke out of the ranks and headed back to the north. The other does stopped to watch her, and the buck followed the single doe.

She headed straight toward Jackie's tree as if she were on a string. The buck followed without hesitation. In a matter of minutes, they were right beneath Jackie, but there was no shot. My heart was pounding. "He's got to see them!" I whispered to myself. Jackie had mentioned that he was having trouble judging the racks on these big-bodied Alberta bucks, but surely he could tell that this one was a keeper.

"Please Jackie," I groaned, "don't let this one get away."

The buck and the doe milled around within 20 yards of Jackie's tree for what seemed like forever until, finally, a shot rang. My eyes were glued to my binoculars. The buck seemed to react to the shot, but he was immediately on the move and out of my sight. A second shot followed, and Jackie was soon coming out of his tree. He followed in the direction the buck had gone and was quickly out of my sight. Fifteen agonizing minutes passed while I chewed on my nails and fretted nervously on the porch. Finally, almost 20 minutes later, a single shot echoed from the cottonwood thicket.

"That's it," I thought to myself. "He must have wounded the buck, tracked him down, and the third shot was the finisher."

At the instant I arrived at that conclusion, Jackie walked in the kitchen door. "Did you get him?" I asked.

"Sure did," he said with a grin like a 'possum eating red ants.

"Congratulations, you've bagged the porch monster! Then that must have been Jody who shot just a few seconds ago."

Jackie agreed. He and Jody were hunting less than 200 yards apart. As soon as Jackie established that his buck was down, he came back to the house, hoping not to further disturb Jody's hunt. We waited nervously on the porch for a half-hour. We were anxious to see what Jody had done, but we were not about to repeat our previous blunder of walking up to his stand too early.

At last we saw Jody walking out of the timber, so we hurried to meet him. As we approached him, he was babbling in a language all his own. "Buddy, I've seen all there is to see in the world of deer hunting this morning!" he crowed.

"Didja get a buck?" Jackie asked.

"I sure did," Jody grinned. "There were no less than seven bucks within 10 yards of my tree for a half-hour! And there was a hot doe in with 'em. One buck bred the doe three times while the others were grunting and milling around under me. They made scrapes and they rubbed the willows and I got to see it all. Three of the bucks were bigger than any living buck I've ever seen! I was trying to decide which one I was gonna take when No. 8 walked up, and he was the biggest one of 'em all. Buddy, I just said 'thank you very much,' and I shot him.

You wouldn't believe it. When I shot my buck, the other bucks never even lifted their heads. They were after that doe, and they could have cared less about anything else. That's why I was so long getting out of my tree. I just sat there and watched them carry on for another half-hour."

It was a truly incredible story. Jody led us to his buck, a fine 8-pointer with a couple of non-typical sticker points. It was easily the best whitetail of his career. Then we walked back to Jackie's buck. It was a grand, symmetrical 160-inch 10-pointer. It was the second best buck of Jackie's career, surpassed only by the 173-inch 12-pointer he bagged in Alberta the previous year.

I examined Jackie's buck, but I could find only one bullet hole. "Which shot hit the buck?" I asked.

Jackie stammered a little and then said: "The second one."

"Are you telling me you missed this critter at 10 yards?"

"I guess that's about it," Jackie replied sheepishly, as Jody and I gave him the gears.

"Well, you're quite a sport," I teased. "It takes a real sportsman to fire a warning shot before you shoot your buck!" We couldn't resist the opportunity to razz the "Buckmaster!"

In spite of a near miss, the fact was that in 20 minutes, while hunting only 200 yards apart, Jackie and Jody both bagged trophy bucks on the first morning of hunting on the Majestic Ranch. Now that's performance.

What followed was equally amazing. The next morning, even though the hunt was over, Jackie was up before dawn, standing at the patio doors. The two yearlings were feeding on the lawn as usual. Then, from out of nowhere came a nice 8-point buck. He was less than 30 feet from the porch. Jackie streaked downstairs to tell Jody, and together they returned to watch with amazement. Jody eased the patio door open and took several pictures of the buck before it retreated into the willows. This was truly a back porch with a view.

That evening, just for fun, I put Jody in an old platform stand in a cottonwood tree and left him there with my rattling antlers. When I picked him up at dark, he was beside himself. He rattled up two bucks at once: a 6-and an 8-pointer. His desire to rattle up his first whitetail buck was doubly fulfilled.

The balance of the week was spent videotaping a show for the Buckmasters Whitetail Magazine television series, which aired in July of 1989 on the Nashville Network. Those who were watching got to see the Buckmaster, the Bullmaster and, of course, me, the Porchmaster, having the time of our lives—not to mention the great bucks that Jackie and Jody bagged, and the many others still running around behind the porch.

I still remember the closing scene. While the camera was running, Jody announced that he had a special present from his Uncle Henry that he wanted to present to Jackie. Jackie knew that something was up, but he had to go along with the gag because the TV camera was rolling. Next, Jody pulled out his lock-blade, Uncle Henry skinning knife. Then he pulled out Jackie's shirt tail and said: "Meet my Uncle Henry!" as he cut off a broad swath of camo and held it up before the camera. We all laughed, even Jackie. It had been a most interesting and successful hunt—one that could never be equaled or repeated.

TWENTY-FOUR

Belching Up Book Bucks
(and Other Sorrows)

In mid-November of 1989, after 18 years in the guiding and outfitting business in Alberta, Canada, the last hunters I would ever guide professionally arrived at my door. James and Betty Robison are from Fort Worth, Texas, and they are both deadly serious whitetail hunters. Foremost, James is a well-known evangelist and television personality, but in November, he and his wife Betty take some time off for their favorite sport: hunting big whitetails.

We hunted small farm plots carved out of the mixed spruce and aspen timber north of Rocky Mountain House, in the central western part of the province. This area is not as popular among non-resident hunters as the eastern part of the province because it is more closed in with timber. But the bucks are there for those with enough patience to hunt them.

The weather had been unseasonably warm and had suppressed the rut, but when the temperature finally dropped to below zero, the bucks began to show up, trailing the does.

James was perched in a tripod in the corner of an oat stubble field while Betty and I covered an alfalfa field a half-mile to the east. As the sun hovered on the horizon, deer began emptying out of the dark timber into the alfalfa field. A dozen does and small bucks appeared first, but nothing that appealed to Betty. She is a dedicated trophy hunter and had already mastered the toughest part of the sport: passing up small bucks.

After the deer fed past us, it appeared that it was over for the evening. Then Betty whispered, "Russ, there's a buck right beside us!" I turned to see a beautiful 8-pointer less than 30 yards distant.

"Where did he come from?" I asked. Betty thought he had come out of the timber a half-mile to the east of the other deer. In any case, he was right in our laps, and now it was all up to Betty.

I learned long ago not to urge hunters to take animals that didn't appeal to them the instant he or she saw it. I could tell the buck was tempting Betty, but it was no runaway. She patiently studied the buck and asked me what I thought of him. I knew that he was a much larger bodied deer than she was used to hunting in Texas. I also knew from previous experience guiding Texas hunters that antler spread was very important. This buck looked like he would go 18 inches inside. His beams were dark and heavy and the rack was perfectly symmetrical. "He's a darn nice buck," I replied.

"I wish I could be sure," Betty whispered. "He looks good, but not great."

Due to the warm weather, this was the best buck I'd seen all November. I decided to encourage Betty to take him because I was concerned that she might not get another chance at a better buck. "He's a better buck than you think," I urged.

"How good is he?" she asked. By now the buck had walked directly out in front of us and was standing like a statue at no more than 40 yards.

"Just pull that trigger," I whispered, "and I'll show you exactly how good he is."

Betty brought her .30-06 to her shoulder in slow motion and took a steady rest. The buck continued to stand stone still, as if he were frozen in place. I had the buck in my binoculars when Betty's rifle cracked. She made a perfect heart shot and knocked the buck off his feet. In a few seconds, he lay still in the snow.

I congratulated Betty on her shot as we walked toward her first northern whitetail. As I expected, when she had a chance to see the rack up close and hold it in her hands, she was more impressed with the buck than she thought she'd be. Its high-tined rack scored 140 and change: a fine 8-pointer. Betty called it right. It was a nice buck, but not a monster by Alberta standards. In any case, it turned out to be the best buck she saw on the hunt.

Soon it was dark, and James returned from his stand to join us and admire Betty's buck. They were awestruck by the deer's body size and the long hair of the northern buck's coat. "They're just a different animal entirely from our Texas deer," James commented.

I agreed. To me (pardon my bias) they're the epitome of what a whitetail is supposed to be.

The next afternoon, James returned to his tripod stand. There were plenty of tracks in the snow-covered oat stubble. And those big drag marks in the snow that looked like cross-country ski tracks were obviously made by a very large buck. We had no better options than to man that stand until it paid dividends. The landowner told us of a huge buck with awesome antlers that he had seen several times in that area. In fact, he had named the buck Ferdinand.

It was ironic. It seemed the farmer saw Ferdinand every time he turned around, but we had yet to see him for the first time. That's whitetail hunting. Those big bucks seem to understand who's after their hide and who's not.

There were fresh rubs throughout the area, so the sign was positive. Now all we required was some good old-fashioned luck.

After James was settled in his stand for the evening, I headed north to examine another area. About a half-hour before dark, I sat down on a log to rest for a few minutes. As I sat there in the heavy timber, I marveled at the beauty of the north woods under the mantle of fresh snow. It was not cold enough to be uncomfortable that evening—just a beautiful evening to be deer hunting.

The crack of a rifle echoed through the timber from James' direction. "What luck," I thought to myself. "James has got himself an Alberta buck!" I waited a few minutes and then headed toward his stand. It was almost dark when I arrived and James was literally babbling to himself.

"You're never gonna believe what just happened to me," he blurted when he saw me.

"Well, let's hear it," I offered, and his bizarre story came pouring forth.

"I was rattling my antlers about a half-hour before dusk," he began, "and a doe came out of the timber and started feeding in the oat stubble. I thought that was great because she'd serve as a perfect decoy for a buck. Then, a little while later a small 8-pointer came out of the timber into the oat field. I was just watching them when I noticed another deer jumping the fence into the field. I knew he was a bigger deer, so I put my scope on him and studied him. I could tell he had a 10-point frame with heavy beams and it looked like he had some sticker points around his bases. I figured him for a 160-class buck. He really wasn't as big as I'd hoped, and with the hunting being as tough as it has been, I thought I might as well take him. I steadied my crosshairs, pulled the trigger and the buck dropped in his tracks at about 175 yards. I decided to watch him for a few minutes to be sure he was down for good, then an incredible thing happened. The little 8-pointer was still in the oat field. After my buck fell, he ran over and began raking him with his horns. I tickled my rattling antlers together to see if I could pull him away from my buck. It worked. He started walking in my direction, finally walking right beside my tripod, then wandering off into the timber behind me.

"After he was out of sight, it was getting late. I decided to get down and walk over to my buck. I dropped my rattling antlers. As soon as they hit the ground, I saw another deer jumping the fence from the timber into the oat field. I could tell it was a buck—a big buck! When he jumped the fence, he ran straight out to my downed buck and began thrashing him with his antlers exactly like the little 8-pointer had done. I put my scope on him and I could see a tall 10-point frame, much larger than my buck. It was getting so dark that I couldn't make out the fine details of his rack, but I just knew that I was looking at a book-class buck.

"I was wishing I hadn't dropped my rattlin' antlers because I might have been able to rattle him up closer so I could get a better look. Then it dawned on me. We'd been joking earlier about burping to imitate a grunt call. I had nothing to lose, so I let out a loud belch and the buck jerked his head up and came straight to me and stopped 20 yards in front of my tripod!

"Well, now I could see everything he had. He was 24 inches inside, five- to six-inch brow tines, and back tines that would go between 10 and 12 inches on both sides. He was perfectly symmetrical with no junk—just a perfect 10-pointer. If he wasn't a Boone and Crockett buck, he wouldn't miss it by more than an inch or two. Man, what a buck! I couldn't believe it. I had just shot a 160-class buck, then the dream buck of a lifetime is standing 20 yards in front of me!"

James continued his amazing tale: "You can't imagine what I went through. First, I shoot a good buck and I'm feeling pretty good about that, then this monster comes out and taunts me. I couldn't believe I was looking at a book deer at 20 yards!

"Finally, he circled me and slipped around behind me, jumped the fence and then stopped and looked back at me one last time before he disappeared into the timber. I could have shot him a hundred times. Man, what a buck!"

By the time I arrived on the scene, James had already examined the buck he shot. It was a very impressive old 10-pointer with many two- and three-inch sticker points around the bases. In fact, there were 20 measurable points in all. Both bases measured an honest 6½ inches in circumference, so the old buck had great mass. It appeared that he was quite old, well past his prime and on the downhill side of life. We speculated about what his antlers might have been in his prime. He was a fine trophy by any standard. Well, by almost any standard—the exception being the heartache buck that appeared after the shooting was done.

Someone once said that whitetail hunting consists mostly of anticipation and memories. If that's true, then James Robison experienced the essence of whitetail hunting. He went home with a lifetime memory of a book buck standing 20 yards in front of him. In addition, there was the anticipation of possibly seeing that great deer again on a future hunt. And as a bonus, he had a gnarly, heavy-beamed 10-point Alberta rack for his collection.

In addition, James learned a new trick: belching up a white-tailed buck. When all else fails, belch! It might not be popular among grunt call manufacturers, but it works in a pinch. And speaking of new tricks, there is one more that can be learned from James' experience. It's the oldest whitetail trick in the book, and one practiced regularly by the very biggest bucks. It's called "Wait until the hunter burns up his tag on a smaller buck, then walk out and break his heart!"

Remember the famous saying, "It's never over 'til it's over"? I think those words were uttered by baseball great Yogi Berra. They might be true in baseball, but they are THE RULE in hunting big whitetails!

CHAPTER TWENTY-FOUR

POSTSCRIPT

I talked to the landowner shortly after James and Betty returned to Fort Worth. He said he was driving down his gravel road, a short distance north of his house, when he spotted Ferdinand browsing along a fence line right-of-way beside the road. He parked his truck and started walking toward the majestic buck, totally unarmed. He just wanted to see how close he could get. He knew this incident would rub salt in our wounds, and he got quite a kick out of the fact that he saw Ferdinand on a regular basis while the visiting hunters were constantly eluded by the smart old buck.

He finally made it to the fence corner, about 50 yards from the unconcerned buck. He remembered James' story about belching at the buck, so he trapped some air in his throat and uttered a loud "buuurp!" Ferdinand jerked his head to attention, looked squarely at the farmer and charged him. The farmer scrambled back to his truck, slammed the door and drove away quickly.

"I couldn't believe that crazy deer!" he exclaimed. "I didn't know what he would have done if he'd caught up with me, but I'll tell you one thing: Burping really works!"

SECTION V

One on One with Whitetails

TWENTY-FIVE

Of Bows and Bucks and Pick-Up Trucks

Whitetails appeared like gray shadows at the edge of the red willow thicket as the sun settled behind the hedge of cottonwoods in eastern Alberta's Red Deer River valley. The most important 15 minutes of the day were at hand. I craned my neck to look behind me and saw the faint shapes of seven deer. Possibly two had subtle halos of antlers above their heads. They seemed to congregate there at the edge of their bedding area until the precise degree of dusk prevailed. Only then did they begin their quarter-mile journey to the alfalfa field where they would feed all night. Their time worn trail wound within 20 yards of the cottonwood tree where I was perched in my treestand. Fifty yards beyond me, the deer trail crossed the fence and the farm road and emptied into the alfalfa field. Slowly I eased around in my stand with my back to the approaching deer. In minutes, they would be within bow range. It was Oct. 1, 1985.

I had been watching the deer enter the alfalfa field for several days before the bow season opened. There were two trails they favored. One was through an open pasture, which offered no hiding place for a bowhunter, and the other was through a sparse fringe of cottonwoods that afforded me the position I now occupied. This was the first day of the bow season, and somewhere in that willow thicket I knew there were several record-class bucks, including one that might even crowd the B&C minimum.

The trail angled slightly less than 20 yards to my left. I sat 20 feet above the ground with my back against the tree trunk. As the deer approached from behind, I could hear the faint shuffling of cottonwood leaves and soon they were milling around almost directly below me. I rolled my eyes as far left as I could and saw the dominant doe step into view. She raised her nose to test the wind and looked cautiously at the alfalfa field ahead of her. Then she checked her back trail one last time and, with a casual twitch of her tail, started toward the field. Behind her came another mature doe and her fawn of the year, followed by two more does. That accounted for five of the seven deer I had seen. When the last doe passed me, I breathed a deep sigh of relief and strained to hear more shuffling of leaves. There was the sound. I could tell the deer were walking briskly, without hesitation. I was sure they were bucks, now confident that all was clear since the does had passed without incident.

Out of the corner of my eye, I saw the first buck emerge. He was a small 8-pointer, but automatically I raised my bow and drew, holding the top sight pin on his right front shoulder. The next buck would soon be standing in his tracks and I was ready. Then the second buck emerged with his head held low. I swung the pin onto his ribs and checked his antlers. He was a 6-pointer. Too small! Not the buck for which I was hoping. I eased the string down and drew a trembling breath. I craned my neck once more to see if there were more deer coming. Two more does, each with yearlings, and one small spike buck passed my stand in the semi-darkness. After they were well out into the alfalfa field, I climbed down and walked back down the road to the truck where my partner, Doug Sproule, was waiting.

"Any luck?" Doug asked. After I gave him my report, he told me he had been up high in the river brakes with a spotting scope, watching the deer enter the alfalfa. Several big bucks had come in through the trail in the open field. It appeared that they knew exactly how safe they were on that trail. There was simply nowhere to set up on them as long as they used that route. It was disturbing to see the pattern developing. Unless the bigger bucks just wanted a change of scenery, they were as safe as a day in jail. It appeared that I was going to have to stick it out in the cottonwood tree and hope that a good buck used that trail before the does figured me out and ended my only hope. From experience, I knew that one slight breeze or downdraft could mean "game over." One or two sittings were about all I expected I could manage before the does betrayed my position. I had already used up one of them.

We contemplated every possible option as we ate supper that night, but we could not come up with any other plan. That one key cottonwood tree was the only perfect ambush, and even that position was subject to very critical wind conditions. As long as the wind was directly out of the east, it would work. But in southern Alberta, where the wind changes continuously, that was asking for a miracle. It was obvious that I could only hunt the stand when the wind was from the east and just hope that one of the big bucks would pick the same day to abandon his guaranteed safety for a stroll through the cottonwoods. Doug and I agreed that the odds were not exactly promising. All night long, the problem kept replaying in my mind. By morning, I felt like I hadn't slept at all. Nothing is more frustrating than a big whitetail buck you can't get at.

I decided not to hunt that morning for fear of spooking deer in the dark that might be near the stand. At 4 p.m., Doug drove me to the spot where the deer trail crossed the dirt road into the alfalfa field. It was only a 50-yard walk to my cottonwood tree from there. I asked him what he was planning for the evening, and he said that he was going back up on the river brakes for some more scouting. Then an idea popped into my head. I asked him to drive the truck over to where the big bucks were crossing the farm road into the alfalfa field and park against the fence, right in the middle of their trail. He looked at me kind of funny, shrugged his shoulders and agreed. Then for good measure I suggested that every 15 minutes or so he get out of the truck, walk around it, get back in and slam the door. Maybe, just maybe, the commotion would turn the bucks back and subtly pressure them into using the other trail. He agreed to the plan and drove away while I climbed into my treestand. The wind was still holding from the east.

Three hours dragged by before the sun sank low enough to get the deer up and moving. Right on schedule, the does appeared at the edge of the thicket as they had done the previous evening. I watched them congregate and start toward the alfalfa in the late shadows. They appeared to be moving more cautiously than the day before, and this time I could see no bucks at all. The big dominant doe came in the lead again and scoured the area with her senses, stopping frequently to test the air. The does trailing along behind her watched her intently for any sign of danger. The same five does and yearlings passed my stand at exactly the same minute as they had done the previous evening. But this time they ran past nervously, reminding me that time was running out for my strategic cottonwood. Through some sixth sense, whitetails have come to fear the presence of man, even when there is no apparent way for them to know he is there.

More does hung back at the edge of the willows as the light faded. I could barely see them through my binoculars, weaving their way in and out of the brush. My neck ached from being twisted back so far over my left shoulder as I watched for any sign of the bucks. Eventually, like living shadows, the does slipped into the open and onto the trail. I turned back in my stand to wait them out, in hopes that a good buck would follow them. A couple of minutes later, I could hear them walking in the leaves, and I eased my head to the left toward the trail. But instead of coming out on the trail, they came out directly beneath my tree. Two does, one yearling and the spike buck I'd seen the previous day milled around below my stand. I sat on pins and needles, afraid to breathe for fear of being discovered. Eventually, they moved out in front of me five or six yards, nibbling and sniffing at every square inch of ground. I was expecting one to get a whiff of something wrong and explode into fits of blowing and snorting. The light was almost gone, and I felt the day would be a success if the does would just leave me undiscovered—buck or no buck. As I sat statue-still, wishing the curious does away, they all suddenly stopped their investigation and focused their attention on their back trail slightly to my right. I could not stand the suspense so I slowly turned my head to look over my right shoulder. I could immediately hear more footsteps in the leaves, then I saw them—five bucks travelling together. There were the same two I had seen the day before, as well as a young forkhorn, a medium-sized 8-pointer and, behind them all, a larger-bodied deer with a much better rack than the rest. I could not turn my head far enough to count points, but I knew instantly that he was an older buck—one of the ones I had seen on the other trail. It worked! The truck trick must have worked!

As I frantically tried to ready myself for a shot, I realized the bucks were approaching 20 yards to my right, on the opposite side of the tree from the trail. I was stuck with a left-hander's shot from a right-hander's position. For the first time, I fully appreciated the luxury of a treestand with a swivel seat. I twisted around 180 degrees to the right with almost no effort. Had I been sitting on a stationary seat, the shot would have been impossible.

The group of bucks moved past my tree in single file with the larger buck at the rear. I took a deep breath and drew the arrow back to the corner of my mouth, then settled the 20-yard pin behind the big deer's shoulder. He stopped on a small knoll with his head high. At that instant, I released the arrow. The second the string slipped through my fingers, I knew the shot was good. As if in slow motion, the arrow disappeared into the deer's ribs. Then there were deer running everywhere; bucks and does were going in all directions. My buck bolted ahead at full tilt for about 40 yards, finally cartwheeling into a clump of buckbrush. He never stirred again. In a few split seconds, the rest of the deer were in the alfalfa field, looking back to see what had spooked them. They still didn't know I was there.

Within a few minutes, it was too dark to see. I wondered if I had just dreamed it or if I had really bagged a good whitetail. I climbed out of the stand and walked the few steps to where the buck was standing when I shot. The arrow was there, sticking in the ground. I picked it up and felt the shaft. It was still wet with blood. So it was not a dream after all! It was too dark to see without a flashlight and mine was in the truck. I walked out to the road on the deer trail and met Doug as he returned from the other crossing.

"What's the verdict?" he asked as he pulled up beside me.

"Couldn't be better!" I grinned. Together we walked back to the stand with the flashlight, and I quickly found the arrow where I had left it as a marker. Then I hurried over to the buckbrush where I saw the buck flip end over end. There he lay, exactly where I saw him last. He was a beautiful 9-pointer with five points on his right side and four on his left, and at that time he was easily my best bow-and-arrow whitetail. The shot had penetrated one lung and passed through the center of the heart. I couldn't have asked for a better one.

I recounted the whole experience to Doug and learned that he had turned back no less than five good bucks by parking right on the crossing. Where the other four had gone was anybody's guess, but one of them had fallen for the trick. He was mine! After supper, Doug asked what I thought the buck would score. In my excitement, I hadn't even thought about scoring him. A quick taping revealed a score in the mid-130s, easily enough to qualify for the Pope and Young bowhunting records. It was a team effort, and it had worked. Most strategies are one-shot deals with whitetails. We tried the same trick a few days later for another hunter, but the big bucks just waited until dark before crossing right behind the truck. The element of surprise had been essential. Given time to digest the trick, whitetails will alter the rules again in their favor. I am reminded to be thankful for one success but not to expect lightning to strike twice in the same place, at least not during the same season.

Whitetails have a way of taking the wind out of your sails, as I found out the day after I killed my buck. I set up another stand in hopes of taking a mule deer in an area where we had seen a good muley buck entering the alfalfa. Ten minutes before dark, I looked down and there was a huge 10-point whitetail buck nibbling at the branches I had sawed from the tree to make shooting lanes. And me with no whitetail tag! I watched him in disbelief a mere 20 feet beneath my stand. He fed there contentedly until it was too dark to see, while my poor heart nearly exploded. Where he came from I'll never know. He just suddenly appeared. I guestimated him at 165 inches. His very appearance seemed to say that just when you think you've put one over on a whitetail, you've got another think coming.

TWENTY-SIX

Almost a Legend

*I*n hunting, anticipation is everything. Before the event, a hunt can be as wonderful as your imagination will allow. However, the reality after the fact is seldom as wonderful as imagined. I know. I've hunted a long time. Some hunts have lived up to my expectations, but few have exceeded them. For that reason, I still marvel at this particular bowhunt, which will probably never be surpassed in my life. It was so incredible that I feel a little sheepish when I tell someone about it because it sounds so embellished. But, dear reader, every word that follows actually happened—believe it or not!

Being more a creature of habit than the deer I hunt, I returned to western-central Saskatchewan to hunt with Caribou Trail Outfitters during the last week of November 1993. I should qualify this statement by saying that I am a creature of habit, so long as I am convinced that I'm hunting where I have a real chance at a quality buck. Success is habit forming. Over the previous four years, I had taken seven good bucks while bowhunting with Caribou Trail Outfitters. Thus, the aforementioned habit.

I was traveling from Fort St. John, British Columbia, to Saskatchewan a day later than planned. It was early afternoon when I climbed into my appointed treestand. A huge non-typical buck had already been seen twice from this stand, and had thus far gone unscathed. The report was that the non-typical was always seen traveling with a medium-sized, typical 8-pointer.

At 2 p.m., such an 8-point buck wandered into view and milled around, finally coming within easy bow range of me. I was amused, but not tempted. I wanted a look at his big non-typical friend.

Eventually, the 8-pointer wandered off into the timber and all was quiet for an hour or so. About 4 p.m., the stillness was broken by a single, thunderous, guttural grunt. It startled me because it was so loud—louder than any deer grunt I'd ever heard.

I waited breathlessly for the next sound. It came 10 minutes later, just like the first. I couldn't locate the source of the sound, but it was obviously very close. The volume seemed too loud to be real, but where exactly was this loudmouthed buck? That was THE question.

A silent wait for an additional 15 minutes finally told the story. The buck was standing directly behind a huge spruce tree about 40 yards from me. He finally raked his antlers against the trunk, and I saw part of one main beam. It was truly awesome, and it was definitely non-typical.

It appeared that I was engaged in a 40-yard standoff with this forest giant. I knew that he was unaware of my presence, but perhaps previous encounters had made him wise to this location. I waited a full hour without further sound or sight of him. Eventually, I assumed he'd somehow slipped away unde-tected. But in case I was wrong and the buck was still there, hiding behind that tree, I didn't want to tip my hand by climbing down and letting him see or hear me. I knew if I wasn't at our rendezvous location at dark, my guide would come looking for me. In my mind, it would be better for him to come walking in and spook the mystery buck than for me to do it by climbing out of my stand. I know that's giving the buck an awful lot of credit for reasoning power, but I just didn't see how he could have left the area without me noticing. It was dead calm. You could hear a pin drop in the big boreal forest, so I wasn't tak-ing any chances.

After dark, as I anticipated, I heard Dave approaching my stand site and saw the beam of his flashlight flicker through the trees. Finally he stood at the base of my spruce tree, shined his light up at me and asked if I was okay. I assured him that I was and began lowering my gear on my pull rope. When all my gear was lowered, I unlatched my safety belt and descended. When my feet hit the ground, as I was about to explain why I was still in the tree, the buck broke and ran and sounded like he was tearing down the forest as he went. I was shocked and some-what unnerved. The buck had been standing like a statue for more than two hours. Who says animals can't reason?

I tried the same stand the next morning, but the sound of timber wolves howling in the woods behind me guaranteed that I would see no more deer there that day.

My guide and friend, Dave Kelbert, suggested another stand dubbed the "Bowling Alley." A very good buck had been spotted there, and it was still at large. At first light, I was ready for action—bow in hand—25 feet up a big pine lo-cated along the edge of a seam where a relatively open stand of aspens met the dense evergreen timber.

At 9:10 a.m., I heard a crashing in the timber behind me and knew instantly that it was a buck thrashing the trees with his antlers. Moments later, a similar crashing occurred in another stand of evergreens about 100 yards in front of me.

"Wow!" I thought. "Two aggressive bucks right here close. This could be very interesting."

Seconds later, the buck behind me made another crash and I looked back over my shoulder to see if I could glimpse him. I spotted movement and, within seconds, a dainty doe came walking out of the green timber, heading my way. She passed within 17 yards of my tree and walked off into the aspens in front of me. Moments later, she spotted another doe about 80 yards away and headed in her direction.

Another crash jolted me back to attention. A peek over my shoulder made my heart jump into my throat. A huge 10-point buck was coming out of the evergreens right on the doe's tracks. He had a dark ebony-colored rack, easily 24 inches wide, with tall dagger-like tines. At a glance, I guessed him as a 160-point-plus buck—truly a buck to die for. To my utter delight, he was following the doe's tracks with his nose to the ground. He would walk right past me just as the doe had, offering me a slam-dunk shot, quartering away at between 15 and 20 yards!

I watched him come closer. He was a magnificent beast, easily better than any buck I'd ever arrowed. Finally, he stepped behind a neighboring spruce tree and stopped.

One more step and he would be mine.

He lifted his head for the first time since I'd laid eyes on him and peered ahead into the open aspens and spotted the doe, which he was following. She was walking off to my left. With a visual fix on her, the buck turned straight away from me and bounded toward her, keeping the spruce tree directly between us as he went.

I felt sick. So close and still no cigar. It was a cruel twist of fate that left me weak in the knees and a bit nauseous.

Soon the buck chased the doe out of sight and I was alone again with a nearly terminal case of the "almost-but-not-quite" whitetail blues.

Then came another crash in the timber behind me. When I looked back, I was astounded to see another 10-point buck walking toward me with his nose in the same doe's tracks. Behind him, also dogging the ground with his nose, was a nice 8-pointer. Now that the hot doe was out of sight, there was little doubt in my mind that both bucks would walk right by me, making perfect targets of themselves.

The dark-antlered 10-pointer was an exceptionally huge-bodied animal with a rack I estimated at 150 inches. His rack was smaller than the first buck's, but he was a bird in the hand, so I prepared to take my shot. When he stepped out from behind the spruce tree that had denied me the first 10-pointer, I drew and held. He stopped for a brief moment before continuing to follow the doe's tracks. Within a few steps, he was in the clear and quartering slightly away from me.

My arrow sizzled through the buck's ribs and stuck in the ground under his offside ear. The sound of the arrow hitting the snow spooked him, and he jumped back toward my tree, facing me. It was obvious that the shot, though lethal, had not inflicted enough pain to even concern the buck. He stood there at 10 yards rotating his ears, obviously listening for further evidence of the foreign sound that had startled him.

It seemed that he stood there for an unusually long time. I knew my shot had passed through both lungs, but the buck still didn't seem the least bit concerned. I finally began to have some doubts about my shot. I was sure I saw the arrow dissolve into the crease behind his right shoulder. I could see it was sticking in the ground.

Just as I was really starting to worry, the buck started reaching out with one hind leg to keep his balance. That was the sign for which I'd been looking. I breathed a sigh of relief. Within seconds, he toppled in his tracks right below my stand.

When I got down for a closer look, I was amazed at his size. His antlers were a shoe-in for the record book, but his body size was equally impressive. Although I couldn't weigh him, 25 years of experience with western Canadian whitetails assured me that he would tip the scales at over 300 pounds. I remember thinking when I first saw him that his body seemed too long, like a couple of boxcars with whitetail antlers.

Dave came to check on me and we celebrated my good fortune and took some photos before he drug my buck out of the woods with his four-wheeler. Afterwards I returned to the same treestand to see if I could burn up my second buck tag. I could still hear the putting sound of Dave's four-wheeler when the unthinkable occurred. Out of the timber before me stepped that first big 10-pointer that almost presented me with a shot. He had obviously abandoned the doe that took him away from me, and now he was heading back to square one where he started. It appeared that he would pass within bow range of me.

"This is too good to be true!" I thought. "If I arrow that buck, I'll be a legend in my own mind."

I stood at full attention in my treestand, with an arrow on my string. The crunching of hooves in the dry snow sounded amplified in the stillness of the forest. He was now within 50 yards, walking fully broadside to me. "If he stops, he's mine," I whispered to myself. And then he stopped. His head was conveniently behind an aspen tree, but his entire body was in the open. I centered my chosen sight pin in the crease behind his left shoulder and released my arrow. The string snap was also amplified in the frozen stillness. As the arrow arced toward the target, I remember watching it fly—knowing it was a perfect shot. However, the sizzling stillness of that November afternoon worked against me. The buck heard the string snap, and since he was 50 yards away, the slight lag time of the arrow's flight gave him time to swing his head toward the sound. Just as his rack swung back over his left shoulder, the arrow arrived. Instead of slipping through his ribs, it centered his right main beam with a resounding crack. The broadhead drove deep into his antler, and he reared up on his hind legs like a spirited stallion. As he tossed his head, the shaft hit a tree, snapping it off behind the broadhead. Then he sprinted into the timber, leaving me with a memory I'll never forget and a broken arrow for a souvenir. He was one of the best white-tailed bucks I'd ever had within bow range. So much for legendhood! Oh well, I was almost a legend.

That night I washed off the "lucky" arrow and resharpened the broadhead. It still spun true, so I put it back in my quiver as my designated lucky No. 1 arrow.

The next morning, I climbed back in the same tree, hoping for a repeat performance. However, it was a different day. There was an east wind blowing and, within minutes, I sensed the area had gone flat. I was right. By 4 p.m., I had seen only one doe and one small 8-point buck. It was the last hour of daylight and I had little faith that a good buck would appear. The truth of the matter was that I was sitting in my treestand, fighting off the brutal assault of an unusually determined nature call. I didn't want to climb down that late in the day with only the best 60 minutes of the afternoon left to hunt. On the other hand, I wasn't sure I could resist nature for that last hour.

The wind was blowing too hard to hear hooves in the snow, so I was taken by surprise when I heard a loud crunch right under me. I looked down just in time to see a wide, chocolate-antlered buck walk behind the same spruce as yesterday's bucks. I jumped to my feet and drew my arrow. Instantly the big 8-pointer stepped into view, and as he turned slightly away, I hit the trigger on my release. The arrow hit with a crack and the buck hopped forward, looked back, then trotted out about 40 yards and stopped again. Within seconds, he tipped over in the snow.

It happened so fast that I didn't even have time to think. All I knew was that his antlers impressed me at first sight, so I took the shot.

When I walked up to the buck, the reality of what had happened settled in on me. It was the second record-book buck in two days, both shot from the same stand with the same arrow! When I walked back to retrieve my lucky arrow, I was amazed to realize that it was stuck in the ground no more than six inches from where it had landed the day before, after passing through buck number one.

This was bowhunting adventure at its finest. As I said in the beginning, I'm almost (but not quite) sheepish about telling this story for fear I will be looked upon as some wild teller of tales. But dear reader, that's just the way it happened.

TWENTY-SEVEN

Third Time's Charm

Pre-season scouting paid good dividends in the little thicket north of Caroline, Alberta, just a few miles from my home. Buck sign was literally everywhere. By late October, it seemed that every second tree had been rubbed. Some were as big around as my leg, and I'm no featherweight. On Oct. 28, 1988, just three days before the rifle season opened, there was fresh snow on the ground. I walked the thicket one last time, and there were scrapes in the snow, every few feet along the main trail. I even ran into two bucks standing like statues in the thick aspen and spruce timber. Our eyes met and for a few seconds we just stared at each other. Finally, they bolted and disappeared. One was just a forkhorn; the other was a small 8-pointer. They looked beautiful standing there in the new fallen snow, but they were not what I was seeking. And they were certainly not the bucks rubbing those trees, eight inches in diameter.

The thicket was about a half-mile square, and it backed up against a small lake. The green timber along the edge of the lake was truly a jungle, too thick to attempt to hunt. But because it was an impenetrable sanctuary, the deer used it as a bedding area. When they left the bedding area, they filtered out through the thicket en route to an incredible smorgasbord of feeding opportunities. To the north of the thicket was a huge alfalfa field. To the west was an oat field, also sown with clover, and to the south, barley was planted. The lake bordered the thicket to the east. I can honestly say that I have never encountered such a buck haven as this. I felt an overwhelming confidence that I would take a great buck from the thicket, but little did I realize how complicated that task was going to be.

THE FIRST ATTEMPT

At dawn on Oct. 31, the whitetail rifle season opened. I did not hunt that morning. I waited until the middle of the day, then went in broad daylight and set up my treestand. By 2:30 p.m., all was in place. I climbed into my stand, 25 feet above the ground in a large cottonwood tree. I chose a location in the heaviest timber in the thicket, where I felt a buck would move about without feeling the least bit exposed. At 3 p.m., I smacked the rattling antlers together, then, after a minute or so of rattling, I put them down and waited. The afternoon was clear and mild. Some of the snow from the previous week was still on the ground. Everything felt right.

Twenty minutes after I rattled, as I sat silently listening for any sounds of an approaching buck, I felt an overwhelming urge to look directly behind me. I have experienced that feeling many times in my hunting career and have come to trust my intuition. I eased the swivel seat around to my right and there, behind me, tiptoeing down the truck trail, was a hunter. My first reaction was anger. No one else was supposed to be hunting this thicket. I had asked the landowner if anyone else had asked him for hunting permission and he assured me that no one had.

I NEVER rattle antlers if there are hunters I don't know in the same area that I'm hunting. It was obvious that this hunter was looking for the bucks he thought he had heard fighting. I sat quietly and watched him as he slipped along. He had no idea he was being watched. I decided to let him pass rather than draw his attention to the fact that I was there. Soon he was out of sight, and after 30 minutes I rattled again.

From the east, back toward the lake, I heard something move. I listened carefully. I heard the sound again. It was getting louder. Perhaps, in spite of the interference of the other hunter, a buck was responding to the rattling. Soon I heard more noise in the thick timber. It was beginning to sound a bit too loud for even the most aggressive whitetail buck. There was a crashing sound and then all was quiet. After a minute or so, I heard the crashing again. Each time it sounded a little closer. Whatever it was, it was most certainly coming toward me.

At last, the crashing was directly to the east of me, less than 30 yards. I knew it could not be a deer, but at the same time, I couldn't imagine what on earth it could be. No hunter in his right mind would try to plow his way through that tangle of alders and spruce trees.

The crashing was only 20 yards away now, and suddenly, amidst the cracking of limbs, a hunter fell face-first onto the ground between two big spruce trees. I could scarcely believe my eyes. He was wearing a plastic camo suit unlike anything I'd ever seen. His every move sounded like the world's largest Safeway bag being dragged through the timber.

After his spill, he dragged himself to his feet, dusted himself off and immediately assumed the assault position, looking around keenly to see if there might be any deaf and dumb deer still in the immediate vicinity. Once satisfied that there were no deer, he began his thunderous advance through the timber. In seconds, he was directly beneath my stand. The temptation was just too great to resist. I cupped my hands at the sides of my mouth and in my most ethereal voice yelled, "Mister, that's never gonna work!"

The pour soul sprang straight into the air with terror on his face. As his eyes met mine, a look of partial relief and embarrassment swept over his face.

"Oh, was that you rattling antlers?" he said ever so casually.

"Why do you ask?" I replied with equal nonchalance, my rattling antlers still in my hand.

While he stammered for words, I asked the question that was most pressing on my mind: "What on earth are you doing down there?"

"Well, uh, I'm pushing the deer out to my partner who's waiting at the edge of the alfalfa field," he said sheepishly.

I couldn't hold my tongue. "You're not pushing the deer out of anywhere! You're pushing them farther into the timber, back to the jungle along the lake! Why don't you take off that plastic suit and just go sit down somewhere and be still? You're never going to see a hair doing what you're doing, and, furthermore, you're going to make it impossible for anybody else to see anything!"

The words were barely out of my mouth when there was a crash in the timber off to the south, followed by the unmistakable blowing and snorting of a departing white-tailed buck.

The hunter on the ground even heard it. "Was that a deer?" he asked with eyes as wide as saucers.

"You guessed it," I replied with disgust.

"Uh, what should we do now?"

Although I felt the overwhelming urge to recommend brain surgery to him, I suppressed my hostility and calmly suggested that it was too late to do anything but go home. He shuffled off toward the alfalfa field and I got down from my stand. I stopped at the farmer's house on my way out and asked him about the intruders, but he had no answers. He said he'd keep a closer eye on things in the future. For that I was thankful. I knew that these guys were never going to kill the big buck I was after — not the way they were hunting. But they could make it pretty tough for me just by being in the neighborhood. And on top of everything else, they hadn't even asked permission.

THE SECOND ATTEMPT

A week later, I figured the enthusiasm of opening day fever might have worn off for most hunters. Perhaps the thicket would be quiet once again. I stopped and talked with the farmer, and he assured me that no one had been around in several days. That was music to my ears.

A southerly breeze dictated that I enter the thicket from the north. It was the long way in, but at least my scent would not broadcast my entry. At 4 p.m., my stand was again attached to the same cottonwood tree. As soon as I latched my safety belt, I cracked the rattling antlers together. Instantly, before I was even finished my first rattling sequence, I heard a truck bouncing across the pasture to the south. It continued to clang and bang along the field until it was about 200 yards from me at the edge of the thicket.

"Now what on earth is happening?" I mumbled to myself.

I found out quickly. I could hear a chain saw whining and then, through the timber, I could see flames leaping into the air. Next came the smoke in great billows, straight into my face. The neighboring farmer picked this, of all evenings, to burn a windrow of timber that had been lying on the ground for years. Choking and hacking, I descended from my perch while smoky tears streamed from my eyes. What was it about this thicket? How could such a wonderful patch of deer heaven be so impossible to hunt? Maybe the deer knew how hard they were to hunt here, too. Maybe that's why they were there! I drove home in utter dismay.

THE THIRD ATTEMPT

I would have written the thicket off except for those huge rubs. There was undoubtedly a great buck in there somewhere. I had to give it one more try. Again I stopped at the farmer's house and asked him how the war was going. He assured me again that no one had been hunting there since the beginning of the season. "What about the burning?" I asked.

"Nope, no more burning," he said.

I hung a set of rutted-up buck tarsal glands on a branch 20 yards downwind of my stand location. If I did draw a buck in with the rattling antlers, if he made the customary downwind circle to test the situation with his nose, he would smell the hocks. They were the real thing, so if he smelled them, he should be convinced enough to come in without reservation. At least that's the way I hoped it would be. With cautious optimism, I attached my stand to the old cottonwood for the third time that season.

"What can go wrong this time?" I wondered.

I looked at my watch. It was exactly 4 p.m. My first rattling sequence lasted no more than a minute. Then I sat quietly for a full half-hour. At 4:30, I rattled again. Soon after my second sequence, I heard the sound I had been waiting to hear: heavy antlers clanking against a poplar tree. I waited. Soon I heard the sound again. Then came the electrifying sound of a buck thrashing the brush. He was coming to me. At last it was working.

He emerged from his bedding sanctuary along the lakeshore, about 75 yards north of me, and slowly began his circle. He was in no hurry, but he was convinced. He repeatedly cracked timber and thrashed his antlers against trees both large and small. Then came a sound to the south of me. I strained my ears and then I heard it again. Yes, it was a second buck. I had two bucks coming to me from opposite directions. It was too good to be true. This was worth the wait and the interference of the first two attempts. I glanced at my watch. It was 4:50 p.m. Both bucks continued to make their opposing circles in an attempt to check everything with their noses before they came to the scene of the rattling. I could tell by how loud and aggressive both bucks were that they were mature. I supposed their circles would eventually bring them face to face. I wondered if they might become preoccupied with one another and deal me out of the game. "Wouldn't that just be my luck?" I thought.

The buck to the north was closing the distance. I estimated that he was no farther than 40 yards. A half-dozen thick spruce trees formed a natural hedge that hid him from my view. The buck from the south was still coming, but he was probably 75 yards distant. The nearer buck was stopped on his side of the spruce hedge, obviously making his final calculations. Another two or three steps would put him in my sights. I could feel my heart beating in my chest, and I inhaled deeply, fighting the intensity of my own excitement. I waited a full minute, but the buck stood his ground. I felt sure he was downwind of the tarsal glands. They were extra stinky, too, so I felt sure he could smell them.

Once I know a buck is coming to the antlers, I don't rattle again. It was now 5:05 p.m. Only a few minutes of shooting light remained. Being in the heart of the thicket made things even darker. Had we come to a stalemate? Was I even going to see the buck after all the anticipation?

I slipped my right hand into my jacket pocket, pulled out my grunt call and eased it to my lips. I inhaled quickly and made two consecutive grunts. I listened and waited. It was the buck's move, and move he did. I could hear him pushing himself forward through alder branches and then the rhythmic crunching of footsteps on poplar leaves. I crammed the grunt call back into my pocket and picked my rifle up off my lap. I saw him as he emerged from the thick spruce boughs. He took two steps and stopped with a large poplar tree blocking his head from my view. He was six feet straight downwind of the tarsal glands I had hung on the branch. I could tell he was studying them with his nose.

"C'mon baby, just one more step!" I silently pleaded.

His body was huge, and my heart was about to explode with anxiety. He was only 25 yards from me, but I still couldn't see his antlers. I fought to stay calm, and he finally took two more steps and stopped. He stood facing me, between two poplar trees, his nose stuck to the hanging hocks. Immediately I saw ten tall tines and good mass. He had no inkling of my presence, but still I dared not move while he was facing my direction.

Suddenly, from behind, the second buck cracked the timber. My buck instantly looked back over his rump, turning his head directly away from me. I threw the .280 to my shoulder, centered the crosshairs between his shoulder blades, and touched the trigger. Before the sound of the shot finished echoing through the timber, the buck was lying still in his tracks. I sat quietly watching my buck and listening as the second buck cautiously retreated back in the direction from which he came. Perhaps five minutes passed and darkness fell in the thicket. From the time I first heard my buck coming until the time I dropped him, 40 minutes had passed.

I got down from my stand and walked over to the buck. It was only 24 steps to where he lay. He was a huge animal and his symmetrical 10-point rack was splendid. I guessed him at about 160 inches. Both sides of his rack were even except for the fourth point on his right side. It was shorter than the same point on the left, and there was an acorn-shaped formation in the tine, probably the result of an injury while still in velvet. I admired him until it was too dark to see. The third time was truly charmed. I couldn't have asked for a more perfect hunt. I leaned my rifle against a tree and walked back to get the truck.

"I'll have to get the farmer to help me load this big fellow into the truck," I mused. "Thanks, Lord, for such a wonderful buck."

TWENTY-EIGHT

Deer TV

As the sun set on the Yellowstone River bottom in eastern Montana on that October evening in 1996, I was in a treestand in an ancient, twisted cottonwood. Over my shoulder was Buckmasters' TV cameraman, Mark Oliver. Does walked single file out of the river bottom like a mule train, en route to the sugar beet fields above us. At about the time you'd expect a buck to appear, one did. We watched him angle toward our stands. As he closed the distance to a mere four yards, there was little doubt this was the buck I'd waited for all my life—an 11-pointer with double drop tines!

I closed the jaws of my release around my bowstring and started to raise my bow for the shot as the buck walked past me and angled away from the tree.

"Don't shoot!" Mark whispered quietly, but emphatically.

My first thought was that he must actually have seen an even bigger buck that I hadn't noticed.

"Why not?" I whispered back, as my heart thundered in my chest.

"Not enough light for the camera!" he whispered. Not at all what I was expecting.

I was stunned. There was the best buck I'd ever been in bow range of and now I'm told not to shoot because the camera can't see it! Welcome to the wonderful world of Deer TV! We were filming an episode for the "Buckmasters Whitetail Magazine" television show.

I felt sick at my stomach when I realized that I wasn't going to get to shoot that buck. You know the feeling—something like hearing your first girlfriend in junior high school tell you she doesn't like you anymore. You think you might die right there on the spot.

Suddenly, the obvious question flooded my mind: "What am I doing here?"

All my hunting life, my mode of operandi had been to outsmart and shoot the biggest buck I could find. Now, having done almost all of the above, I had watched this glorious trophy stroll out of my life. Suddenly, I hated Deer TV. Appearing on TV meant nothing to me, but that buck sure did. I could see that TV and me weren't long for this world.

Meanwhile, the next morning a huge buck walked right in front of Buckmasters' founder and TV show host, Jackie Bushman, at 10 yards and stopped broadside, offering him the shot of a lifetime at what would have certainly been his best-ever bow buck. From over his shoulder came that dreaded whisper from cameraman Gene Bidlespacher: "Don't shoot." Again, there was not quite enough light for the camera. Jackie described the buck as a huge heavy-beamed, mainframe 10-pointer with some extra "stuff" on his brow tines. Foiled again by Deer TV!

In less than 24 hours, both of us had let the best bucks of our lives walk. My question was: "Wouldn't it be better to shoot those monsters, even if the camera couldn't pick it up? Then we could film the walk-up scenes, letting the viewing audience see what we shot, after the fact?"

"Viewers want to see the real thing. They want to see the shot," Jackie said. "If we have to shoot a smaller buck just so the viewing audience can see it happen, then so be it. That's what viewers want—the real thing. To the viewers, seeing the shot authenticates the hunt they're watching."

While I admired his dedication to his TV audience, I was mentally planning my future hunts to be as far from a TV camera as possible. I had never considered my hunting time as live entertainment for a viewing audience. In my mind, hunting has always been a private, solitary endeavor, just between the deer and me. Now, adding a potential viewing audience and a cameraman to the equation, hunting was not going to be the same. It was not just hunting for hunting's sake. It was hunting for the sake of entertaining others. For untold years, I have reported my triumphs and defeats on the written page, after the fact, but never interrupted by readers because they had to wait until the story was written and published. Suddenly, that concept became a luxury unavailable to those who choose to hunt before the TV camera's eye.

As the week passed, I saw numerous small and comparatively insignificant bucks, at least when compared to the double drop-tined 11-pointer I saw that first evening. My heart certainly wasn't in taking a small buck, knowing what was still walking around in that cottonwood river bottom. I kept hearing Jackie's mandate in my mind: "We're here to shoot the best buck we can in front of the camera . . . . That's what Deer TV is all about."

Up until then, as a non-TV hunter, I always had the option of shooting nothing if I didn't see the buck I wanted. But, for the first time in my life, I felt obligated to shoot a buck, even if it weren't the one I wanted. It was a strange and somewhat foreign concept, and it ran against the grain of my personal hunting ethic. I began to realize how important the right of refusal is to me. The bottom line was that Jackie had to produce 26 deer hunting TV shows in a very compact time frame while the seasons are open. That amounts to a lot of pressure.

"You've just got to get your mind adjusted to what we're here for," Jackie reminded me. "This is not hunting just for fun—this is Deer TV, complete with pressures and deadlines. If a buck walks by in bow range with enough light for the camera, you take the bird in the hand."

While it didn't set right in my mind, I recognized I was there on company business, so I'd have to comply, whether I liked it or not.

On day four, a respectable 8-pointer walked by in easy range, with plenty of daylight. It was already past 8 a.m. "Should I take him?" I whispered to Mark, hoping he'd say no.

"It's up to you," he whispered back.

I knew what that meant. I nocked an arrow.

"Okay, I'm going to take him," I whispered to Mark. I could already hear the soft "clunk" of the camera engaging. I knew I was "on the air."

When the buck turned his head away from me to nibble on something, I came to full draw, anchored and released my arrow. My initial assumption was that I hit the buck where I was aiming—through the heart. At the sound of the arrow, the buck jumped ahead behind some thick brush, out of my sight. I waited for a crash in the brush, but all remained quiet. After waiting and watching for a minute or so, movement caught my eye on the trail 60 yards to my left. It was my 8-pointer walking casually down the trail, nibbling on leaves and acting astoundingly healthy for a buck just shot through the heart. I climbed out of the cottonwood to examine my arrow. It showed no signs of having touched the buck. I was stunned. I had never missed a "lay-down" shot like that, much less before a TV camera. Now I really hated Deer TV. My only consolation after missing the easiest shot in the history of bowhunting was that at least my tag was still in my pocket. "Maybe, just maybe," I reasoned with myself, "I'll still get a chance at my double drop-tined buck." Surely there had to be a redeeming reason for missing a shot like that. I certainly hoped so. The good news, from a TV point of view, was how entertaining it was going to be for a million deer hunting viewers to watch ol' Russ miss the easiest shot in history. Some consolation!

After the morning hunt, Mark and I headed up the hill where cameraman Elliott Allen was waiting with the truck. Elliott announced that Jackie had arrowed a beautiful 10-pointer that morning and that they were still filming parts of the show in the river bottom. We arrived to see Jackie beaming over a gorgeous record book 10-pointer. It was his career best with a bow. I congratulated him with a newfound appreciation for the accomplishment. It was all on film, and a heckuva buck at that.

"When it all finally comes together, it makes all those frustrating moments worthwhile," Jackie smiled.

"Yea, everything came together nicely for me this morning. I missed the easiest shot in the world, and we got it all on video. It sure make those frustrating moments worthwhile," I said. He laughed. I didn't.

Jackie said that he and Gene were watching a group of seven or eight bucks and several does feeding under a small umbrella-shaped tree on the riverbank about 100 yards distant. "We were hoping that they would feed our way, but they seemed pretty intent upon feeding where they were. Then we saw this 10-pointer working his way toward us, obviously keeping his distance from the main group of bucks. It was plain that he didn't want to go anywhere near them. The buck came by my stand on the wrong side for a southpaw, so I had to twist around to take a right-handed shot, which meant Gene had to swing his camera around the other side of the tree, too. Somehow I got the shot off at about 10 or 12 yards, and Gene got it all on film! Like the old saying goes, 'Even a blind sow finds an acorn once in awhile,'" he grinned.

I couldn't wait until my acorn appeared.

The next morning, Jackie and Elliott flew home. Mark, Gene and I stayed behind for one last-ditch effort. Mark and I decided to man Jackie's and Gene's lucky stands in hopes of getting a look at that group of bucks they had seen the previous morning. Sure enough, just after daylight, the bucks came back and fed under the little umbrella-shaped tree. There were several excellent 8-pointers, two good 10-pointers and a heavy-beamed, mainframe 10-pointer with long, split brow tines on both sides, making him a 12-pointer. I studied the bucks from 100 yards through my binoculars. While they were all shooters, the big 12-pointer was to die for. The bucks did pretty much exactly what they'd done the morning before for Jackie and Gene. They fed for about 15 minutes, then crossed a dry wash and disappeared into the brush en route to their bedding area on a high-water island.

After they disappeared, Mark and I walked over to the mystery tree where they had been feeding. It turned out to be an American elm, and it appeared that the deer were feeding on its fallen yellow leaves. I needed to find an ambush site closer than 100 yards for the following morning. Fortunately, there was a huge cottonwood tree just 30 yards from the base of the elm. Unfortunately, it was twisted and leaning at such an angle that there was no way to set up a treestand in it, much less two of them. The only possibility the ancient tree offered was standing space for one man in a fork about 30 feet high. To make matters worse, the trunk was leaning so badly, there was no way to climb it with any kind of conventional climbing apparatus. I studied the tree for a long time, knowing it was my only hope. I could envision myself standing in that high fork, belted to one side and secured with another safety rope wound around the fork, about waist high, like a crow's nest on a sailing ship.

Mark had to fly home the following morning, so now it was just up to Gene and me. That afternoon, I showed the tree to Gene and told him my plan. "I'll borrow the rancher's big extension ladder," I began. "We'll set it up to reach that fork this afternoon, then, in the morning in the dark, I'll climb up there and let down the ladder. You can carry it off and hide it before you get in your stand, where I was this morning. You'll just have to film the whole episode from 100 yards. What do you think?"

Gene looked at me quietly for a moment, then gazed up at the twisted cottonwood and back at me. He shook his head from side to side. "You know it can work, don't you?" I insisted. He just kept shaking his head. I knew that he knew it could work. It was crazy, but it was our best and perhaps only option!

On Saturday morning, as planned, I climbed up the extension ladder into the fork of the "impossible cottonwood." Once secured aloft, I let my end of the ladder down with a rope and Gene carried it off in the dark. For insurance, I was wearing a remote lapel microphone. Gene would be 100 yards away, wearing headphones so he could hear me. The plan was, if the group of bucks came back, to whisper to Gene when I first saw them coming and to advise him of which buck I was going to shoot, so he could be ready with the camera. It was an optimistic plan to say the least, but time was running out and this was our last hope.

My bow was on a hanger on the backside of the big fork in which I was standing as daylight broke. If the bucks came in on their previous schedule, they should appear in about 20 minutes. There was already plenty of light, and I was amazingly optimistic. I was daydreaming when I heard the crunch below my stand. I looked down and watched two does and the big 12-pointer walk right under me, heading briskly for the elm tree. Caught totally flat-footed, I grabbed for my bow, slid my hand into the sling, released my homemade rubber band arrow holder and clipped my release on the string. By then, the buck was a full 30 yards away and still walking. I rushed the top pin of my pendulum sight behind his right shoulder and hammered the trigger on my release. Before I could get my wits about me, it was finished. I heard my arrow connect, and the buck bolted into the nearby willows. Suddenly, he reappeared to my left with his head low. I knew he was hit hard, but for insurance I nocked another arrow and shot again, managing a double-lung hit. The buck jumped back in the willows and disappeared.

After it was all over, I realized that I had never even turned on my microphone. There had been no time. The buck was just suddenly there without warning. I had committed the unforgivable Deer TV sin. I had shot a buck off-camera. I shuddered to think what Gene would say. After some lengthy deliberation, I decided to turn on my mike, apologize to Gene and hope I would be forgiven. To make matters worse, when I looked into my shirt pocket, the red light on the mike was glowing red, which meant that it had been on the whole time. All I would have had to do was whisper, "Here he is!" or just anything, and Gene would have had a chance. I begged my deepest apologies into the mike, hoping Gene would still speak to me. He had no microphone, so I knew he wouldn't be able to talk back to me. Then I waited. It was still early, and deer were still filtering through the river bottom. I knew Gene wouldn't bring the ladder back to get me until all the potential filming was finished. After two agonizing hours, Gene came with the ladder and some wonderful news. He saw the buck just before I did, got the camera turned on in time and filmed the whole event. I climbed down the long ladder and headed for the spot where the buck was last standing. Before I got there, Gene peeked over the bank and saw the buck lying there below him. It was the same buck Jackie had to pass up that first morning because there wasn't enough light for the camera. What an irony! Jackie was going to croak when he realized I shot the buck he couldn't shoot. As a prank, I planned to sneak back into the office and just lay the rack on his desk for him to discover. I knew he'd be wondering how my hunt ended.

Gene and I spent Sunday filming some filler segments for the TV show. Monday, we began our long series of flights back to Alabama. I called my secretary from the Billings airport, hoping to check in without spilling the beans. She asked if I'd gotten a buck, but before I could answer, Jackie's voice replaced hers. "Did you shoot my buck?" he demanded.

"Er, well, uh, I guess I did," I replied.

"You dog," he said. "Well, now we're even." I knew what he meant. Many years ago while I was guiding trophy whitetail hunters in Alberta, Canada, Jackie hunted with me and shot what was at that time his best-ever whitetail. It was a mainframe 10-pointer with double brow tines, making it a 12-pointer. That great buck still serves as the image for the Buckmasters logo. Now, thanks to Jackie's willingness to let my Montana 12-pointer walk for the sake of Deer TV, I bagged the best bow buck of my career. Ironically, both bucks were 12-pointers with split brow tines on both sides.

As the saying goes: "All is well that ends well," and this hunt certainly ended very well. Be that as it may, when I remember that double drop-tined buck walking by at four yards and hearing the two most dreaded words I've ever heard in a treestand—"Don't shoot"—I'm more convinced than ever that I'm not cut out for Deer TV.

TWENTY-NINE

Come Rain, Sleet, Crows or Chain Saws

orning No. 10 broke overcast and drizzly, pretty much a carbon copy of the previous nine days. I was perched 25 feet high in an oak tree overlooking a river bottom that flanked a well-worn deer trail at the base of a 40-foot high, timbered ridge. Behind me another deer trail crossed a small creek and joined the ridge-bottom trail within easy bow range. Either trail would bring deer within spitting distance of my climber.

It was my first time to hunt Iowa. I was already three days past the original week I'd allotted for the hunt, but the longer I hunted the more convinced I became that this was a whitetail bowhunter's paradise. Surrounding soybean and corn fields offered unlimited groceries for the whitetails. Hardwood ridges and heads chock full of red and white oaks showered the ground with acorns. Knowing this, it doesn't take a rocket scientist to understand why Iowa regularly produces a disproportionate share of the nation's top trophy whitetails.

My invitation to bowhunt in Iowa came from Sam and Judi Collora. I got to know the Colloras after Sam arrowed his "Buckmasters Whitetail Trophy Records" No. 1 Typical buck (in the BTR's compound bow category). It scored 204⅞. I went to Iowa to score the buck and subsequently covered his historic hunt in a couple of magazine articles. We hit it off, and I was honored with an invitation to their hunting cabin for a bowhunt in southeastern Iowa. The problem was drawing a license. I'll get to that a little later.

A crow flew over in the dim gray sky and began circling me and screaming at the top of its miserable lungs. Within seconds, it was joined by nearly a hundred of its comrades. Crow No. 1 had spotted an owl in a tree next to me, and suddenly there was no more peace in the valley. The crows, in a wretched cacophony of screaming and squawking, dove at the bewildered owl as it sat hunkered on a limb.

The owl dodged the onslaught as long as it could. Periodically, it would flutter to another tree with a feathered entourage right behind. The sound was deafening, and I prayed they would take their business elsewhere, but my prayer went unanswered. The rodeo continued for more than two hours. By 9 a.m., I was about to lose what little remained of my mind. "Why me?" I wondered.

Things went from bad to worse at 9:30 a.m. The farm owner cranked up his chain saw and began cutting firewood nearby. In fairness to him, although he had granted me unlimited access to his land, he didn't know I was hunting nearby that morning. If he had, I'm sure he would have refrained from cutting wood. Between the crow show and chain saw, I was kidding myself. No deer in its right mind would venture into that river bottom. So, I did what any sane hunter would do. I got down, took my stand off the tree, loaded up my bow and gear and started down the trail where I was to meet my hunting partner, Kevin Fisher, at 10 a.m. I took one step and glanced down the ridge trail just in time to see three does heading straight toward me. I squatted behind some brush in hopes of not being seen, but it was too late. They saw me, abandoned the trail and headed straight up and over the ridge. When they were out of sight, I looked back down the trail just in time to see a huge-bodied buck turning back on its tracks. I could see enough antlers to know that he was a good, mature buck, but not enough to venture a guess about the number of points he had. He was definitely a shooter, and I was kicking myself for bailing out of my stand 30 minutes early.

If I had stayed, all of these deer would have passed me at five yards or less. "The big 'If' again," I thought to myself in disgust. "How many times do I have to learn this lesson?"

"Yeah, but the crows and the chain saw," self argued. It was a weak argument. The big "If" had spoken.

Kevin showed up minutes later, and I told him what had happened. He was a gentleman and chose not to rub salt in my wounds. None of the deer I saw crossed the creek trail behind my stand. Instead, they crossed farther to the north. Upon closer inspection, I found two even hotter creek crossings where I spotted the buck turning back, and Kevin found a third crossing where the main ridge trail crossed the creek. I placed my stand on a tree equidistant from all the obvious trails and within easy bow range of each. We concluded that this was probably a late-morning trail or travel corridor. I manned the location that evening and had two small bucks pass by while heading north. My conclusion after morning and evening shifts: deer were moving from south to north in the mornings and opposite in the evenings. I planned to be there before daylight the next morning and stay until noon—come rain, sleet, crows or chain saws.

The next morning, I was back with renewed confidence. The first deer, a lone doe, didn't show until 9 a.m. She was approaching the ridge trail from the north, which meant she would ford the shallow water and then have to climb a very steep bank to follow the trail. About halfway across the creek, she stopped and seemed to reconsider the climb. She walked approximately 50 yards down the middle of the creek and chose one of the two easier trails. She walked right below me and picked the trail only five yards in front of me. The tarsal glands on her hocks were stained nearly black, so I knew she was well into the rut. When she began tossing her head like a frisky colt and kicking up her heels, I knew she was red hot. My confidence level soared. It was Nov. 10, just at the peak of the rut and the last day of my hunt. There was no doubt in my mind that a buck would eventually be following her.

Another mature doe and two yearlings crossed the creek and paraded by me on the same trail 20 minutes later. I didn't see another deer for nearly an hour. I glanced to my right at 10:25 a.m., just in time to see a buck wading out into the creek where the hot doe had originally started to cross. The buck apparently had followed her trail to the creek and assumed she had gone straight across onto the ridge trail. Suddenly, he lunged ahead to get up enough steam to climb the steep bank. I can still see the image in my mind as he topped the bank, his heavy shoulder muscles rippling, reminding me of a quarter horse. He was a big animal, obviously mature, moving at a brisk pace with the prevailing north wind behind him. It was all happening so fast; I didn't even try to count points. I saw more than enough antler to satisfy me, so I stayed at red alert with my release on the string, just waiting for him to walk past my tree.

When he was directly in front of me, I felt the wind reverse momentarily. In the process, the buck smelled something that broke its concentration—presumably me. He stood stock-still and began testing the wind by throwing his head back and forth. At one point, he looked straight at me. My heart stopped. I was peeking down through the riser of my bow, which I was holding in front of my face.

"C'mon old boy, don't leave me now," I whispered to myself. The moment was positively electric, and I could feel my heart gearing down for the added RPMs.

The buck advanced another cautious step and stopped, still searching the wind with his nose. Finally, the wind resumed from the north and seemed to calm him. He dropped his nose to the trail and began walking slowly forward, now only five steps from where the hot doe's route intersected with the ridge trail. I let him walk past me until I knew I could move. Then I drew my arrow, placed my sight pin behind his left elbow for a heart shot and released my 31-inch, aluminum "Lincoln Log." Upon impact, the buck thundered off into the timber, but I knew the deed was done.

As soon as he was out of sight, I sat down for a moment to unwind. It was then that I realized just how excited I was. I don't remember the last time I got that revved up on a shot. After catching my breath, I descended, picked up the buck's trail and walked directly to where he had dropped on the bank of the river. He was a magnificent, heavy-beamed 11-pointer and fully mature. The deer was never weighed, but he appeared to be 260-275 pounds live weight. According to my notes, he was the 25th buck to come within bow range since my hunt had begun. Other than one awesome, irregular buck I saw, well out of bow range, this was the best buck I had seen. Points and score were not the issue. What I wanted was a respectable, mature Iowa buck. I couldn't have been more pleased.

In retrospect, my Iowa hunt was surely the most pleasurable and memorable bowhunt I've had in years. I love the land, how it looks, smells and feels. It is custom made for whitetails and bowhunters, although Iowa has shotgun and muzzleloader seasons, too. But the state, at least in the southeast, begs to be bowhunted. And the people . . . Well, if all Iowans are like the folks I met, it's the most hospitable place on earth.

Now, about my license . . . I applied in the non-resident draw, but my bubble was burst when I got my "Dear John" letter from the Iowa Department of Natural Resources, along with the return of my license check. As far as I was concerned, Iowa and I were not to be. However, Judi Collora, dubbed "Bullet" by her husband (undoubtedly for her speed and accuracy), didn't give up on me. I didn't know at the time, but Judi wrote to folks in high places and pled my case for one of the coveted Governor's Celebrity Licenses. Unbelievably, the request was granted. As far as I can tell, the only thing that ever elevated me to celebrity status was receiving that coveted hunting license. I don't know what Judi said in her letter on my behalf, but I'm trying to hire her as my full-time public relations manager. When she received my license, she gift-wrapped it and sent it to me in the mail. Imagine my joy when I opened it. So, after experiencing the disappointment of losing, I was now a winner and chomping at the bit for Nov. 1.

When I arrived, Sam and friends Kevin Fisher and Ted Aicher took turns taking me to hunting spots too delicious for words. My greatest dilemma was simply deciding where to start. I was the proverbial kid in the candy store, and I wanted a taste of everything I saw.

Despite the privilege and wonders of bowhunting Iowa's giant whitetails, what will live on long after that great hunt fades from memory will be the heart of the matter: the relationships established and friendships made. I will remember the countless games of Rummy with Sammy (Sam's son) and Kevin's daughter Casey at the cabin at night. What great kids! I still think Sammy was dealing off the bottom of the deck! I'll be ready for him next time.

I'll never forget Kevin's cooking. This jovial prince of a man should have been a chef. Meals were phenomenal. Hunting with Sam, Kevin and Ted was an honor. I've never met more honorable hunters, and I was always aware that they were offering me their best. It is a true friend who offers you the spot he would be hunting if you weren't there. I know Sam put me in the area where he'd seen a buck to rival his great trophy of 1996—a buck that he'd been hunting diligently. How's that for unselfish? I left Iowa with much more than a trophy buck. I left with the treasure of a lifetime—friendships and fond memories. In the end, that's all that really matters. Thanks again Iowa, Colloras, and all the dear, deer friends who adopted me and treated me like family. And as for you, Judi, the offer still stands for the public relations position.

THIRTY

Palmetto State Surprise

"**M**r. Thornberry, I'm Rusty Shannon and I want to invite you to come and hunt on our family's property in South Carolina this season. When do you think you could come?"

I was taken aback by the bold invitation. Rusty was obviously serious about the invitation, considering he'd driven all the way to Montgomery, Ala., from his home in South Carolina to extend it. My 1998 hunting calendar was already overflowing, but something in Rusty's voice convinced me it would be a big mistake to turn down the invite. To my utter delight, my son, Darren, was invited to come, too.

"Sure Rusty, I'll find a way to work it into my schedule, and I'm sure I'll be bringing Darren with me," I said.

It was early October when I headed for South Carolina, and I was totally unprepared for what I was about to experience. The Shannon family greeted me like a long-lost son and, before any hunting got underway, I was having the time of my life. It was worth the drive just to get to know them. Glenn and Francis Shannon are the mom and dad of the family. Rusty and Billy are the adult sons who handle the hunting operation, and adult daughter Cathy shows up regularly to assist Francis with the meals that defy description. Suffice it to say that I foundered myself on the mustard-fried venison, and, pardoner, if you haven't had cheese grits swamped in tomato gravy, you just haven't lived.

The property was a gorgeous blend of mixed Southern hardwoods, including red and white oaks, water oaks and even some live oaks. Since 1998 was an off year for the white oaks in that area, the deer were gravitating to the water and red oaks. As I found out later, in the absence of white oak acorns, their ultimate preference was live oak mast. There were numerous winter wheat fields carved out of the hardwoods for planting, but in the clearing process, the Shannon's left all the big oak trees standing. So, in the midst of the winter wheat were mature oaks dropping their acorns to the additional benefit of the deer.

The rut was obviously well under way as is typical by the end of October in South Carolina. We did some scouting and hung our portable treestands deep in the hardwoods where the buck sign was plentiful. Rusty and I both took stands in the same tree. He wanted to try to video me taking a buck with a bow. Initially, we were deep in the hardwoods, overlooking a natural travel route to an adjacent winter wheat field. On our first couple of tries we could hear deer all around us, but they never came into bow range. We finally decided that we needed to move closer to the wheat field. We ended up setting our stands in a tall red oak right out in the field. Tracks indicated that deer were feeding under this particular tree, but more important was the opportunity to watch the tree line along the hardwoods to monitor which trails the deer were favoring as they entered the winter wheat.

The next morning, our first in the new location, we saw lots of deer, including some within bow range of our tree, but no mature bucks showed. By 9 a.m., the deer pretty well cleared out of the field and we decided to go get some breakfast. Rusty was already halfway down the tree when I spotted a real whopper. I hissed at Rusty to stop his descent and pointed out the buck 75 yards away at the edge of the timber. Somehow Rusty managed to inch his way back up the tree and into his stand without spooking the buck. Eventually, the buck fed to within 50 yards of us and I studied him with binoculars. I could count 15 points. He was a mainframe 9-pointer with a long drooping tine growing out over his right eye and splitting on the end. He had three stickers on the bottom of his left main beam and a kicker on a back tine. He was a glorious sight, and I was instantly obsessed with hunting that buck. If I made good on him, he would easily be my career-best bow buck.

I hunted the area diligently. Eventually, I moved my stand to a big water oak nearer the edge of the hardwoods and saw the buck twice more, but never within bow range. The rut was now in full swing and every shift in my stand produced sightings of new trophy-class bucks I hadn't seen previously. On the last morning of my hunt, a gorgeous mature 11-pointer strolled along behind a hot doe and passed within 20 yards of me. He was a great trophy, but, for some unknown reason, I let him walk. Next, an old warhorse with dark ebony-colored antlers emerged from the hardwoods with his nose to the ground and passed within 30 yards of me. I studied his massive rack and counted 13 unbroken points and half again as many broken tines. His main beams grew out beyond his nose. He was obviously ancient, and his hide sagged on his body like an old man in an overcoat two sizes too big for him. I studied him in awe, but somehow, in my obsession for the 15-pointer on which my heart was set, watched him walk out of my life. It was then I realized that I was suffering from some form of altered reality. Rusty wasn't with me that morning, which was probably best. If he'd seen the bucks I'd passed up, he might have run me off the place.

It was at this point that I had a serious talk with myself. "What the heck are you doing?" I asked myself. "Why on earth would you pass on two bucks like that? They were both better than any buck you've ever taken with a bow!"

I had to think about the question for awhile before I could come up with an intelligent answer. The truth was that I was seeing such fantastic bucks that I hated to shoot one and end it. There was just no telling what kind of buck would appear next. But in spite of that, after my talk with myself, I agreed that should any of those bucks give me another chance, it would be on a first-come, first-served basis.

I almost shamefully reported what I had seen to Rusty and Billy, and I don't doubt that they were silently questioning my sanity. What the heck—I was, too.

"Did you see that 15-pointer again?" Billy asked.

"No, not this morning," I replied.

"Well, there's another place I'd like to show you," he said. "I've seen a couple of really big bucks there, and they seem to hang around one particular tree. I've seen them in that spot several times while driving through that area. I'd like to show you the place, and if you want to hunt there for a change of scenery, you can. And if you don't want to, you can hunt right where you've been hunting. I just want you to see this place."

That afternoon, Billy drove me to the spot. The magic tree turned out to be a live oak loaded with acorns in the corner of another winter wheat field. By then I had observed the deer's obvious preference for live oak acorns. There were tracks, droppings and empty acorn hulls all over the ground, and more fresh acorns waiting for the next hungry deer. I looked around and spotted a tall, straight, young red oak that I could get into quickly with my climbing stand. I told Billy I was game to give the place a try. By 4:30, I was 25 feet up the red oak in my climber, waiting anxiously in hopes of seeing the bucks Billy had described.

Within 30 minutes, the first doe and yearling arrived. They emerged from the hardwood forest edge and walked straight to the live oak and began to feed. More does emerged and fed alternately on the winter wheat and acorns. Then, to my utter amazement, a large-bodied buck appeared at the edge of the timber. Through my binoculars, I instantly recognized the split tine drooping over his right eye. My 15-pointer was here. That's why I hadn't seen him at the other location. What a deal! I might just bag that rascal after all!

He quickly located a promising doe and stayed glued to her tail. She zigged and zagged and played coy doe games, and the buck worked her like a prize cutting horse. They were about 45 yards out with 10 to 15 minutes of shooting light remaining. Surely in that length of time the doe would lead him into range.

I heard a crunch in the timber to my immediate left and looked down to see what I thought was a heavy-beamed, 8-point buck emerging. I could see he was very massive. He went straight to the umbrella-shaped live oak and began to feed. I had looped my binoculars through their strap over the frame of the upper section of my climber. It was getting dusky, and I knew I should look at the 8-pointer with binoculars to be sure of what he was, but there was that 15-pointer, still out there with that hot doe. Finally, I eased the binoculars quietly through their strap and freed them. The 8-pointer was now behind the live oak tree so I eased the binoculars up to my eyes for my first good look at him. Even through the branches of the live oak, I could see points going everywhere. There was a drop tine, a split brow tine, several sticker points and mass befitting a Saskatchewan buck! Panic hit me. This buck was by far superior to the 15-pointer I had been hunting. I had to take him before it was too late! I slipped the binoculars around my neck and slid them around so they were hanging between my shoulder blades. Now I could draw, but the buck was walking away with the live oak between us. I felt nauseous. This was the best buck I had ever been within bow range of, and I was letting him get away after having him at 20 yards, broadside and in the clear. What cruel irony!

"Darn these old eyes," I whispered under my breath. My low-light vision had really gone downhill in the last few years. Age and too many hours in front of a computer had taken their toll. In my younger days, I'd have seen every point and would have known at first sight exactly what I was seeing. As I lamented the lost opportunity, the 15-pointer finally chased his doe back in the timber and out of sight. My heart sank. The whitetail god is cruel.

Then, incredibly, the black-horned buck turned 180 degrees and started feeding right back in my direction.

"Oh, let it be!" I whispered. Step by step, the buck was coming, pausing to feed between steps. Finally his head emerged from behind the live oak. I tried not to concentrate on his rack. I could feel my pulse rate quicken and had to talk myself down to ward off a full-blown case of buck fever. "Hurry old boy," I mentally urged. His shoulders were now exposed. After an electrifying eternity of waiting and hoping, the buck stepped free of the live oak at 20 yards, head down, still feeding. I raised my bow, drew and mentally blocked out the whole world as I centered my pendulum sight pin behind his shoulder. When all the elements came together, I tripped the trigger on my release and watched my luminous green vanes dissolve into his ribs. I knew he was mine.

He bolted into the timber and within seconds I heard the crash as he fell. My body involuntarily shuddered as the spellbinding excitement vented itself, finally beyond my control. It was dark by the time I found the buck. When the beam of my flashlight fell upon his rack, I was further astounded. This was the first buck of my career whose rack was, in fact, even bigger than it appeared in life. The rack was a mainframe 8-pointer, but he had a double brow tine on the right side and a drop tine on the left main beam, along with assorted sticker points bringing his total scorable points to 18. Both bases measured 6⅛ inches. He was most certainly the trophy of a lifetime—taken not in Iowa or Saskatchewan, but right there in Lone Star, South Carolina!

Billy drove up 15 minutes later and was as thrilled as I was. So was all the Shannon family. The celebration was cut short by the urgency of my trip back to the Columbia airport, where I was to meet Darren's flight from Montgomery. He was already waiting for me when I arrived. I told him about my buck and the others I'd seen, and he was ecstatic. Maybe this would be his trip of a lifetime, too.

The next morning, I set Darren up in a huge water oak on a ridge than ran out into the winter wheat field where I'd originally been hunting the 15-pointer. I had not hunted this stand location, but I had seen plenty of activity there. The last thing I told him before he climbed into his treestand was to be very selective because there were many young bucks that could sure fool you. He assured me that he would look them over well.

It was sort of awkward because for someone who has never taken a buck with bow and arrow, any number of the bucks he'd see would be terrific. I didn't want to put too much pressure on him, but he had grown up in my deer camps in Alberta back in my outfitting days and he knew what a real trophy buck was. Even though he was new to bowhunting, I knew he wanted to take the best buck he could.

From my vantage point in a treestand 100 yards away, I watched several deer feed under Darren that morning, including a young 11-pointer that was destined to be a real bell-ringer. I'd say he was a 3-year-old at most. Darren passed on him as I suspected he would.

That evening, I suggested that Darren take a stand in another big water oak, only 20 yards from the main trail where I had seen several big bucks entering the winter wheat field. It was the stand from which I would have hunted had Billy not taken me to the other location. I was going to sit in another oak only 30 yards away so I could watch the fun, up close and personal. What a thrill it would be to watch my son bag his first buck with a bow. I had been with him when he took his first rifle buck at 15, and I think I was more excited than he was.

Unfortunately, the wind changed slightly that afternoon, making my chosen observation stand a bad risk. The deer would wind me before they got within range of Darren, so I decided to observe from a shooting house in the corner of the field, a couple of hundred yards distant. By 4 p.m., Darren was in his stand. It was more than 30 feet high. It wasn't that he needed to be that high for any reason other than the dictates of the tree itself. I had to climb 30 feet before there was a place where I could hang his stand. When I sat down in the shooting house, I was disappointed to realize that though I could see the tree in which Darren was sitting, limbs blocked my view of his stand. I could see the tree all the way up to the bottom of the treestand, but I couldn't see Darren at all. Bummer!

Thirty minutes before dark, a buck walked out of the timber a mere 10 yards to the right of the shooting house where I was sitting. He was an immature buck, but his rack was incredible. At least four of his nine tines were over 11 inches long, and his last point on the right beam doubled in a v-shaped formation. He was an awesome animal, heading directly toward Darren's location. "Mature or not," I thought, "there would be no shame in taking that buck."

It appeared that the buck was going to actually wind up right under Darren's stand, but at the last minute a hot doe emerged from the timber and trailed him away before he ever got within bow range.

Several does and small bucks began spilling out into the winter wheat from the opening in the timber under Darren. Several were within easy bow range. Suddenly, all the deer in the wheat field snapped their heads to attention and looked straight into the timber where the main trail emptied out under Darren's stand. In an instant, a big mature buck appeared. I raised my binoculars and immediately recognized the buck as the big 11-pointer that had walked within 20 yards of me two mornings ago — one of the two bucks I passed up that inspired that conversation I had with myself. I knew Darren was seeing him, and I also knew that Darren would know this was "the one." My heart leaped into my throat. "He won't take that shot. The buck's facing him," I mumbled under my breath. The buck stepped farther out into the winter wheat field and lowered his head, making a quarter turn in Darren's favor. "Maybe now," I thought, but the buck turned back facing Darren's stand and continued to feed. What followed was simply spellbinding. Every turn the buck made put me further out on the edge of my seat. As he fed, he turned this way and that, favoring a shot, but each time turning back to face Darren. After 10 minutes, I was a nervous wreck. At least the buck was oblivious to Darren's presence. I wondered how my son was handling the "close-but-no-cigar" routine. Then, suddenly, the buck turned completely broadside. I held my breath and tried to steady my binoculars. The buck suddenly lurched forward and took off on a dead run across the wheat field. I kept my binoculars glued to him, and then I saw a crimson spot appear behind his shoulder, just before he disappeared into the timber. I heard the crash from 250 yards.

I was out of the shooting house like a shot and hotfooting it to the base of Darren's tree. When I looked up at him, I could see questions in his eyes. It was his first animal with a bow, and I understood that he wasn't yet sure of the results of his shot. I mentally flashed back to the first deer I shot with a bow—a mule deer buck in western Alberta. It wasn't until I actually walked up on the buck lying still on the ground that I was fully convinced of what I had done. Now it would be Darren's turn.

"How'd you feel about the shot?" I asked.

"Well, I think it was good," he replied rather nervously.

"I guarantee you it was good. I saw the blood right behind his shoulder as he dove into the timber, and I heard him pile up."

"Really?" he said with more confidence spreading across his face.

I walked over and pulled his arrow out of the ground. It was drenched with bubbly, pink blood. "You double-lunged him," I said as I held the arrow up for him to see.

"Wow!" he said as he reached for his pull rope.

As we followed the buck's trail across the wheat field toward the timber, Darren explained that he actually drew on the buck once, then had to let down his arrow. "I figured he would catch my movement and blow the whole deal when I had to let down on him," he said. "He gave me a shot just for a second, but before I could release, he turned back facing me. Somehow he didn't catch me letting down. Finally, he gave me a full broadside shot and I took it."

At that moment, we spotted the buck lying dead just inside the hardwood thicket. I watched Darren's face as he soaked up the reality of what he'd done, then congratulated him on a heckuva shot and a great buck. We took some photos and headed back to the house to show the Shannons his good fortune. We celebrated properly that night.

THIRTY-ONE

Geronimo's Deer

From a half-mile away, we could see the buck was good. I couldn't count points through binoculars at that distance, but plenty of antler was evident. He was working his way up a ridge from the pila (dammed-up water hole) where he'd come for water in the heat of the afternoon. "Macho venado" (buck whitetail), grinned Octavio, the foreman. "Muchas puntas!" (Many points). Nayo, my outfitter, was also impressed, and since he was the expert, I was anxious to get a closer look.

We had seen another exceptional buck that morning at no more than 80 yards. He was quartering toward us through the thick mesquite on the valley floor. We held tight and waited for a clear view so we could glass his rack. In the shadows, it appeared that one brow tine was broken off at the base. Otherwise, he would have been a tremendous 10-pointer—a "book" Coues' deer (properly pronounced "Cows"). He turned broadside, offering an easy shot, then turned away and disappeared back into the mesquite. Only then, at that last instant, did we see the other brow tine that had been hidden by shadows. He was the buck I had come to Sonora, Mexico, to find, but it was too late. My disappointment was softened by the fact that it was only the first morning of my hunt.

Now in the amber glow of an early January afternoon, we headed toward the ridge where we spotted the second great buck of the day. We had seen eight mature 8-pointers during the course of that first day, any of which would have been wonderful trophies, but I had my heart set on a 10. In this Coues' deer paradise, I was confident that a 10-pointer was feasible.

When we arrived at the base of the ridge, Nayo's plan was to climb slowly and quietly to the top and peek into the draw beyond. The terraced ridges rose from the valley floor like stair steps, each ridge rising higher than the last, and beyond each ridge was a draw. It was typical topography for these beautiful, cactus-clad mountains of crumbling granite that the Coues' deer call home. This was the land where Geronimo and his warriors fled to take refuge when the U.S. Cavalry was hot on their tails, an enchanted land of mountainous, multi-colored granite, punctuated with palo verde, encinos, mesquite trees and octillo cactus—all beneath a canopy of cloudless blue. I admit expecting to see smoke signals rising from a distant mountaintop at any time. It was a rugged and beautiful land, reminding me of country I'd seen in cowboy-and-Indian movies as a kid.

The sun was still clinging to the horizon, drenching the landscape in bronze, as we tiptoed up the ridge, scanning every deer-shaped rock formation, bush and tree. One thing was already apparent to me: Coues' deer are true masters of concealment. By simply standing still they seem to disappear from the face of the earth. Then, when you think there are no deer there, they explode like a covey of quail and tear over the top of the next ridge at warp speed, leaving you with egg on your face.

Such was the case as we topped the first ridge, scanning the draw below and the hillside beyond. To me it was vacant real estate, but Nayo's educated eye spotted the buck climbing up the next ridge. "There he is!" Nayo whispered urgently. "He going over the top!"

I saw a flash of brown as the buck topped the ridge, and I shouldered my .25-06. It was almost like shooting quail. I couldn't count points, but my brief glance at the buck's wide, ebony-colored rack told me all I needed to know. He flashed into my crosshairs and, as instinct commanded, I slapped the trigger. The report of the rifle was still reverberating through the hills as Nayo and his two guides stood looking at me with questioning eyes that seemed to ask: "Why did the gringo shoot? Is he crazy?"

The deer was nowhere in sight. I took the only shot possible as he crested the ridge, quartering away at full tilt. Even if my shot were perfect, his momentum would have carried him out of our sight. The distance was something beyond 200 yards, and while the shot now seemed stupidly optimistic, I still felt confident. I have taken some long running shots in my day, but only when that little voice in my subconscious says, "NOW!" That voice had spoken and, somehow, despite the unfavorable odds, I believed I could make the shot.

Nayo's guides split up and flanked us right and left as we dropped into the draw and climbed up to the top of the next ridge where we'd last seen the buck. I walked straight to the spot where the buck had been at the instant I shot. Thirty feet beyond, he lay dead. The 115-grain Nosler Partition bullet had entered behind his last rib, quartered forward through his heart and exited through the front of his right shoulder. Instinct had prevailed, and I had my first Coues' deer, a proud 10-point buck that would have soared into the record book if not for several major broken tines, obviously due to fighting.

"Man, you're lucky!" Nayo said. "That was a heckuva shot!"

"Even a blind sow finds an acorn once in awhile," I replied.

"Too bad his rack is broken," he continued. "He would make the book easy if those tines weren't broken off."

"He makes my book of great memories anyway," I said. I couldn't have been happier with him.

It was the end of a phenomenal first day of hunting. I had seen more than 100 Coues' deer, 10 of which were bucks—all but one mature 8-pointers or better . . . all wonderful trophies by anyone's standards. From what I've heard from other Coues' deer hunting enthusiasts, I had obviously fallen into the hunting mecca for the Odocoileus virginianus coues'i.

Nayo Balderrama is a wildlife biologist by education, and while doing a game survey on the 20,000-acre La Montosa Ranch, 250 miles north of Tucson, he was astounded to find a Coues' deer to every 15 acres, with a 1-to-5, buck-to-doe ratio! Since the La Montosa Ranch was virtually unhunted, the numbers of mature, trophy-class bucks were unbelievably high. Now, in Nayo's third year of outfitting on the ranch, which allowed the taking of a maximum of 10 bucks per year, I was experiencing Coues' deer hunting as good as it gets.

Jack O'Connor had whetted my appetite for hunting Coues' deer 30 years ago, but recent horror stories of hunts gone bad and rogue outfitters kept me at bay. Finally, a friend of mine from Idaho, Pat Prentice, called me and told me of his personal involvement with Nayo Balderrama of Hermosillo, Sonora, Mexico. Finally I had the trustworthy connections for which I had waited so long.

My buddy and hunting partner, Ted Keaton, of Greensboro, N.C., accompanied me on the hunt. It was Ted's first time out for Coues' deer, too. A shot across a deep canyon turned out to be 300 yards instead of 200 and broke his buck's foreleg just below the brisket. Right after the shot, the deer dropped into the tall grass, and it wasn't until the guides went to recover the animal that they realized he wasn't dead. The buck jumped up right in front of the guides and ran over the top of the mountain and out of sight. It was nearly dark, and the tracking job would have to wait until the next morning.

Nayo assured Ted that he'd recover the deer. His secret weapon was a hound named Pirata ("pirate" in English), named for the black patch over one eye. "We've never lost a wounded deer, thanks to Pirata," Nayo assured us.

The next morning, Ted, his guide Brigitta, Pirata and I were back on the mountaintop. It took us more than an hour to find a small trace of blood in the dry, rocky soil. Brigitta had Pirata on a leash and led him to the small spot of blood. With makeshift sign language and limited Tex-Mex lingo, I told Brigitta to turn the dog loose. When he did, Pirata turned 180 degrees from the direction the deer was travelling, and, in seconds, he was in the bottom of the draw below us and out of sight. The last sound I heard of Pirata was his distant bawling as he topped the next mountain and disappeared over the top heading for places unknown. Ted came up out of the draw and reported seeing Pirata jump a deer and chase him completely over the next mountain and out of sight. He also reported that the buck was running like the wind, and appeared to be anything but wounded. (So much for Nayo's confident claim.) The dog allegedly tracked mountain lions, coatimundies and wounded deer. Nayo swore the mutt never chased a healthy deer. Now, there was nothing to do but painstakingly follow the scant sign left in the dry sand and granite soil and hope it led us to the deer.

After an hour, we had gained only 200 yards as we painstakingly followed tracks and pin-sized smudges of blood on dry grass down off the mountain into the timber-lined draw. At the bottom of the draw, in a boulder-strewn dry wash, the sign disappeared. We were at a loss and wondering what the next step should be when I heard Pirata's faint, hoarse barking in the distance. I called Ted and Brigitta over, and we all listened intently. The crazy hound had obviously chased a deer all the way around the mountain and seemed to be coming back in our direction. After a few minutes, it became clear that the sound was stationary. Pirata was at bay.

We were hustling down the dry wash along the base of the mountain toward the sound when we came to a fork in the wash. Suddenly Pirata's voice gained volume and we realized he was much closer than we had thought. The main wash continued ahead along the perimeter of the base of the mountain. The other veered off to the right, leading up into a box canyon fold in the mountain. Another 300 yards and we were right below the action. Pirata had the buck backed out on a ledge with no place to go, just 75 feet above us. Pirata bawled furiously as he dashed back and forth, keeping the buck hemmed up on the ledge. With every move the hound made, the buck whirled to face him. Brigitta looked quickly through his binoculars and motioned to Ted that the buck had a broken front leg.

That amazing dog had been right all along, and now the proof was at hand. Ted steadied himself and, when the buck offered him a view of his ribs, he fired and it toppled off the ledge, landing at our feet. Ted's first Coues' deer was a gorgeous 10-pointer. We took some photos, field-dressed the buck, then Brigitta tied its front and back feet together, slung it over his shoulder and we walked back down the wash to the road where we would be picked up at noon. Pirata was the hero, worth his weight in pesos, after all!

The other three hunters in camp were also doing well, each taking very respectable, mature bucks with racks knocking on the record book's door.

We stayed in the old La Montosa home place, once the ranch headquarters for a thriving cattle business. Now Coues' deer were worth more than Mexican cattle, and the heirs of the ranch lived in town, two hours from there. The elegant old casa was made of stone with very high ceilings to allow the intense heat of summer to rise away from the occupants. In each bedroom was a fireplace for the cooler winter months. Electricity was provided by a large generator during the day, which was shut off at night. The house had modern bathrooms and showers and, best of all, no telephones. Francesca Paz, the cook, made meals fit for a king, which included her famous saddle blanket flour tortillas that were nearly two feet in diameter, paper thin and deliciously tender. Nayo's wife, Sylvia, also helped with hospitality and meals, and their son, Nayo Jr., politely assisted with guiding and other camp duties. It was a family operation. From a worldwide professional hunting perspective, their operation was second to none.

I don't remember a hunting trip in my life being so pleasant in every way. The weather was out of this world. Nights got down in the 30s with daytime highs reaching the mid-70s. You couldn't buy a cloud the entire time we were there, and the countryside was breathtakingly beautiful. Coues' deer hunting reminded me of sheep hunting, but without the pain. The mountains seldom reached more than 4,000 feet, so there was still plenty of breathing air for middle-aged, desk-bound editor types like me. I will never forget sitting on a mountainside, glassing every nook and cranny for traces of the elusive little venado, and straining to hear a sound—any sound. There was none. There was no distant humming of high-way traffic, no airplane noise, only the overpowering silence and calmness that seemed by its presence to shame civilization. I had forgotten this world could be so wonderfully still.

On one memorable afternoon, Ted and I hiked a quarter-mile up the draw above the casa to a small lake created by damming up the deep, narrow draw and trapping the runoff of spring rains. Nayo promised us it was full of bass. We took his son's rod and reel and a couple of surface plugs and took turns catching bass until we were satisfied. We finally just laid back on the grassy bank and watched flock after flock of pintails, mallards, canvasbacks, widgeons and redheads landing on the water and Coues' deer coming down to drink. It was relaxing at its finest. I'm sure the exceptional population of Coues' deer on the La Montosa was due to the amount of water available. The ranch owners had spared no effort to build earthen dams in major draws to trap rainwater. Deer didn't have far to go to get a drink, no matter what part of the ranch they inhabited.

I had the option of taking a second buck, so I spent the last two days looking for something to top the one I already had. That turned out to be a tall order. On the next to last hunting day, we spotted two excellent bucks on a ridge-top 300 yards due west of the ridge on which we were standing. I knew it was due west because the bucks were backlit by the setting sun, creating so much glare in my scope that I never could shoot. It was cruel. There stood ol' Macho, broadside and still, silhouetted in the center of a blazing sun. By the time the sun slipped behind Macho's ridge, he was gone.

The next morning, we returned to the same area and spotted an end-all 8-pointer, as well as several other excellent 8-pointers. This one in particular was amazingly wide. "Seventeen inches!" Nayo said (incredibly wide for a Coues' deer). The buck was rubbing a tree and making a scrape 300 yards across the canyon with no clue of our presence. I settled back, took a rest in the fork on my shooting sticks and centered the crosshairs behind his shoulder. He appeared almost golden in the rich morning sun. There was plenty of time, and the shot was duck soup. For some reason, however, I couldn't do it. I recognized that this was a buck of a lifetime and a classic way to end a phenomenal hunt. But something in the pit of my stomach said no. We watched the gorgeous animal for 15 minutes before he walked out of sight. All was quiet. I knew Nayo and his guides were expecting me to shoot, and for good reason. I could feel their disappointment. "Guys, that was a wonderful deer," I explained. "Everything about this hunt and this particular opportunity has been incredible, and you've all served me well. I don't know why I couldn't shoot that buck. He was beautiful and a tremendous trophy. For some reason, I just couldn't do it. But I'm not the least bit disappointed. I've had a wonderful hunt."

With that, we hiked back to the truck and headed toward camp. Nayo and I were in the cab. Guides Octavio, Poncho and Brigitta stood in the bed of the pickup behind the cab. There wasn't much conversation now. The hunt was over, and our minds were slipping back to the noisier worlds that awaited us. Only a quarter-mile from the casa, I heard the soft whistles of the guides in the back of the truck. That's how they signal when the see a deer. Nayo eased the truck to a stop and we looked in the direction they were pointing, but saw nothing. "Probably a doe," Nayo said nonchalantly. But the guides kept exclaiming "Macho, macho," while pointing toward a clump of encinos. I knew macho meant buck, so I said, "I'm going to have a look," as I opened the truck door and stepped outside. I slid a cartridge into the magazine and bolted it into the chamber as I walked to higher ground and looked toward the grove of encinos 75 yards distant. Immediately, I saw the forms of two deer standing in the shade of the gnarly little live oaks. I shouldered my rifle and saw antler—lots of antler. A high-tined buck was tending a hot doe. In much less time than it takes to write these words, I realized this was a great buck. Instinctively, once more, as my crosshairs snapped into the center of his chest, that little voice said "NOW!" and I pulled the trigger.

Nayo was stunned at the report of the rifle, his eyes full of questions again. It all happened so fast. "Macho," I said teasingly as I turned back toward Nayo. "Mucho macho—muchos puntas . . . diez puntas!"

"Man, you're lucky! I've never met such a lucky hunter," Nayo exclaimed, extending his hand and congratulating me on my second 10-point (diez puntas) Coues' buck. It was crazy. It was destiny. Now I realized why I couldn't pull the trigger on that big 8-pointer. The "fat lady" simply had not yet sung.

While the Coues' whitetail is a tiny member of the whitetail family, his nature and his habitat make him a "must do" for any soul who truly desires to experience the grand scale of whitetail hunting. After having hunted whitetails from Texas to Saskatchewan and all points between, I can say emphatically that until you've hunted Coues' deer, there's a huge slice of the whitetail experience missing from your pie.

When I recall my fondest memories of the mountains of Sonora, in my mind's eye I see deer stepping out of shadows into the sunlight, appearing as if by magic from hillsides I would have sworn were devoid of deer. I see the shy Montezuma's quail chortling beneath the encinos, and endless flocks of white-winged doves fluttering from bush to bush ahead of me as I walked in search of venado. I see the morning sun, spilling like thick amber honey over the mountaintops, filling the valleys with rich wondrous colors. And I see myself resting against a large boulder on top of a granite ridge, glassing the vast expanse, searching every nook and cranny for the glint of sunlight on an antler or the twitch of an ear. And I remember the gentle warmth of the January sun, penetrating to my inner depths as I reveled in the stillness of golden silence that wrapped itself around that timeless land.

POSTSCRIPT

Back at the airport in Hermosillo, preparing for our flight back to Phoenix, Ted and I were asked to present our stamped visitors' visas to the agent at the airline ticket desk. For reasons that none of us could imagine, the Mexican Department of Immigrations had not stamped Ted's visa when he entered Mexico. That meant that he was in Mexico illegally. My visa was stamped, but his wasn't, and we went through immigrations together. Go figure. Suddenly things got tense. We all knew that Ted could be in a heap of trouble. I started humming the old Kingston Trio tune: "Tijuana Jail." Nobody laughed.

Nayo saw that there was a problem, so he marched up and asked what was wrong. We explained what we knew, which wasn't much. Then he snatched the document out of the ticket agent's hand and ordered us to wait there for his return. He marched down to the back door of the Immigration Department, pried it open and disappeared. If he'd done that in America, all the alarms in the world would have gone off and he would have been arrested on sight. A few minutes later, Nayo and the immigrations officer came marching back out the same door, past us and out the front door of the Hermosillo Airport, disappearing somewhere into the parking lot. About 10 minutes later, they came back into the airport. The officer went back into immigrations and Nayo walked up and handed Ted his stamped visa. "You're okay now," Nayo announced matter-of-factly.

"What's the deal?" Ted asked.

Nayo explained that he had taken the visa to the officer who, not wanting to appear to have failed to take care of business in the first place, was belligerent at first. He even told Nayo that Ted could be put in jail for not having the document signed. That's when Nayo earned every penny we paid him and then some. He began to negotiate with the officer. That's when they went together out into the parking lot. "So what did you do?" I asked. "What did you have to pay to keep ol' Ted out of the Hermosillo slammer?"

"I offered him a hindquarter of a Coues' deer," Nayo replied.

"And he took it?"

"Sure," Nayo said. "He was happy with that."

It was truly another world. Nayo had cut through federal bureaucratic red tape and a civil servant's ego with a hindquarter of venison. Only in Mexico!

Ted breathed a sigh of relief. "This could only happen to me," he grinned.

THIRTY-TWO

All the Hungry Hunters

Memory directed my footsteps along the narrow, winding game trail in the blackness before dawn that September morning. Cautiously, I felt my way through the buffaloberry thickets, feeling ahead of me for the daggers on their branches. My destination was a gnarled, ancient cottonwood that the prairie winds of southern Alberta had twisted and shaped over the years. The spongy bark felt like dinosaur scales as I climbed the tree to my perch, 25 feet above the ground. Now to wait quietly for dawn and the return of the deer to their bedding area. At the time, it seemed as if nothing could go wrong that day.

My cottonwood stood a mere 30 yards from the bank of the Red Deer River, in a bottleneck of timber between the alfalfa fields a mile to the west and the impenetrable buffaloberry thicket bedding area slightly east of me. The thicket is so dense that a man cannot walk upright through it. Even the deer must travel through low tunnels to enter their briery fortress.

I settled in my treestand and hooked the safety belt to the tree trunk. Then I pulled my bow, arrows and daypack up with a safety rope. In a matter of minutes, I was well situated. My pack hung out of the way on a limb above me, and my bow dangled from a convenient broken branch less than an arm's length from my left hand. The ritual was complete. Dawn would break in less than a half-hour.

Out on the broad lazy river, the geese were beginning to stir. The river is a legal sanctuary for them in the fall—no shooting within a mile of the banks – and, subsequently, the big Canadas congregate there by the thousands in September.

A thin pink ribbon was beginning to outline the eastern horizon, and I could feel that involuntary rejoicing of the heart at the promise of new light. There is a sacred appreciation in a hunter for the first rays of dawn. They are his assurance that nature will do her part without fail.

Slowly the pink ribbon intensified, eventually transforming to scarlet rays which stretched up and ignited the clouds. The guttural groaning of a single goose exploded into a chorus of hundreds, then thousands as they woke and stretched their wings. A coyote yipped an octave above the din of honking geese, and then more coyotes, near and far, joined in the song. There was the choking crow of a cock pheasant from somewhere in the thicket. Then the still air breathed a sigh as the thermal currents began to rise, and a soft breeze stirred the twisted branches of the old cottonwood. I felt an overwhelming urge to yell out and join the symphony of welcome to the new day. Instead, I closed my eyes and feasted upon the sounds.

As the light improved, I turned away from the sunrise to study the alfalfa fields. Through binoculars, I could see the dark spots that I knew were deer. They were moving gradually my way, feeding as they walked. I guestimated they would be passing me en route to the thicket within 20 minutes. Everything was working on the perfect schedule of a mid-September morning.

A clattering of wings lifted the first flock of geese into the air above the river, and then all I could hear was the thundering of beating wings and their honking cries. They rose in lazy circles at first, as if they were just getting organized into flocks. Then they picked a direction and left the river. Many of them skimmed the top of my cottonwood, so closely at times that I felt like ducking my head. In three or four minutes, they were gone, off to breakfast in the nearby stubble fields.

As the quiet settled over the river valley one more, my thoughts returned to the oncoming deer. On the dry cottonwood leaves behind me, I could hear the regulated patter of footsteps approaching. Slowly I turned my head toward the trail to my left. A bushy coyote was trotting along, and it appeared as if he would come right past my cottonwood – the ultimate test of how well I was concealed. If a coyote didn't spot me, no deer would. Suddenly the coyote skidded to an abrupt halt, not unlike a good pointing dog. He either smelled or heard something in the buffaloberry. Without a sound, he disappeared into the bushes. Now he was hunting, and he moved as silently as a shadow.

Back to the west, I heard more footsteps on the cottonwood leaves. The pattern was slower than the coyote's, and I was sure it was a deer. Many trails braided through the sparse cottonwoods and dense underbrush. For the most part, the deer would be invisible to anyone on the ground. But from my high vantage point, I could see the openings in the trails. The trick was to be looking at the right opening at the right time. Fortunately, I could also hear the deer on the dry leaves and monitor its progress until it came into view.

It was walking steadily toward me on a trail that passed 30 yards from my tree and intersected at right angles with the trail that led directly to me. There were two openings where I would be able to see the oncoming deer before it was within bow-and-arrow range. The first was about 60 yards away, and I glued my eyes to it. Suddenly, the opening filled with a magnificent white-tailed buck—a 10-pointer with long brow tines. His main beams reached beyond his ears by two inches, and I guestimated him as a 160-class buck.

He stopped in the opening, as if to let me feast upon him with my eyes. His sleek body seemed to glow a radiant gold in the rich morning sun. I eased my left hand toward my bow and gently lifted it from the limb in slow motion. The buck moved out of the opening, still coming my way. My hand trembled slightly as I took a deep breath and nocked and arrow.

The buck was moving steadily. I watched him pass through the second opening without hesitation. Within seconds, he would enter the opening and offer me a confident shot. His footsteps grew louder. I gripped the bowstring and began to draw when his footsteps stopped just short of the opening. I held the string until the muscles between my shoulders began to burn. Finally, I could hold no longer and let off on the string.

Immediately, the buck took one cautious step forward and was in the center of the opening, standing broadside and testing the air with his nose. Everything was perfect. I began a slow and steady draw for the shot of a lifetime. Then calamity struck. The brush exploded as a panic-stricken cock pheasant ripped through the buffaloberry. Right behind him and also airborne for a second was a bushy coyote. My wonderful white-tailed buck bolted for the thicket and evaporated into a wonderful memory of what might have been.

I was so dumbfounded that I accidentally let the string go at half draw, and the arrow dribbled helplessly to the ground. How could so much go so wrong at precisely the moment of truth? Never had I been so close to such a magnificent buck. I couldn't have asked for a more perfect shot. Why did the coyote have to find the pheasant right then? Why . . . Why . . . Why?

Footsteps continued to move through the timber. Several does and yearlings passed on the trail where the buck had been, and a small fork-horned buck appeared on the river a mere 20 yards away, but after what I had seen, I was not interested in junior bucks. Eventually, the movement of deer ceased as they filtered into the safety of their buffaloberry sanctuary. No more bucks passed. It was too much to hope for another chance like that in one morning—perhaps in one lifetime.

The sound of a lone goose pulled my eyes to the river again. I wondered why he had not followed the flocks. He was swimming around and calling as if wondering where everybody had gone. Then, from out of nowhere, came the attack. A mature bald eagle swooped down with its talons extended. Just a millisecond before they connected, the goose dove beneath the surface. The eagle pulled out of the dive and regained altitude, and the goose bobbed back to the surface. Immediately, the eagle repeated its incredible dive, only to be foiled by the perfect timing of the disappearing goose. It happened again and again. The eagle made at least a dozen attempts, but the goose, which I assumed could not fly, continued to dive beneath the surface just in the nick of time.

Next, the eagle began to circle overhead and watch the goose on the river for a few minutes. Then it dove again, but this time, instead of pulling out of the dive, it plunged headlong into the water, stubbornly trying to beat the goose at its own game. The goose was still quicker.

It was comical to see the eagle sprawled helplessly on the river with its tail high in the air and its beak in the water. Then, to make matters worse, the goose surfaced five feet away and proceeded to honk at the eagle at the top of his lungs. Through the binoculars, I could see the aggravated determination in the eagle's eyes.

By thrashing its huge wings, the eagle managed to get airborne again, only to repeat the comical performance. It dove face-first into the river no less than eight times and never touched so much as a feather on the goose. In the end, the waterlogged predator was unable to get airborne and had to flop onto a sandbar to dry. The goose continued to swim around and honk. I'll never forget the picture in my mind of that drenched eagle, standing on the sandbar with his wings outstretched, dripping dry while enduring the humiliation of the incessant honking of his would-be breakfast. I had to laugh at the look in the eagle's eyes. It was a look of pure contempt.

I glanced at my watch – 9:30. The deer were finished moving for the morning, and it was time to head home for breakfast. Then I looked down from the stand and was astounded to see a mule deer doe and her twin yearlings bedded directly beneath my tree. If I climbed down, I'd scare the daylights out of them, and that's a no-no in bowhunting. If one deer figures out your stand, it will blow your cover. So I'd just have to stay put – maybe for hours—until they left. My stomach growled, reminding me that I was getting hungry. How ironic, I thought. It's been a tough morning for all the hungry hunters. We've all missed breakfast!

THIRTY-THREE

Old Contenders

*B*eing longer of tooth and grayer of beard, the icy grip of this November morning chilled me deeper than it had in my youth. That same wondrous flame of anticipation burned deep within my soul, as it had without flickering for almost 50 years. But half a century had changed some things. The desire was still there, but the walk through knee-deep snow was harder. My feet felt heavier. I was more aware of numb fingers and the sting of the icy air on my cheeks.

Just being out of the woods wasn't the same incentive that it had been in days past. These woods were as familiar as my living room. I knew them intimately. I wasn't propelled by the same fuel anymore. Just seeing or getting a shot at a deer wasn't the issue. It was the picture framed in my mind that lured me into the forest one more time—the picture of that great, ebony-antlered 10-point buck I had seen the previous year. I rattled him on the last day of the season. He came in quietly behind my tree and stood stone still for almost a half-hour. By craning my neck, I could look back and see him standing there in the deep snow, only five yards behind me, like a bronze statue of the ultimate whitetail. I scarcely breathed for fear he would hear me. His body was immense and muscular—obviously in his prime—the unmistakable bull of the woods. His heavy 10-point rack was perfectly symmetrical and stretched far beyond his ears. His tines rose like swollen daggers. Never had I seen such a whitetail!

Though I hadn't seen him before that day, I knew he was there. Two years of scouting told me so. Huge aspens, as big around as my thigh, were rubbed raw. Some of his scrapes were as large as pickup truck beds. Finally he was in my sight. My heart labored in my chest. It was the ultimate reward for a lifetime of bowhunting.

I fought for self-control—not even daring to look over my shoulder at him. I had to be calm and under control, or all would be in vain.

Then I heard the snow crunch under his first step.

Another step!

He was coming out under my left hand! Rolling my eyes left, I waited for him to walk into view. More crunching sounds and he was there, a mere 20 yards out and still slightly behind me. He stopped again, and looked to his left, allowing me the opportunity to lift my bow and draw. For the first time, I noticed that the tip of his right ear was missing. Perhaps he lost it fighting. I couldn't imagine a deer brave enough to contest him.

Anchoring the top pin in the center of his deep chest, I loosed my arrow, which clipped a tiny spruce bough I hadn't even noticed. The arrow took a downward dip and stuck deep into the frozen earth below his chest. In two bounds, he was gone. My breath came in jerking gasps and my body trembled and felt suddenly warm. Never had I been so close to such a magnificent deer.

Yes, that was the picture that lured me into the woods again. It was the hope of another chance to see that incredible creature that inspired me to trade the warmth of my bed for 20-below temperatures. I had seen thousands of bucks in my life. All were beautiful, but none like this.

Plodding on in the snow, I was aware of aging bones, less eager for discomfort with each passing year. I could foresee a day when the hunt would make way for easier pursuits. But I had to try again. The buck was still there. His sign betrayed his reclusive nature.

I climbed the trunk of the familiar white spruce, wiped the frost from the seat of my treestand and sat in it. Once belted in, I raised my bow, nocked an arrow and hung it on a neighboring limb. Last, I pulled my rattling antlers out of my daypack and secured them in place to wait for dawn.

It was a full half-hour before a rose-colored hue began to silhouette the treetops to the southeast. The air was still, and my breath rose as small frosty clouds, turning to silver upon my beard. How many sunrises had I seen from a treestand? Uncountable! Still, it was new and fresh—almost sacred. What a privilege to meet the dawn. A chorus of distant coyotes broke the frigid silence. I closed my eyes and let them sing to me. It stirred something deep within. This was very special. I suppose there really was more to it than just that magnificent buck, like the sounds, the smells and the solitude. The rewards poured out before my eyes—deep blue shadows bordered by sunlit diamonds glistening on the snow. How wonderful it was to be alive, to see another sunrise, to breathe the frosty air. How precious, this thing called life. Perhaps even more precious as the beginning fades and the end comes into view.

When I could see well enough to shoot, I picked up the rattling antlers and tickled them together briefly. I was amazed at how the sound sizzled on the cold, still air. Ten minutes later, I clicked the antlers together again, and, as I did, I heard a crunch in the snow, deep in the dark timber before me.

Laying the antlers aside, I lifted my bow from its hanger. A deer was definitely walking steadily toward me. The dry snow continued to crunch and squeal beneath its feet. Then silence. I could almost picture what it was doing—waiting and listening for another trace of sound . . . one more clue.

Long, silent minutes passed before the snow crunched again. The deer sounded close. My eyes strained into the timber, and I was suddenly conscious of my heart beating loudly. The anticipation was the thing. How incredible! What was life without anticipation? That's what hunting was—a world of great anticipation. It was the crucial element that so often waned as life slipped into humdrum routines. But in the hunt, it was always there. Every hunt was preceded by great anticipation. That's why I was there. I had something wonderful to hope for and to anticipate.

Motion caught my eye deep in the green timber. Small streams of golden light, prying through shadowed boughs, fell in stripes upon his back as his form emerged from the depths of the spruce thicket. He was coming in my direction with his head low. Something was different. With each step, his shoulders seemed to sag. He was limping.

I could tell he was a large-bodied buck, but his rack was much smaller than that of the old monarch I was seeking. Now I had to make a decision. There were still three days of the hunting season left. Should I take this buck or continue to hold out for his superior?

At 30 yards, the buck came to the edge of the spruce thicket and stopped again. I could finally see his rack well. He had four stubby points on his left beam, and on his right side the forward third of his main beam was broken off. He appeared to have been in a severe battle. Tufts of hair were ruffled or missing all along his right side, and his right foreleg was obviously injured. He had trouble putting his weight on it. I could see frozen blood on his right shoulder where it appeared that he had been gored by another buck.

Eventually, he took a few more steps in my direction and stopped, quartering toward me with his right side. Now, at 20 yards, I could see that he had also lost his right eye in the battle. The poor buck was truly in desperate shape. A raven swooped over the trees above him, croaking loudly, as if to prophesy his doom to the scavengers of the forest. I resented the noisy intrusion. The buck lifted his head toward the sound and shifted his weight again to relieve his injured leg.

Then I saw it. Unbelievable! The tip of his right ear was missing. This was my buck! I could hardly believe it. He had gone downhill so dramatically. I was flooded with emotions. Suddenly I felt overwhelming compassion for him, especially knowing what a majestic creature he had been. I had seen him in his prime when he was strong and proud, when he would have sailed into the record books. Now he was a broken down old man, blind in one eye and limping.

I felt a stinging of tears. "What's happening here? Get a grip on yourself," I said under my breath. "Since when did you get so soft?"

As I considered his fate, I realized that being partially blind and having a damaged foreleg would spell almost certain death for him that winter. Should I spare him the agony of starving or being ripped apart by wolves and shoot him while he was standing there offering me a broadside shot?

I raised my bow slowly and put the 20-yard pin on his ribs. He stood there with his blind side toward me, sifting the air for his next bit of information. He was old and tattered; gray in the muzzle. His breath flowed from his half-open mouth in short white puffs; his ears rotating routinely like radar. He looked tired, but still the flame burned within him as he searched for the sounds of the fighting bucks, which I had imitated with my rattling antlers. He was still a warrior at heart. He still believed he could win.

He shifted his weight again, still favoring his damaged right leg and began turning away from me. If I was going to shoot, I had to take my shot now. He stopped again, now quartering away from me, and looked back in my direction.

I felt a strange kinship with the old buck. I wondered if he knew how close the end was for him. Perhaps not! I hoped not. Maybe his world was simpler without the awareness of time and its passing. The end would come for him without anticipation, prolonged fear or dread. One day it would just come.

I eased my bow down and rested it on my knees, no longer wanting to shoot him. In truth I wanted to help him. Perhaps shooting him would have been a kinder act, but I couldn't do it.

He reminded me of an old prizefighter who had been a great champion, but refused to retire. How sad to watch an old champion sacrifice his dignity! But the old buck had no choice. He was programmed by urges beyond his comprehension. Mother Nature provides no retirement plans for old contenders. She alone would decide his fate.

He dropped his head and walked back on his tracks into the spruce thicket. I wished him peace in his last days. I was glad to have seen him in his prime. That's how I chose to remember him. That's how I would choose to be remembered.

A chill ran down my spine, making me realize how long I'd been sitting absolutely still. My fingers were so numb I had to peel them from my bow. It had been an unusual morning. I felt again those urges beyond my comprehension, and experienced anew how wonderful it is to be living—to be alive. No, not just to be alive, but to feel alive. How precious, this thing called life, as the beginning fades and the end comes into view.

THIRTY-FOUR

Trophies of the Heart Trilogy

taring out through the fog across the endless prickly pear flats, the world was a ghostly blend of gray and drab green. The low mesquite brush, huisache, catclaw and cactus blended into an inhospitable tapestry of intrigue, where the deer lived. My great-uncle Ben David, a Southern Baptist preacher, sat on the bench next to me in the box blind, 15 feet above the ground. I still remember how the smell of his Old Spice aftershave blended with the buck lure that was sprinkled liberally on his weary old Stetson and the aroma from his stubby cigar. I never saw him smoke a cigar. I guess he mostly just chewed on them. It was a wonderful aroma. It was the smell of deer hunting to me. I was about 11 then.

Occasionally, he would put his big hand on my knee and squeeze, and, in a soft whisper, ask me if I could see any deer. It was his way of keeping me focused on the hunt. He always knew when my attention span was waning. But when he whispered, his voice always sounded so full of assurance that I would quit fidgeting and renew my search for the elusive whitetail. I really wasn't even sure what one looked like. I had never seen a live deer. Uncle Ben said whitetails were the greatest game animals in the world, so naturally I was eager to accept when he invited me to go with him on a hunt.

I still remember the old gray thermos sitting in the bottom of the blind. The paint was all worn off, and it was full of dents. It must have been on hundreds of deer hunts. And I remember my fascination with the bullets Uncle Ben used. They were short and rather fat looking. The tips were rounded, and the lead formed a little star right on the nose of each bullet. The writing on the end of the box said .35 Remington.

Uncle Ben wore cowboy boots. He looked kind of like a cowboy, too—like a sheriff, sitting there with his rifle resting on the edge of the blind as if he were waiting for an outlaw to try to rob the stagecoach. But more important to me, he was a hunter. He was the first deer hunter I had ever known. I wondered if I'd ever be able to go deer hunting with a gun of my own. Even though it was all new to me, I knew I wanted to shoot a deer someday.

Suddenly, Uncle Ben jerked the rifle to his shoulder and aimed out into the foggy morning. I strained to see what he was seeing. Then I saw it. There was a buck chasing a doe through the brush. They seemed to glide as they zigzagged through the brush with the buck always right on the doe's heels.

While the rifle was swinging, Uncle Ben fired and simultaneously bit off the butt of his cigar. The rest fell to the bottom of the blind, and he spit the other end over the side. The buck crumpled in his tracks and was instantly out of sight.

"You got him Uncle Ben!" I shouted in a voice louder that I meant for it to be. Without taking his eyes off the spot where the buck fell, he reached down with his big right hand and squeezed my knee and said, "Was a pretty good ol' buck, wasn't it?"

I followed Uncle Ben through the damp, thorny brush until finally the buck was lying there before us. It was beautiful. It was magical. Where did he come from, and where was he going? I sat on the ground beside the sleek animal for almost 15 minutes while Uncle Ben went to get the truck. I felt its smooth hair and counted the nine ebony-colored points that formed a majestic crown above his head. This beautiful creature lying beside me held the secret and the allure of all wild things — a wonderful secret that would forever be a mystery. Whatever his wonderful secret was, I knew I had to pursue it. What could be more wonderful than to have my own rifle and hunt for a deer of my own?

On the drive home, we met a car going the opposite direction with a buck tied over the fender. "There's goes another deer hunter with a buck," I said as I craned my neck to see the deer. "Was that buck as big as yours?" I asked.

"Well, I didn't get that good a look at it," Uncle Ben said, "but it's not the size that really matters in deer huntin'. Everybody likes to get a big ol' buck if they can, but what's important is the experience. That's somethin' you can enjoy for the rest of your life. Just like seein' that ol' buck out there in the pasture at sunup, chasing that doe back and forth. We'll never forget that sight, will we?"

I nodded my agreement. I would never forget it.

The little open-sighted 6.5mm Swedish Mauser felt powerful in my hands. It was the first time I had hunted with a firearm larger than a .22. The rifle had been on layaway at the local Army Surplus Store while I mowed lawns all summer to accumulate the cash to pay for it. It was November at last. I was 14 years old and on my first deer hunt. It was a feeling so wonderful that it could only be described by the chills of excitement running down my spine as I crept along the creek bank in the damp morning air. The earthy, sweet-and-sour smells of fall hung in the air, and birds began to stir. I caught the white flash of a cottontail's tail as he scampered from beneath my feet. Something larger suddenly crashed through the underbrush in front of me; then all was silent. Finally, in the distance I could hear a sneezing sound. Over and over it sounded. I walked slowly, trying to move without making any noise. In my young mind, I was Daniel Boone. At last I was a deer hunter, too.

A half-mile farther, as I followed the meandering creek, I spotted two deer—a buck and a doe. They were at the bottom of the bank next to the creek, probably drinking when they spotted me. For a long, breathless moment our eyes met and the world stood still. I froze with one foot in midstride. Somehow I knew that to move would end this incredible encounter.

The buck lifted his nose high and appeared to be sniffing the air as far above the ground as he could. The doe began stamping her right front foot and making that same sneezing sound I had heard earlier. So that's what it was. Deer make that noise.

My left leg ached from holding my foot in the air for so long. Suddenly, the doe whirled and bounded up and over the bank and into the thick brush with the buck right on her heels. It all happened so fast, there was no chance for a shot. But I had seen my first deer on my first deer hunt with my own rifle in hand. It was as wonderful as I had imagined.

I secretly wished that I had Uncle Ben's experience. He probably would have thrown the rifle to his shoulder and dropped the buck before he had time to run. Soon youthful optimism promised other opportunities, and I decided not to worry about what Uncle Ben might have done. This was my hunt, and I'd have to get my first deer my way, whatever that was.

When I reached the opposite bank from where the deer had been standing, I sat down and rested my back against an ancient oak tree, facing the hole in the brush where the deer had disappeared. I rested the little carbine across my lap. In my ignorance, I waited for the deer to return to the same spot from where I had frightened them. How little I understood about whitetails back then.

Within 10 minutes, the doe stuck her head out of the brush, not 40 yards in front of me. And then the buck appeared. I was stricken with a brand-new feeling that was something between fear and excitement. The net result was an electric sensation vibrating through my body that made my hands tremble, and, for some reason, I couldn't catch my breath.

"I must be having a 'buckacher,'" I thought. I'd heard Uncle Ben talk about having a "buckacher" (his term for buck fever), but I really never knew what he meant. How would I ever be able to shoot a deer like this? I had to get control of myself.

As I struggled for control, to my amazement the two deer didn't seem to notice me, even though I was sitting in the wide open directly in front of them. I caught my first breath since they appeared as they started cautiously down the bank before me. For the first time, I could see that the little buck had six points, plus a little point near the base of one antler.

More than anything in the world I wanted that buck. Now they were no more than 30 yards from me.

I could see they wanted to drink from the creek. The doe would drop her head as if she were going to drink, then she would jerk it back up as if to see if she could catch me moving. But I remained as still as a stone. Finally, she relaxed, flipped her tail from side to side and started to drink. The buck dropped his head to join her.

I thought my heart would explode as I eased the rifle to my shoulder in slow motion. The buck lifted his head suddenly, looking right at me. I froze again until my arms burned. When he dropped his head again, I continued to move the rifle into position. As I moved the iron sights onto his shoulder, my body shuddered involuntarily, and I began to shake harder than ever. I gasped for air. When the sights bounced into position, I yanked back on the trigger. As I did, I remembered Uncle Ben's instructions: "Squeeze the trigger slowly," he had said. I couldn't imagine such control at that moment.

The little carbine exploded the silent creek bank with a report that seemed out of proportion to its size. The buck's front end fell, but his rear legs remained standing while the doe disappeared in an instant. I yanked the bolt open and drove another cartridge into the chamber and fired again. The buck was still there with his front end on the ground. Then he started to regain himself and he was up on all fours. I fired again. "Dear God," I prayed, "please don't let him get away!"

Suddenly the buck seemed as good as new and scrambled up over the bank and into the brush. I fired my last shot at his waving white tail as he vaulted straight away from me through the creek bottom jungle. As the last shot echoed down the bank, the buck disappeared. All was quiet except my heart and my breathing. I wasn't sure I would survive.

The aching desperation of losing the buck subsided slightly when I spied an unnatural white spot on the ground where the buck had been running. There was nothing white in these woods. It just might be him. Maybe my last shot was good after all.

Quickly I sprinted down the creek to a place where I could ford. When I was directly across the creek from the big oak tree, I turned into the brush and searched for that trace of white. There it was! I crawled on my hands and knees toward the spot through the tangle of vines and limbs for 40 yards, then I saw one leg sticking up in the air. It was my buck!

The Alabama rain drizzled from the roof of the box blind where my son, Darren, and I sat in the dark, awaiting first shooting light. Across his lap was the sleek .243 I had given him a month earlier for his 15th Christmas.

"Do you think we'll see anything in this rain?" he asked.

"We've got a good chance," I answered. "It's the end of January, and the bucks are trailing the does."

Within 15 minutes, the soggy darkness began to fade to gray. We could see the long green pasture of grass and clover bordered on both sides by hardwood timber. Our box blind was ideally situated to observe any deer moving back and forth across the pasture between the hardwoods.

Within 10 minutes after first shooting light, I spotted a deer in the distance emerging from the timber on our left. A quick look through binoculars identified the deer as a doe. I nudged Darren and pointed toward the doe. "Get on her," I urged. "A buck might be right behind her."

Darren rested his rifle on the windowsill of the blind and watched her intently as she eased out into the opening and crossed it without hesitation. Soon she was out of sight. "Sure hope a buck shows up," Darren whispered.

"Me too," I replied. This was Darren's first hunt. I truly hoped he would get his chance. Selfishly, I wanted to be with him when he got his first buck.

I relived the anticipation of my youth as I sat there with my son, wondering if today would be the day. The silent minutes passed, save the dripping of rain from the roof of the blind.

"Dad, there's another deer," Darren whispered. I looked through my binoculars and saw antlers at the very instant Darren saw them.

"It's a buck!" he whispered with renewed excitement. "How far is he?"

I estimated 200 yards. "Just keep your crosshairs right behind his shoulder and when he stops, squeeze one off."

I felt my heart quicken as I watched Darren ready himself. It was just a young buck to be sure, but my adrenaline flowed as if I were watching the world record. I fought to control my own breathing. How strange! It hadn't been like this for me in years. Suddenly I was 14 again. I shuddered silently with the thrill of anticipation. It was MY first buck all over again!

The buck appeared to be walking right on the doe's tracks, and, like her, he kept a steady pace. "What if he doesn't stop?" Darren asked anxiously.

"Get ready, I'm going to whistle at him," I said.

I made a sharp, shrill whistle, and the buck stopped in his tracks and looked in our direction. "Take him now," I urged. I heard Darren take a deep breath to get steady, and the buck started walking again. Darren let his breath go in a heavy sigh.

I whistled again, and again the buck stopped and looked our way. "Better get him this time," I whispered, holding my breath.

I watched over Darren's shoulder as his breath became short and jerky. I could remember the feeling so well. It was as if it were yesterday. Then the buck was walking again.

I whistled a third time and the buck stopped just shy of the timber. "Get on him quick, it's your last chance," I whispered. Secretly, I hoped the buck would hold just one more time. I could feel Darren's anxiety.

At the crack of the .243, the buck lunged forward, running low to the ground. I knew the shot was good.

"Did I get him?" Darren asked anxiously.

"You got him," I replied, feeling greatly relieved.

After congratulating Darren and assuring him that his aim was true, we climbed out of the blind and headed down the pasture. The rain made it impossible to find, or even to expect visible blood. In fact, it was very hard to be sure of just where the buck had been standing. I realized that finding him could be very difficult under the circumstances, but I didn't let my concerns show. I knew Darren would be shattered if he lost the buck, especially knowing that it was hit.

"Think we'll find him, Dad?"

"Sure we will," I said with forced optimism. "He probably just made it into the timber and dropped." I made a loop through the edge of the timber but saw nothing. A second loop proved fruitless as well. By then, I was believing the worst. I could feel Darren's hopes sinking as we walked along the edge of the timber.

"There he is!" Darren exclaimed. He was lying in the deep grass, halfway between the timber and where he was shot. He'd only gone 35 yards. A wide smile spread across Darren's face. I hugged and congratulated him on his first buck and a heck of a good shot. The bullet entered right behind the right shoulder and centered the lungs.

I waited silently as he came to grips with the reality of taking his first deer. He dropped to his knees and ran his hand over its sleek hair and felt the rack. I knew what was going through his mind. He looked up at me and said, "Pretty neat, huh?"

"Pretty neat," I agreed.

We paced off the shot at 180 yards as we walked back to get the truck. He had done well on his first buck.

We walked on in silence for a moment, then Darren said, "It's not much of a trophy, is it?"

I could tell he was measuring his bucks against the big northern bucks he'd seen brought into my Alberta hunting camp when he was younger.

"Son, never measure your deer hunting against anybody else's," I said. "We're out here hunting for the experience—the love of the experience. Deer hunting is not a contest with other hunters. It's just between you and the deer. The thrill of the hunt and the experience with nature is the thing. Deer hunting is its own reward. Bagging a buck is just the icing on the already delicious cake. What really matters is the experience and the memories you carry home in your heart. Those are the greatest trophies of all."

He nodded in agreement, but I knew that it would be years before he fully understood.

"Is he as big as your first buck?" he asked.

"Yes, as a matter of fact, he's quite a bit bigger," I said.

We walked on silently for a moment.

"Pretty neat," he grinned from beneath his soggy cap.

"Pretty neat," I agreed.

About the Author

Russell Thornberry was born in Corpus Christi, Texas, in 1944. After a hunting accident ended his hopes for a football career in 1964, he entered the folk music scene, touring with the New Christy Minstrels. After his discharge from the U.S. Army, he traveled to western Canada to visit a friend. There he met and married Sharleen Gibson. He decided to live in Canada to pursue new musical opportunities, which included concert tours, his own music television series, and several solo, contemporary folk music albums as a singer/songwriter, for which he received six BMI Awards.

During this period in the early 1970s his outdoor interests led him to yet another career. He spent eighteen years in Alberta as a big game guide and outfitter for trophy white-tailed deer, black bear, moose, and elk. As he gained prominence for producing giant Alberta whitetails for his clients, he was also establishing himself as one of North America's prominent outdoors writers and authors, contributing to virtually every noteworthy hunting magazine in North America. In addition, he has also written and published numerous books on outdoor topics, including *Trophy Deer of Alberta; The Art and Science of Rattling Whitetail Deer; Bucks, Bulls, and Belly Laughs; Hunting the Canadian Giant;* and *Buckmasters Whitetail Trophy Records.*

In the early 1970s, Thornberry established an alternative antler measuring system for trophy white-tailed deer. Since then, his "Full-Credit Scoring System" has been widely adopted all across North America. Thornberry's scoring system was adopted by the Buckmasters organization, which in 1996 published the first edition of *Buckmasters Whitetail Trophy Records,* based on Thornberry's system. The second edition, containing five thousand entries, was published in the fall of 1999.

Today Thornberry serves as editor-in-chief of *Buckmasters Whitetail Magazine* and lives in Wetumpka, Alabama, with his wife Sharleen. They have two grown children, Michelle and Darren, and five grandchildren.